IMAGES
of America

UNIVERSITY CITY
MISSOURI

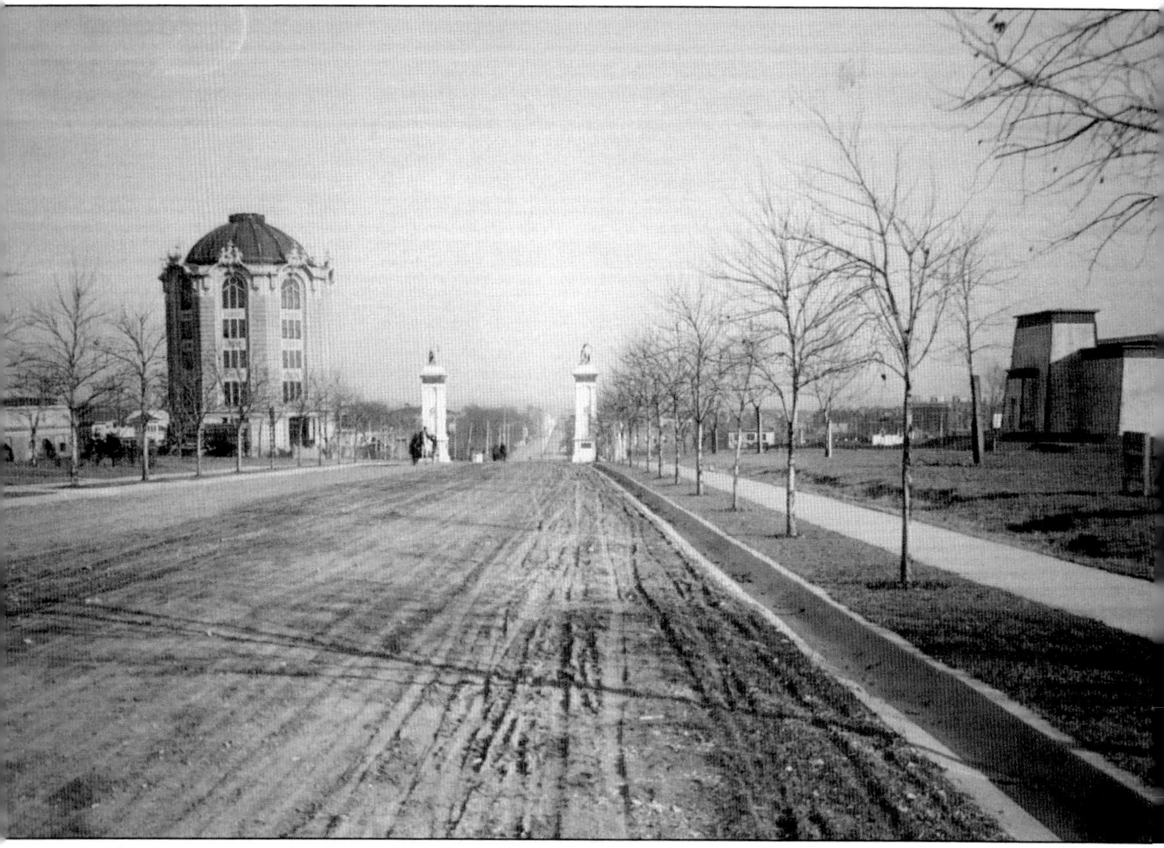

Above is a view of Delmar Boulevard looking east, c.1909. (Photo Courtesy of the Archives of the University City Public Library.)

IMAGES
of America

UNIVERSITY CITY MISSOURI

John A. Wright

ARCADIA
PUBLISHING

ISBN 978-0-7385-2006-3

Published by Arcadia Publishing
Charleston, South Carolina

Printed in the United States of America

Library of Congress Catalog Card Number: 2002107332

For all general information contact Arcadia Publishing at:
Telephone 843-853-2070
Fax 843-853-0044
E-mail sales@arcadiapublishing.com
For customer service and orders:
Toll-Free 1-888-313-2665

Visit us on the Internet at www.arcadiapublishing.com

A portion of the proceeds from the sale of this book will be donated to the University City Education Foundation.

This book is dedicated to the memory of Darwin Portman, who was a friend and lover of University City and someone who exemplified the true meaning of friendship and brotherhood.

Pictured here is the Seal of University City.

Contents

ACKNOWLEDGMENTS

I would like to express a special thanks to Sue Rehkopf, Charles Brown, Michele Ludwig, Eileen P. Dugan, and Carol Prieto for their invaluable assistance and for being available for never-ending help. Special thanks also go to Patricia Whitener and my wife, Sylvia Wright, for their invaluable assistance.

Thanks also go to the following individuals and institutions for their help and support in making this book possible. The individuals are: David Bowser, Sandra Marsh, Susan Lielenberg McGinn, Wallace Klein, Patricia Perryman, Michael Thacker, Joy and Larry Lieberrman, Linda Ballard, Kay Drey, George Murphy, John and Edna Whitefield, Richard Reynolds, Jack Kirkland, Betty Thompson, Esley Hamilton, Duane Sneddeker, Audrey Newcomer, Sister Charline Sullivan, Billye Crumpton, Ellen Ross, Andrey Newcomer, Fred Epstein, Rabbi Tzvi Freedman, Sister Mary Jeremy Buckman RSM, Ph.D, RN, Alfred J. Fleischer, Elise Glickert, Sheila Lumpe, Tony Taylor, Peter Wollenberg, and Jacquelyn and Ladorn Creighton. The institutions are: St. Louis Archdiocesan Archives, Sisters of Mercy Archives, Jackson Park PTO, Mercantile Library, City Hall of University City, St. Louis Public Library, University City Fire Department, University City Police Department, Sisters of St. Joseph of Carondolet, University City Historical Society, University City Public Library, The Green Center, and Washington University Archives.

Words of appreciation go to the following members of the University City Education Foundation for all the hard work they have done on behalf of the children of University City: Joseph Adams, Mary Ellen Campbell, Naima Wartts, Mary Wertsch, Miriam Wilhelm, Susan Carlson, Judy Goldthree, Michelle Gralnick, Ernest Greer, Phil Klasskin, Sandy Marsh, Jon Mendelson, Traci Moore, Barbara Santoro, Mary Schuman, Calla Smorodin, Mary Ann Square, and Al Van Amburg.

Introduction

The area we now know as University City was once owned by the Chouteaus and other early St. Louis settlers under French and Spanish land grants. Before the territory was settled, Old Bonhomme Road, later named Olive Street Road, which ran through the region, served as a path from St. Louis to Howell's Ferry on the Missouri River. In 1851, a local company acquired the road and converted it into a plank road with toll gates. Taverns later opened and measured off the miles from the toll gate to the Sixteen Mile House. Soon farmers began working the land along Olive and gradually changed the road from a Mississippi River to Missouri River route to a market route.

University City's beginning can be traced to its founder, Edward Gerner Lewis' Publishing Company and its relocation to the area. Lewis had outgrown his printing facilities in St. Louis and needed larger quarters. Always being an individual of grand ideas and schemes, Lewis conceived of building a new printing facility surrounded by a residential area, which he would eventually incorporate into a city and serve as its mayor. It happened that his dreams coincided with the 1904 World's Fair, occurring in St. Louis. Lewis used the Fair to promote his publishing business as well as his real estate developments. To attract Fair visitors, Lewis placed on top of his publishing building the most powerful spotlight of its kind. Intrigued by the searchlight, visitors strayed from the Fair and visited Lewis' empire.

In 1906, when University City was incorporated, Lewis became the first mayor. He had grandiose plans for the city, which included moving the new Cathedral to the city, transferring the state capital to the city from Jefferson City, building a subway from Eads Bridge to University City, and opening the first postal bank in America. Lewis wanted his city to be a cultural and learning center. However, his dreams began to fade amidst allegations of fraud and he left University City in 1912 for California.

After Lewis' departure, property values dropped because much of the land owned by Lewis was put up for sale. The city, however, continued to grow through the Roaring 20s and beyond.

In 1930, the City of University City purchased Lewis' publishing building and press area, which now houses City Hall and the Police and Fire Departments. The Lewis Center now houses Washington University's School of Fine Arts and luxury apartments.

The city's first subdivision, University Heights, represents the highest point in Lewis' planning. The stately homes—located on streets that bear the names of well-known institutions of higher learning such as Yale, Columbia, Amherst, Cornell, Dartmouth, and Harvard—helped to carry out his university theme. Most importantly, the homes have been preserved.

The city's population began to change from Gentile to Jewish in the 1920s, and again during the 1960s, when the first African Americans began to move to University City. During this period, real estate agencies attempted to red-line the city and profit from white fears. The city responded with anti-block-busting legislation, which banned the use of "For Sale" signs and passed an Occupancy Permit Ordinance to enforce housing codes. However, despite city efforts, a number of businesses and residents left the city for newer suburbs.

The city faced up to the problems and redefined itself and emerged stronger for its diversity, which can be seen in the make-up of the city's population, ethnic restaurants and businesses, and religious institutions, which include 24 churches and synagogues. University City is also the home of an Eruv District, which allows Orthodox Jews within the area to perform certain activities on the Sabbath.

Today, University City is a highly sought-after community in which to live. It is centrally located—15 minutes from both downtown St. Louis and Lambert International St. Louis Airport and close to most cultural institutions and events. The city is also an excellent place in which to invest. Property values increased 44 percent between 1997 and 2001.

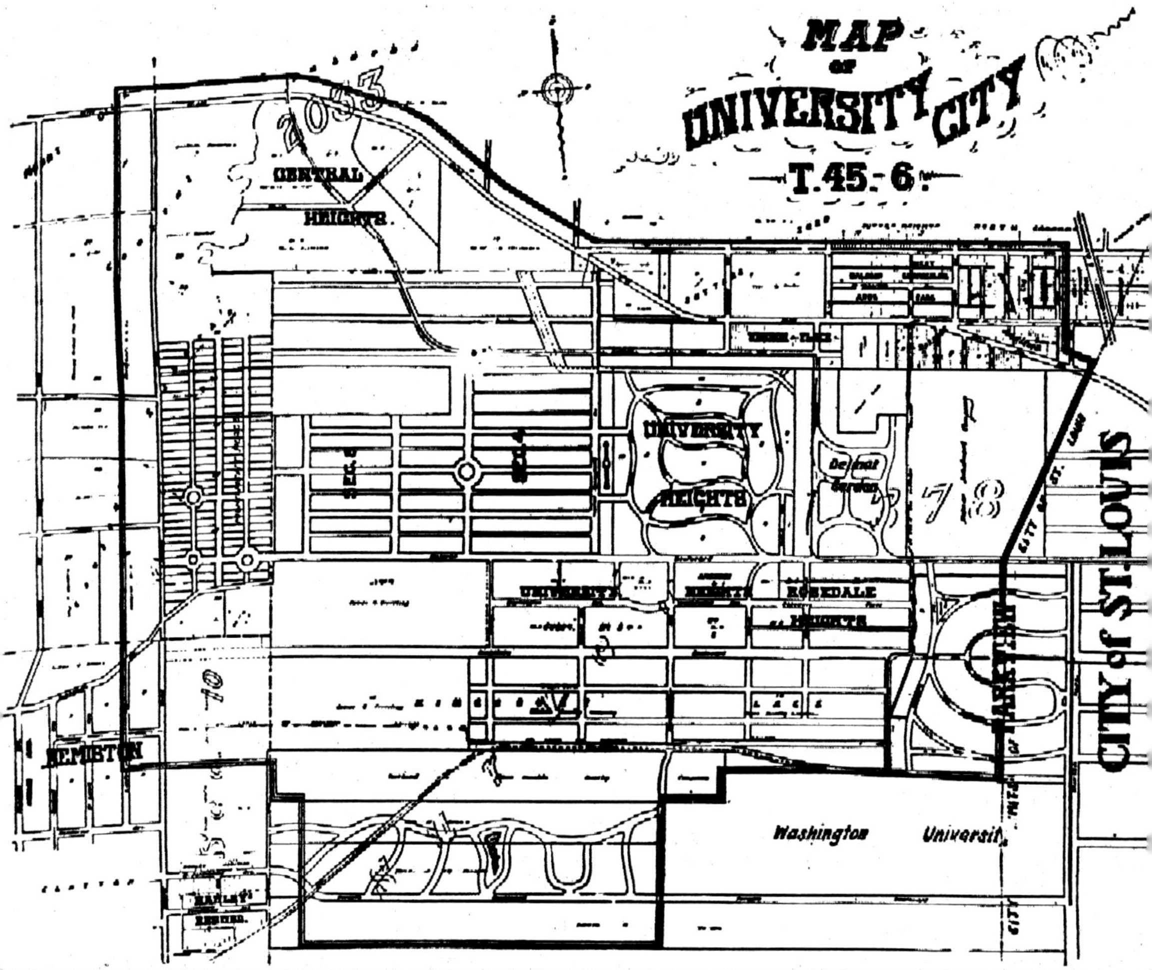

A 1912 Map of University City. (Map Courtesy of the Archives of the University City Public Library.)

One

Before University City

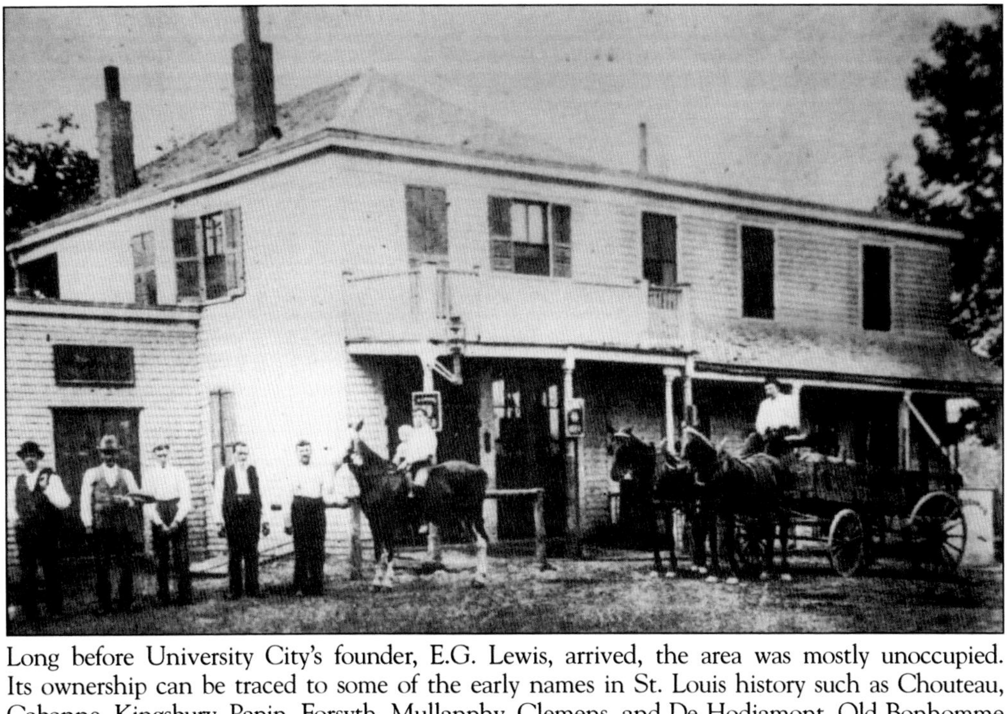

Long before University City's founder, E.G. Lewis, arrived, the area was mostly unoccupied. Its ownership can be traced to some of the early names in St. Louis history such as Chouteau, Cabanne, Kingsbury, Papin, Forsyth, Mullanphy, Clemens, and De Hodiamont. Old Bonhomme Road, which ran through the area, was a link for St. Louisians to the Mississippi River.

In 1851, a group of area businessmen incorporated the Central Plank Road Company and acquired Old Bonhomme Road. They later established a new route and toll road to the river using the present Olive Street Road. The first toll house was located near Grand and Olive and taverns were used to measure off the miles to the Sixteen Mile House. The Sutter Post Office and Seven Mile House on the Old Plank Road (now Olive Street Road), pictured above, served the area from 1887 to 1903. (Photo Courtesy of the Archives of the University City Library.)

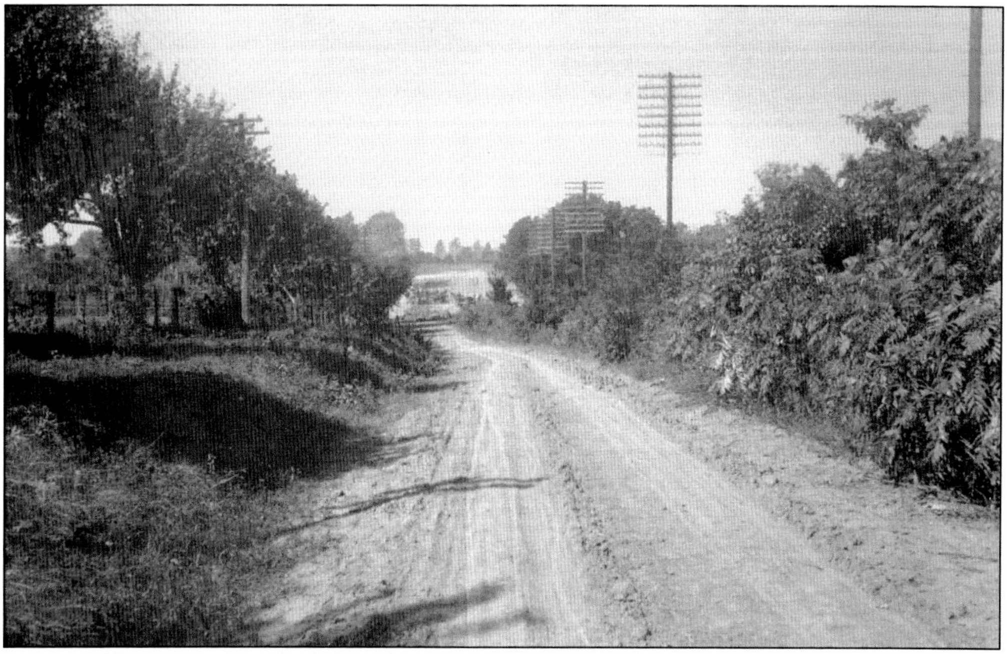

In 2001, Olive Street Road celebrated its sesquicentennial. The thoroughfare began as footpaths used by Native Americans to hunt game. The paths were later joined to form a road to connect Howell's Ferry with downtown St. Louis. In 1906, when University City was incorporated, most of the land along Olive Street Road was still farmland. Occasionally, one would come across a residence or a farm house. The Central Plank Road Company, which operated the road as a toll road, turned it over to St. Louis County in 1858 when they found it hard to maintain and operate. (Photo Courtesy of the Archives of the University City Public Library.)

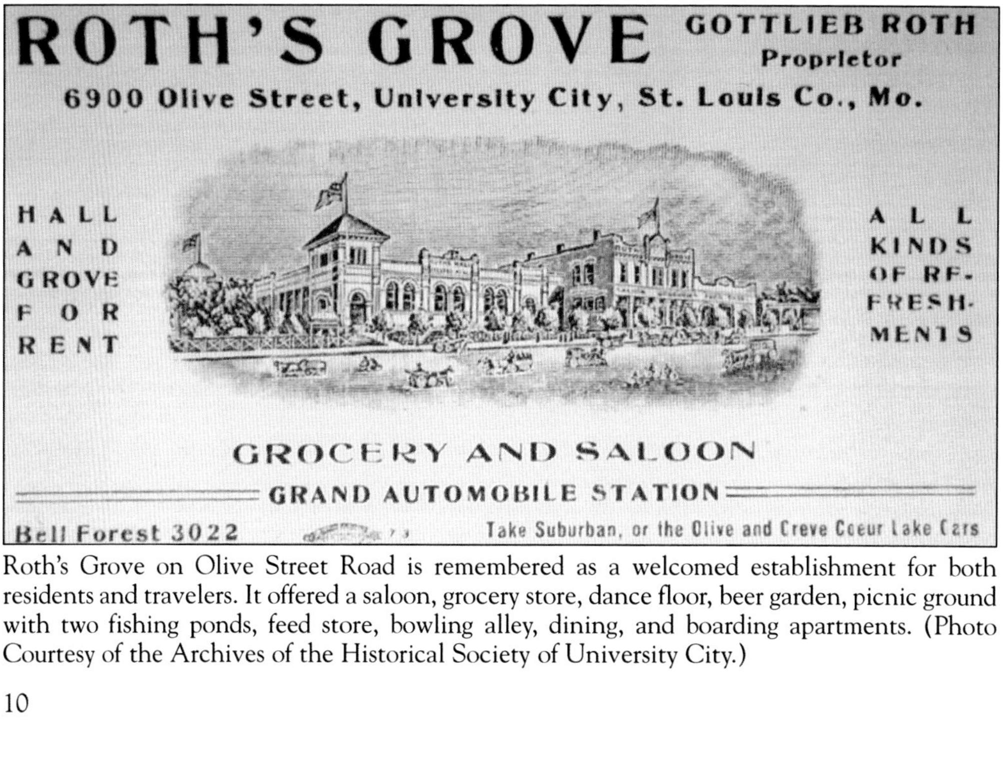

Roth's Grove on Olive Street Road is remembered as a welcomed establishment for both residents and travelers. It offered a saloon, grocery store, dance floor, beer garden, picnic ground with two fishing ponds, feed store, bowling alley, dining, and boarding apartments. (Photo Courtesy of the Archives of the Historical Society of University City.)

Among the early residents of the area were Jacob Klein and his wife, Ursula. They posed for this picture in the 1880s. The Klein's farm covered most of the land that became Ruth Park. (Photo Courtesy of the Archives of the Historical Society of University City.)

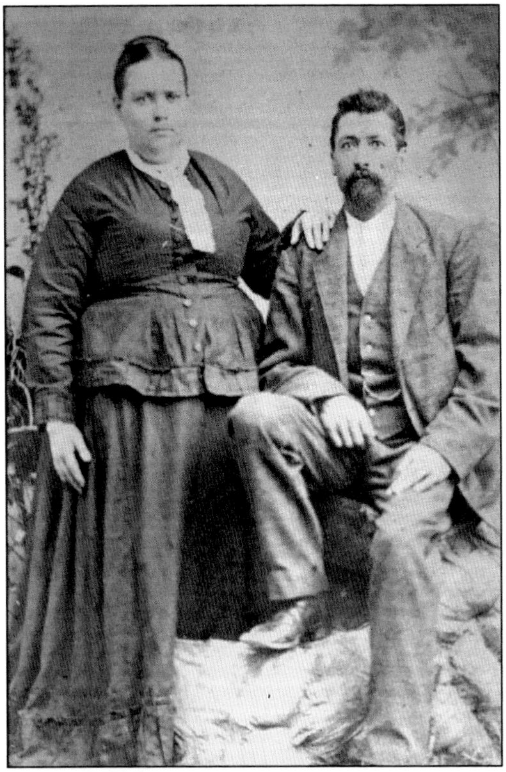

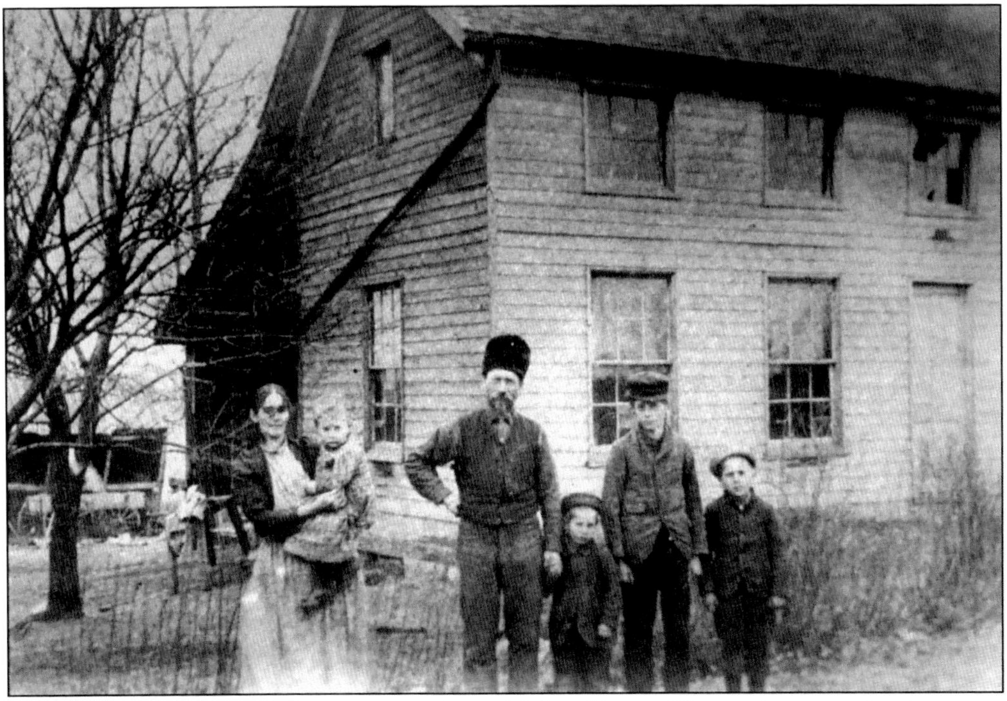

Another early family of the area was that of John George Kurtz, who owned a home on Blackberry Lane. (Photo Courtesy of the Archives of Historical Society of University City.)

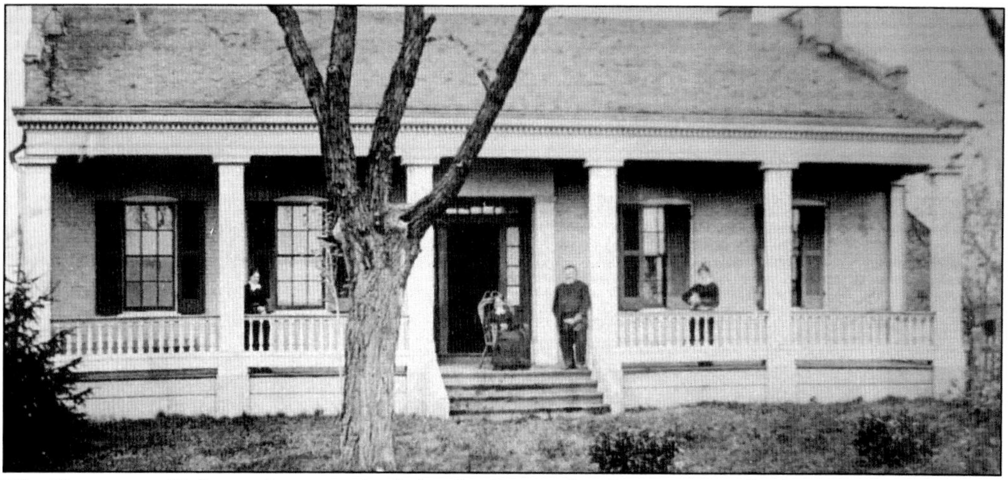

The "homestead" shown here was built by the Sutter family in 1850. The house was the center of their dairy farm located northwest of the intersection of Sutter and Bartmer Avenues, just northwest of the old Sutter Avenue Presbyterian Church. Sutter Avenue originally was the road that led to the Sutter homestead. The farm was destroyed by fire in 1894. (Photo Courtesy of the Archives of the Historical Society of University City.)

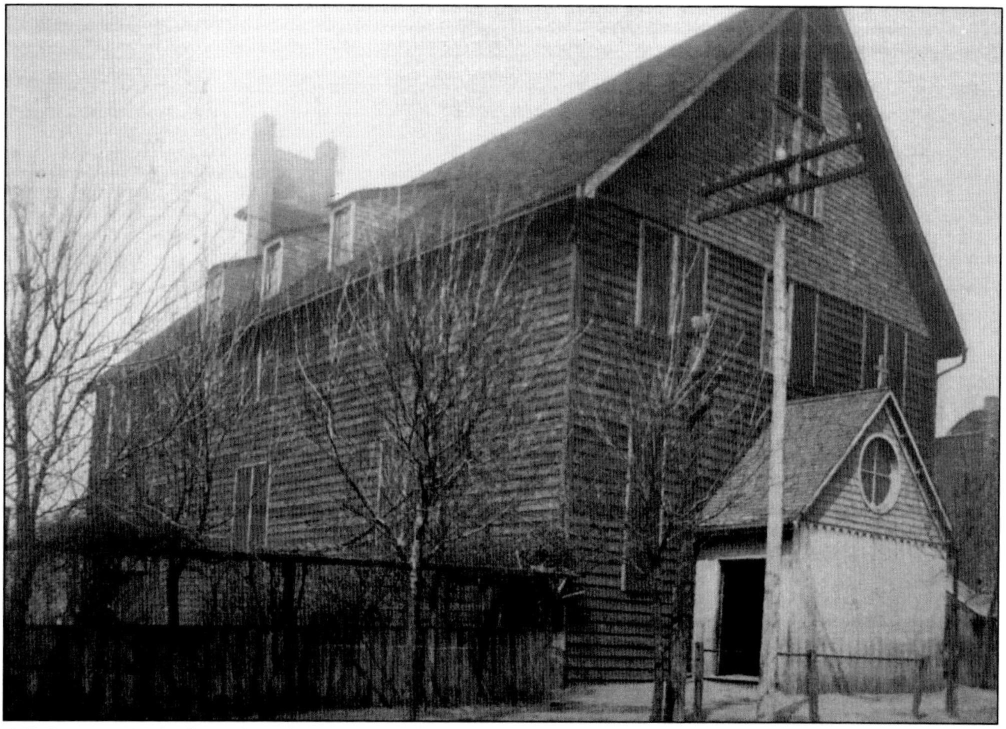

All Saints Catholic Church was established in the area in 1901. This two-and-a-half-story, wooden church-school-rectory was located at 63rd and Maple not far west of where the Norfolk and Western tracks cross Skinker. After it burned in 1917, construction was started on a stone, three-story school building at Westgate and Clemens. Religious services were held in the school hall until 1936 when the church was completed. (Photo Courtesy of the St. Louis Catholic Archdiocese Archives.)

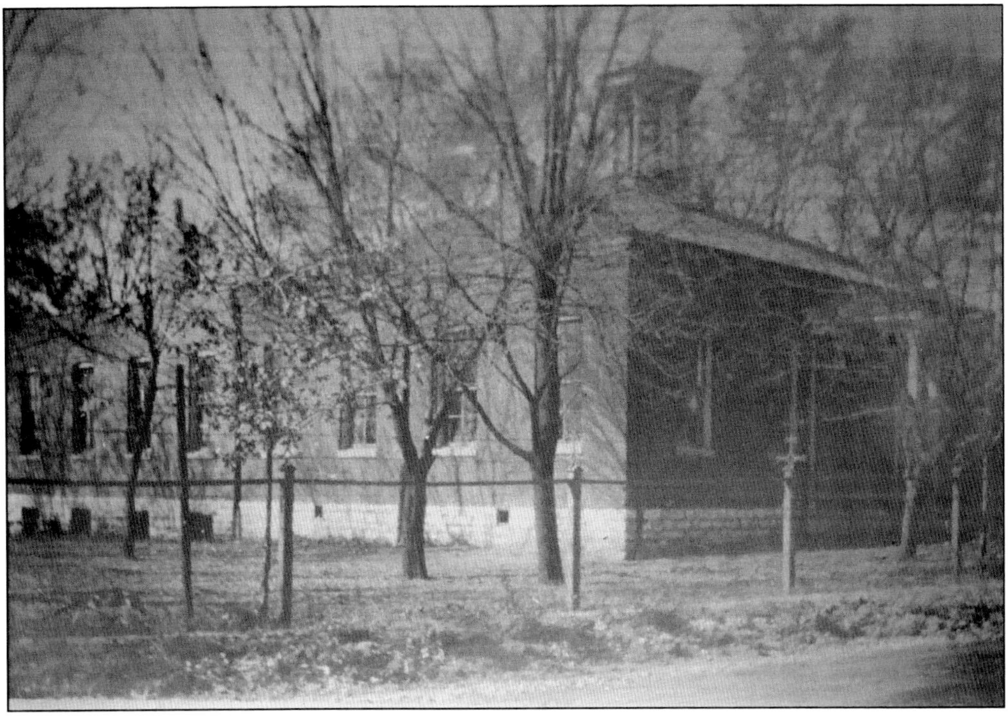

The Ferguson School, which was opened in 1868, was located just east of the old fire station at Pennsylvania Avenue and Olive Street Road. Until the separation of the City of St. Louis from the county in 1879, the school operated under the administration of the St. Louis Board of Education. The school was named for D.K. Ferguson, president of the Mechanics Bank of St. Louis, who donated the land for the school. Parents provided the materials and money for construction. (Photo Courtesy of the Archives of the University City Library.)

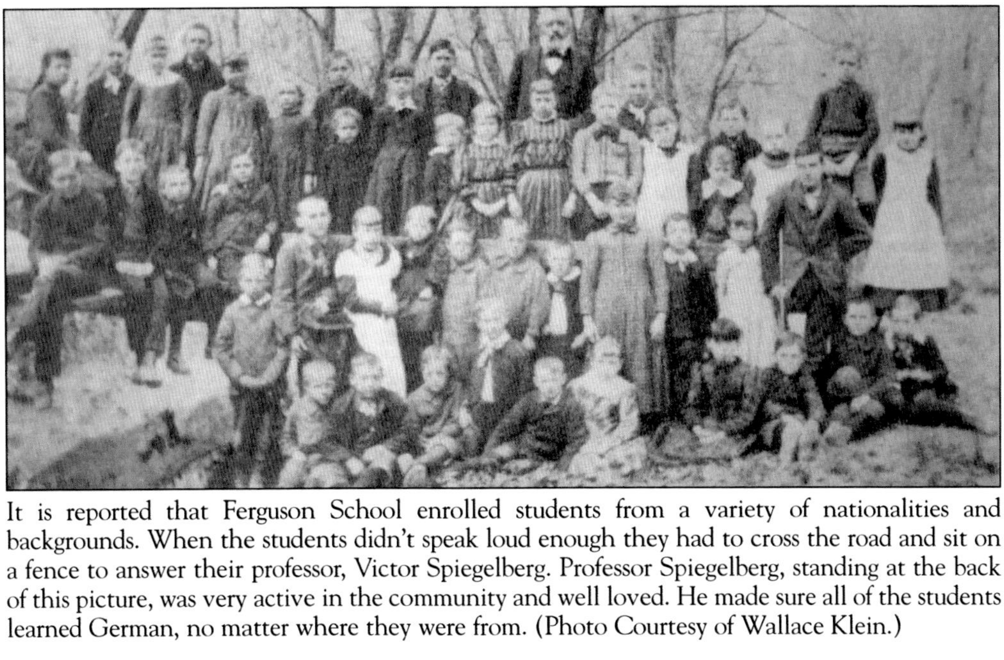

It is reported that Ferguson School enrolled students from a variety of nationalities and backgrounds. When the students didn't speak loud enough they had to cross the road and sit on a fence to answer their professor, Victor Spiegelberg. Professor Spiegelberg, standing at the back of this picture, was very active in the community and well loved. He made sure all of the students learned German, no matter where they were from. (Photo Courtesy of Wallace Klein.)

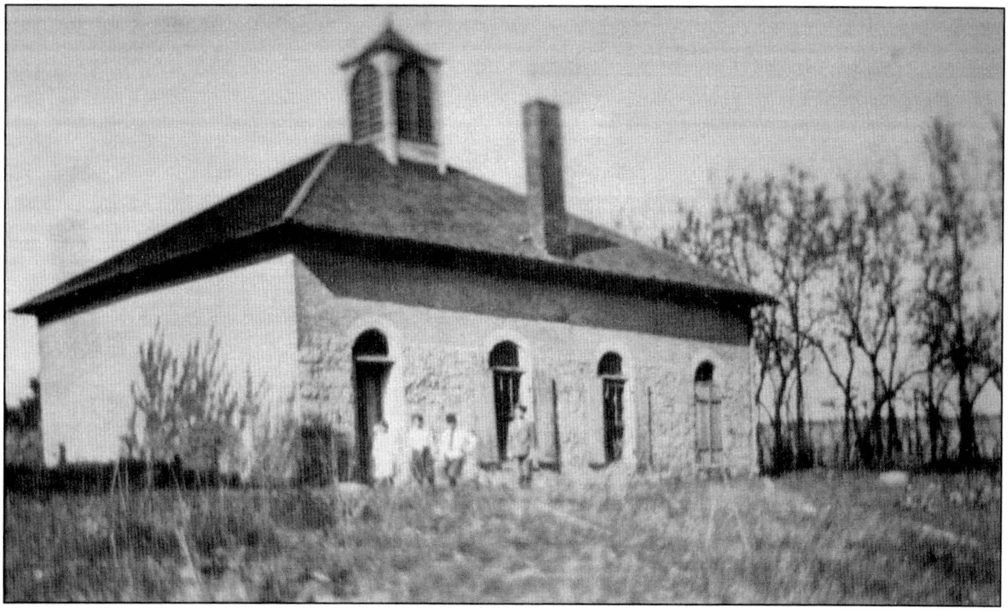

Children in the Mount Olive community around North and South Avenues and Olive Street Road attended this Mount Olive School built in 1890s. The school was later moved to 7800 Olive Street Road. (Photo Courtesy of the Archives of the University City Public Library.)

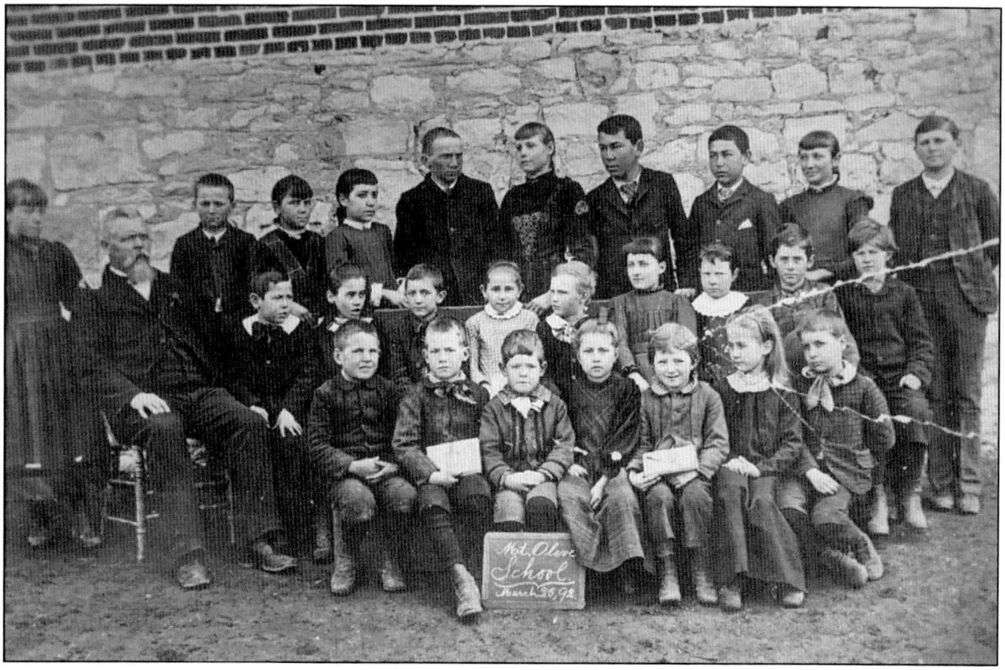

Students attended the new Mount Olive School at 7800 Olive until it closed in 1931. The teachers and pupils who had not gone to Daniel Boone the year before were transferred to Nathaniel Hawthorne. The building was later used by American Legion Post 143. (Photo Courtesy of the Archives of the University City Public Library.)

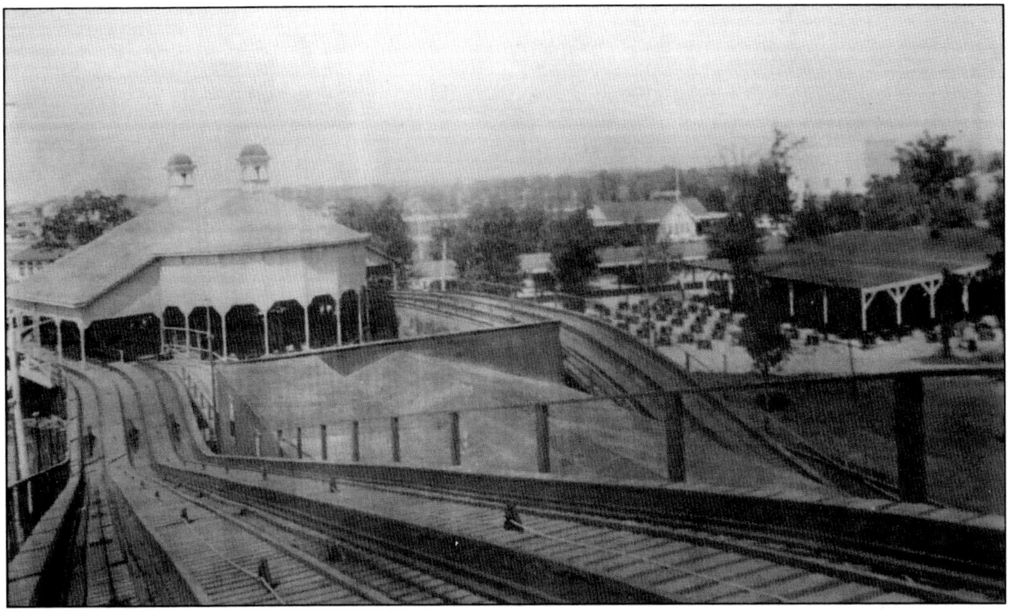

A new racetrack and amusement park on Delmar, next to the city, brought a large number of visitors to the community. The entrances to the track, which straddled the boundary between the city and county, were named Eastgate and Westgate and are the sources of the two street names. The amusement park, known as Delmar Gardens, operated the roller coaster in this picture, along with a variety of restaurants and open air dance halls. (Photo Courtesy of the Archives of the University City Public Library.)

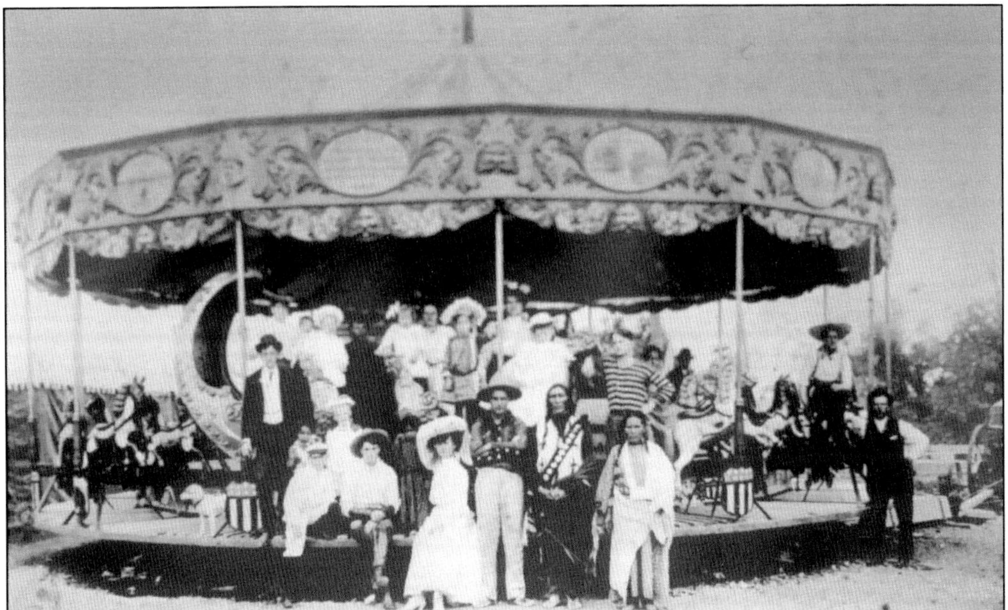

The amusement park's theater attracted a large number of well-known performers such as the ones in this picture from the Buffalo Bill Road Show. (Photo Courtesy of the Archives of the University City Public Library.)

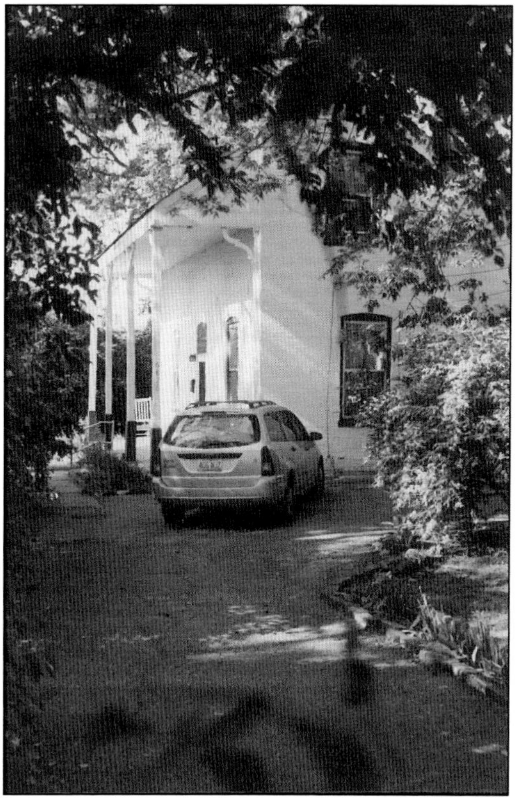

The ravages of time have taken their toll on many of the landmarks that once served the area we know as University City but, fortunately, a few of them still exist. For example, the Sutter-Meyer House (pictured on the left) was built in 1850 and is reported to be the oldest residence in University City. The house is located at 6826 Chamberlain Court. Other surviving notable landmarks include five Jewish Cemeteries: the United Hebrew Cemetery at 7701-7855 Canton, purchased in 1855; B'nai Amoona Cemetery (pictured below) at 848 and 930 North and South, purchased in 1871; Chesed Shel Emeth Cemetery at 7570 Olive, purchased in 1922; and Ohave Sholom Cemetery at 7410 Olive, purchased in 1949. (Photos by John A. Wright.)

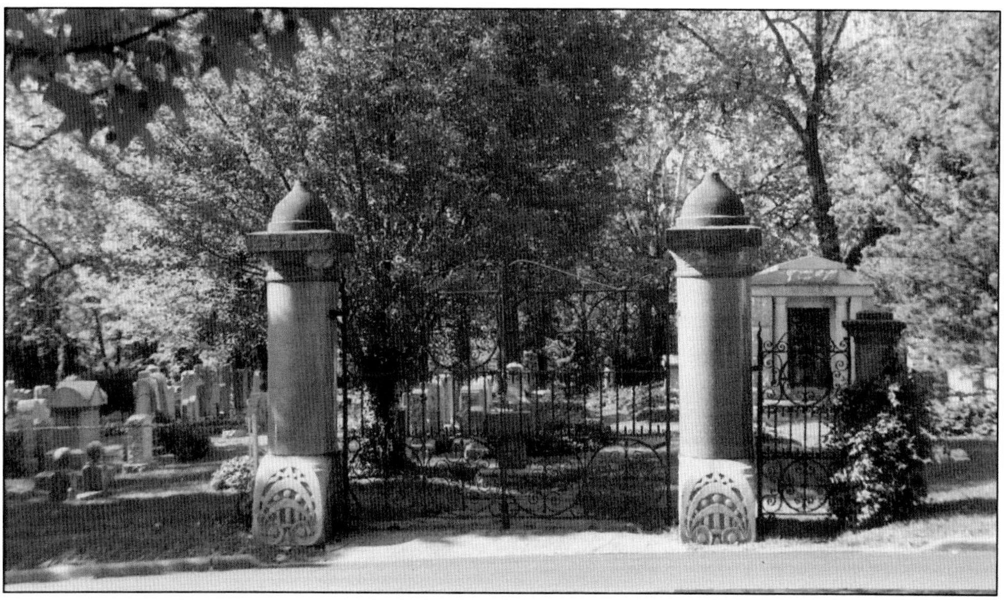

Two

THE MAKING OF A CITY

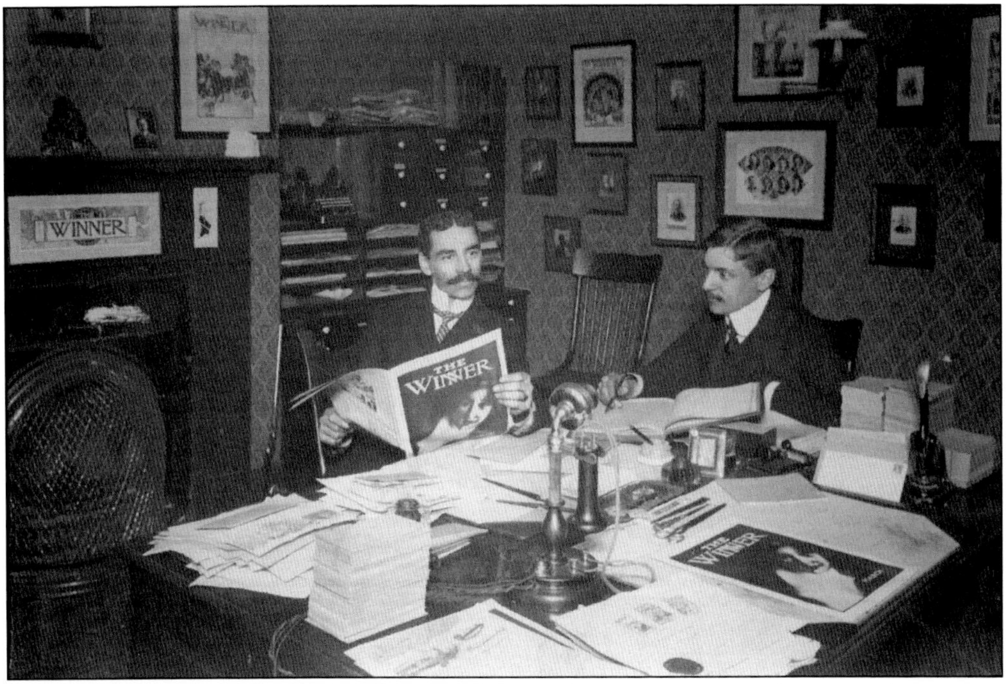

In 1899, Edward G. Lewis, the son, grandson, and great-grandson of Episcopal ministers, purchased a cheap, popular magazine named the *The Winner*. He reduced subscription rates, lowered advertising rates and targeted female readers by changing the magazine's name to *Woman's Magazine*. After a short period of time the publication had one of the largest circulations of any magazine in the country.

The needs of Lewis' publishing company soon outgrew its rented facilities in downtown St. Louis, making a larger facility a necessity. Lewis' ideas and dreams led him to build a publishing plant with a residential district surrounding his offices, which he would eventually incorporate into a city and serve as its first mayor. (Photo Courtesy of the Archives of the University City Public Library.)

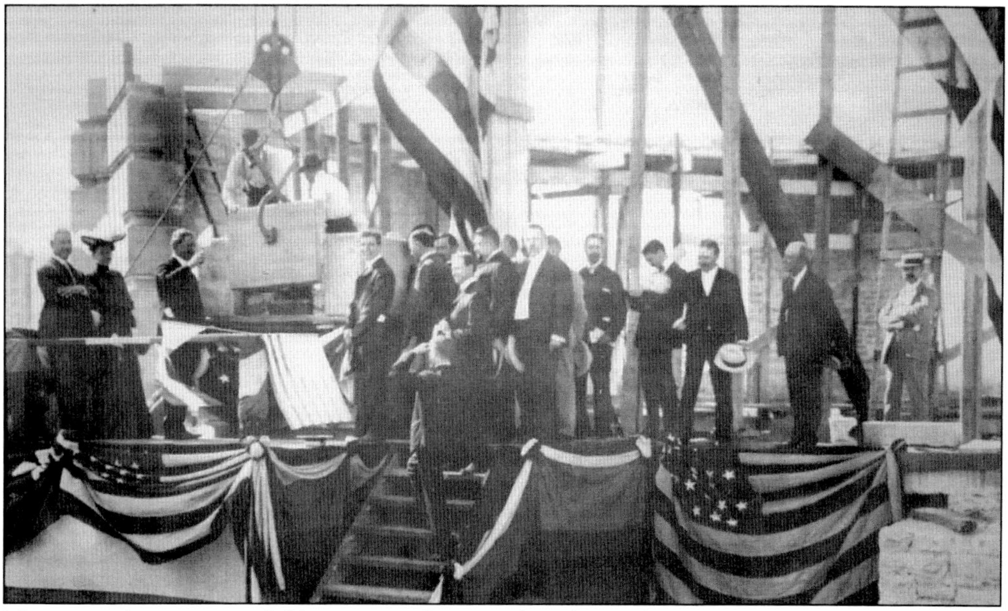

The very beginning of University City is found in the incorporation of the Lewis Publishing Company and was coincidental with the building of the World's Fair of 1904. Governor D.R. Francis, president of the Louisiana Purchase Exposition, is seen here at the laying of the cornerstone of Lewis' new publishing headquarters on August 28, 1903. (Photo Courtesy of the Archives of the University City Public Library.)

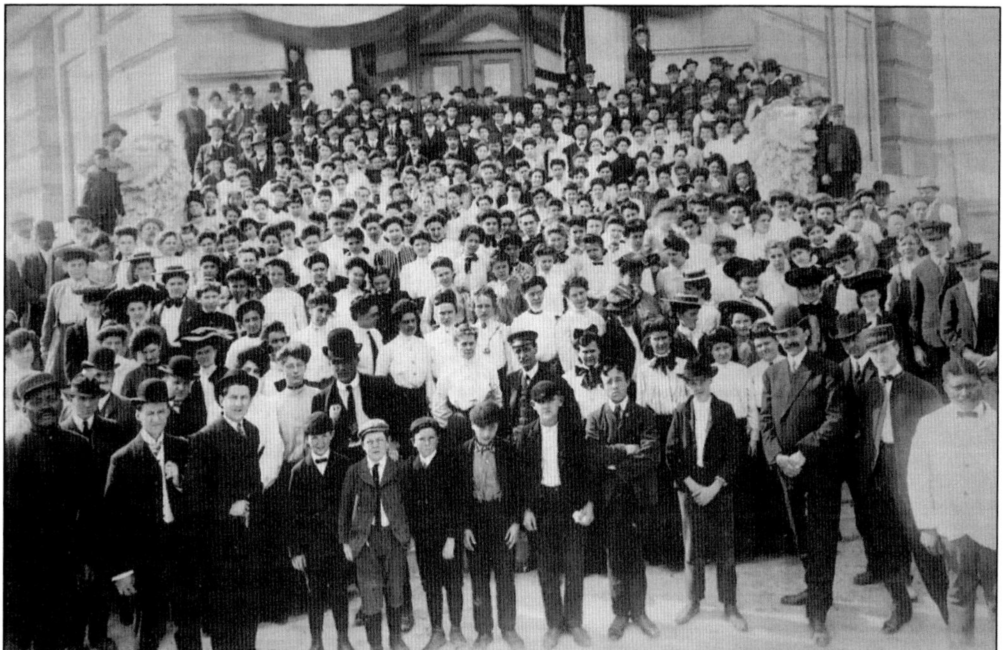

It took nearly two years to complete the buildings of the Lewis Publishing complex. They were finished in time, however, for the opening of the World's Fair in 1904. Once completed, Lewis hired the above staff to support his efforts. (Photo Courtesy of the Archives of the University City Public Library.)

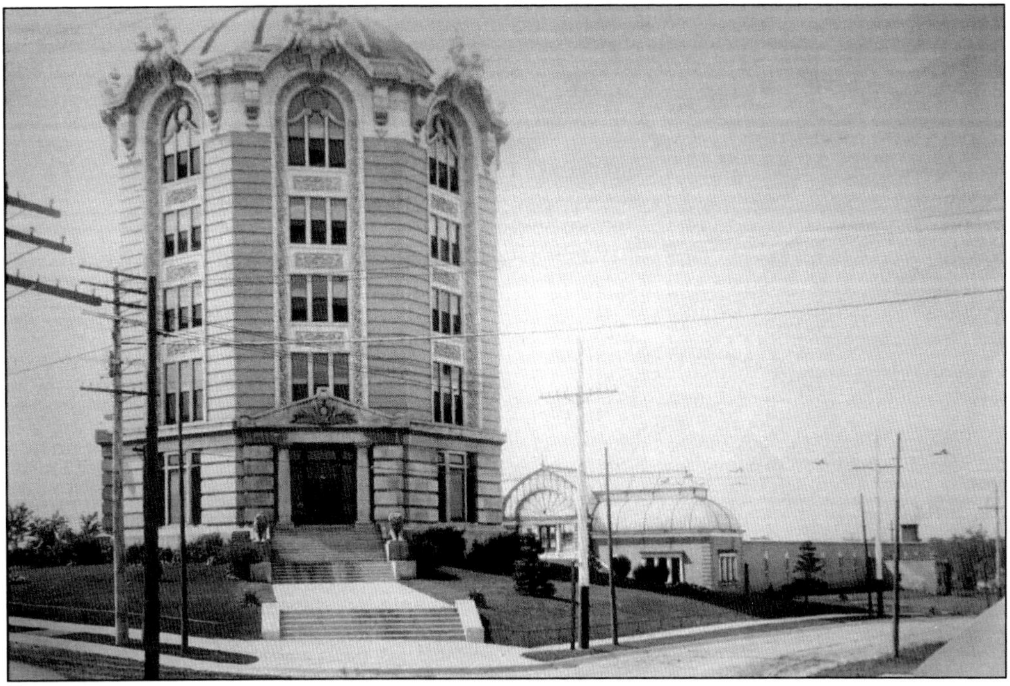

Lewis' octagonal tower office building, which now serves as City Hall, stands 135 feet tall and 85 feet in diameter. This gray building, of rustic limestone and brick, was trimmed with elaborate terra cotta molding and sculptures decorating the top. (Photo Courtesy of the Archives of the Historical Society of University.)

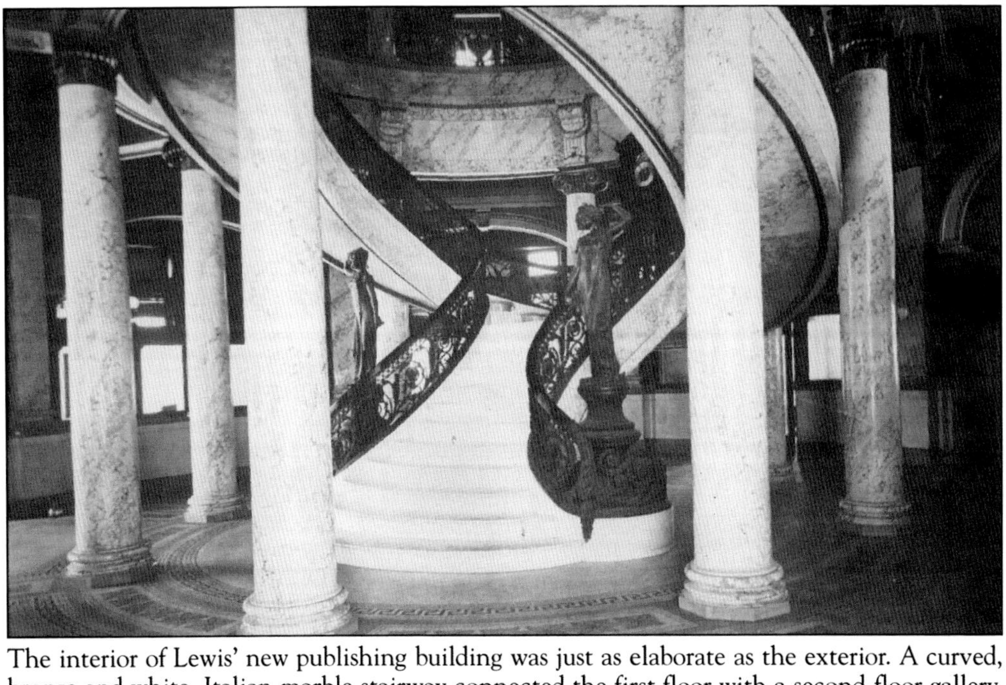

The interior of Lewis' new publishing building was just as elaborate as the exterior. A curved, bronze and white, Italian-marble stairway connected the first floor with a second-floor gallery. (Photo Courtesy of the Archives of the University City Public Library.)

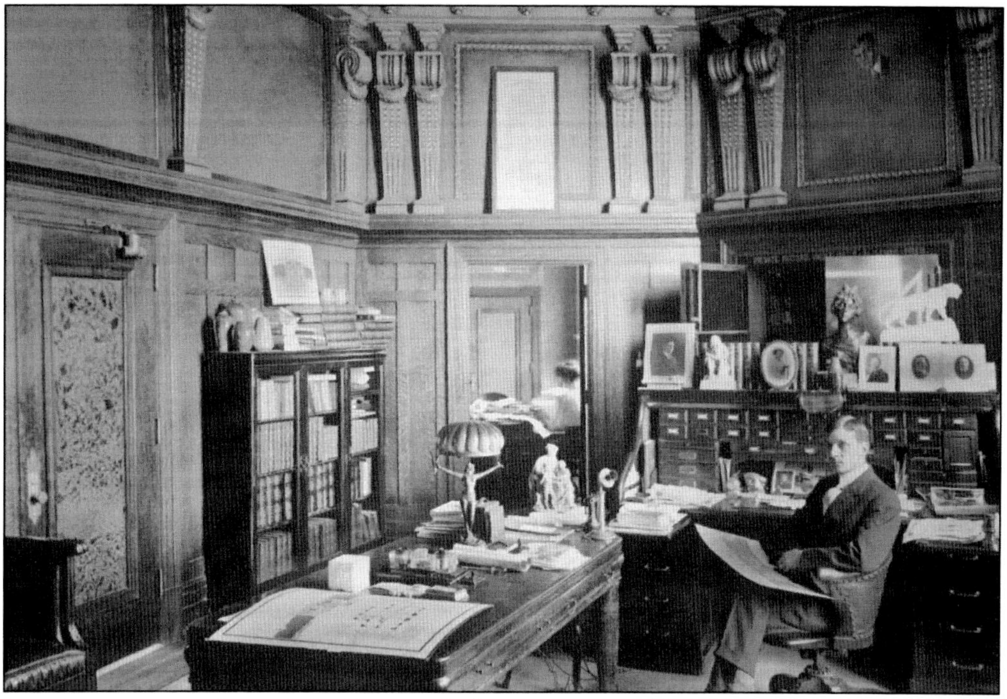

Lewis' private, wood-paneled office was befitting a successful publisher. Lewis is seen here sitting under his portrait. Most of the *Woman's National Daily* editorials, another publication by Lewis, were penned upon the old red mahogany roll-top desk. Lewis preferred this room over his "sanctum" in the Woman's National Daily Building. (Photo Courtesy of the Archives of the University City Public Library.)

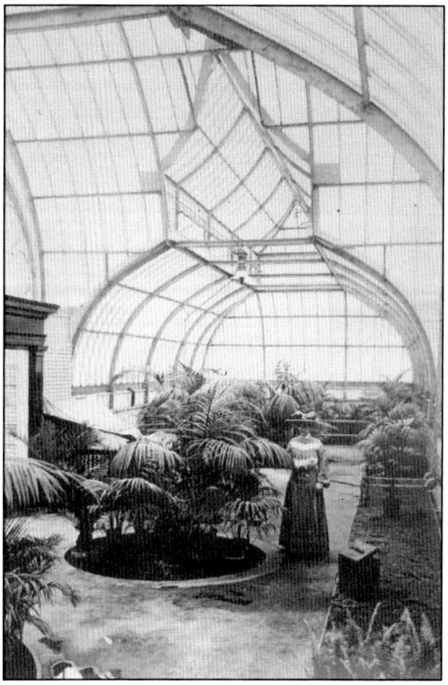

Lewis constructed this lovely conservatory at the entrance to his printing plant. (Photo Courtesy of the Archives of the University City Public Library.)

Lewis had the world's largest searchlight installed on top of his office building. It is rumored that Lewis procured it from the Czar of Russia, who had ordered it for use during the Crimean War, but it was never delivered. Cradled within a specially-designed elevator system, this 16,000-watt beacon illuminated the sky at the opening of the World's Fair and each night thereafter. (Photo Courtesy of the Archives of the University City Public Library.)

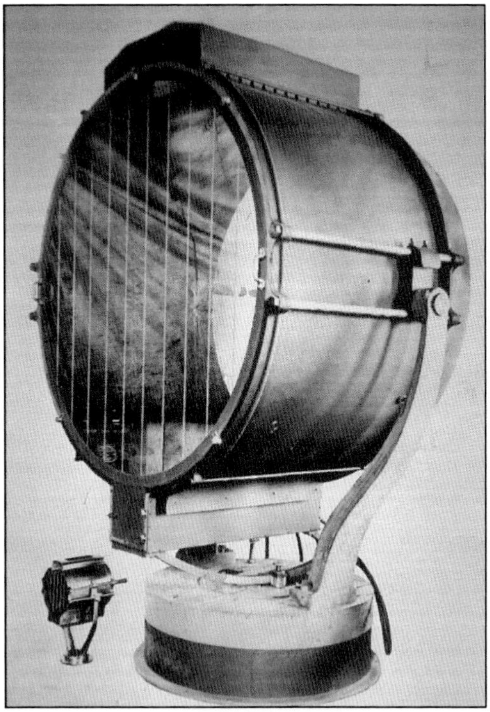

The powerful, 7-foot-beam searchlight atop the publishing company office was used to attract large numbers of curious Fair visitors who followed the light to its source. When they arrived at Lewis' office they were invited to tour the facilities and almost all left with a magazine subscription. (Photo Courtesy of the Archives of the University City Public Library.)

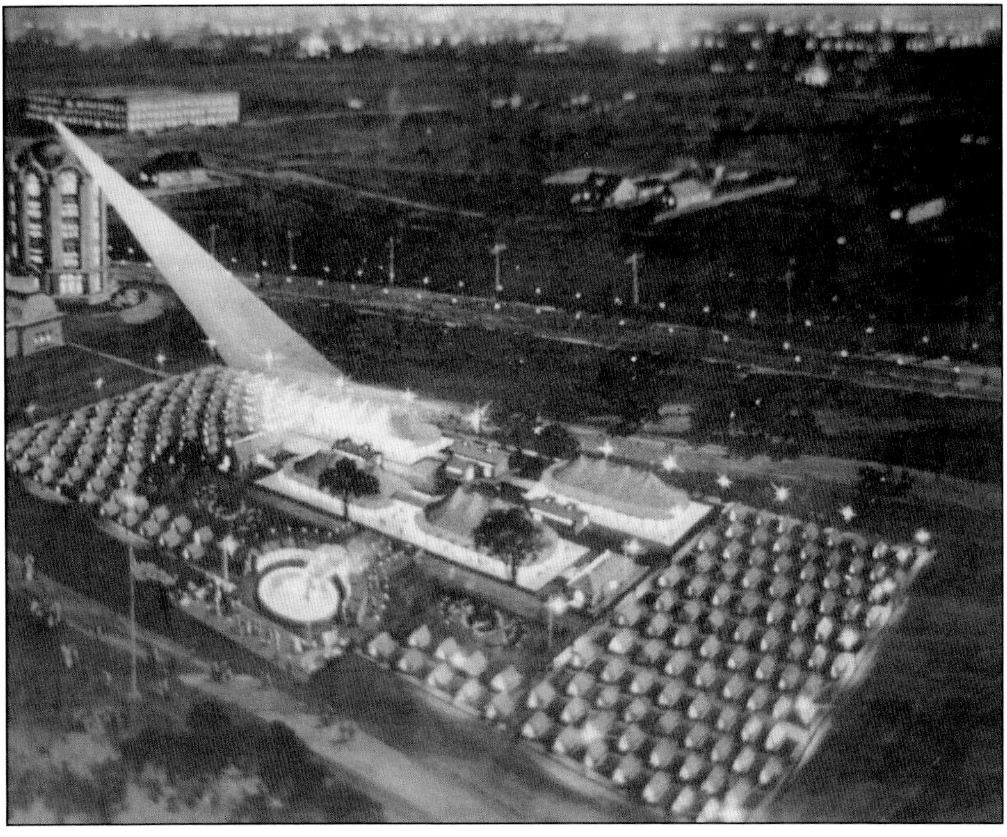

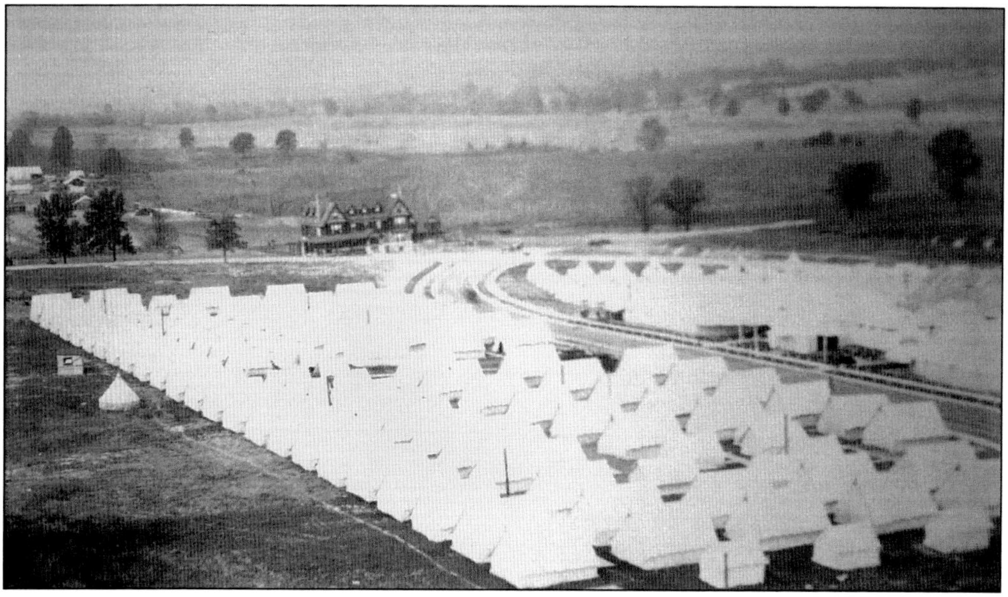

On the land designated for Lewis' real estate development, he had a tent city set up and named it Camp Lewis. The camp provided housing for Fair visitors for 50¢ per night, per person. Lewis wanted to use the funds from the venture to help develop the area. He set up approximately 400 small, white tents with board floors, chairs, electric lights, and iron beds with springs and comfortable mattresses. (Photo Courtesy of the Archives of the University City Public Library.)

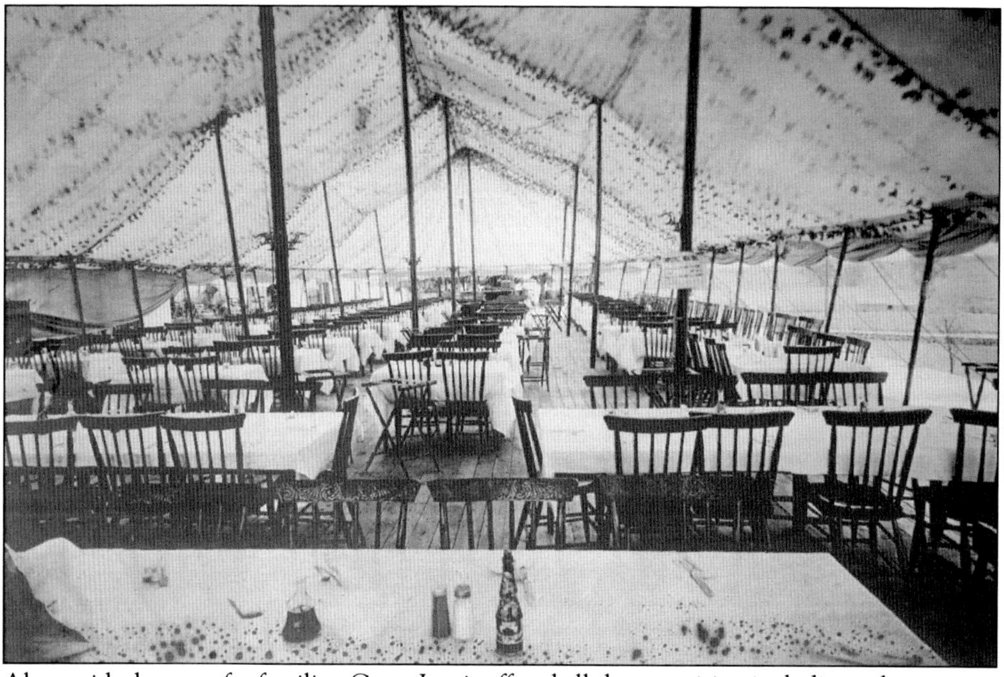

Along with the tents for families, Camp Lewis offered all the amenities, including a dining tent, nursery, barber shop, reading rooms, recreational tents, post office, hospital, and showers. A fully-staffed nursery tent was also available. (Photo Courtesy of the Archives of the Historical Society of University City.)

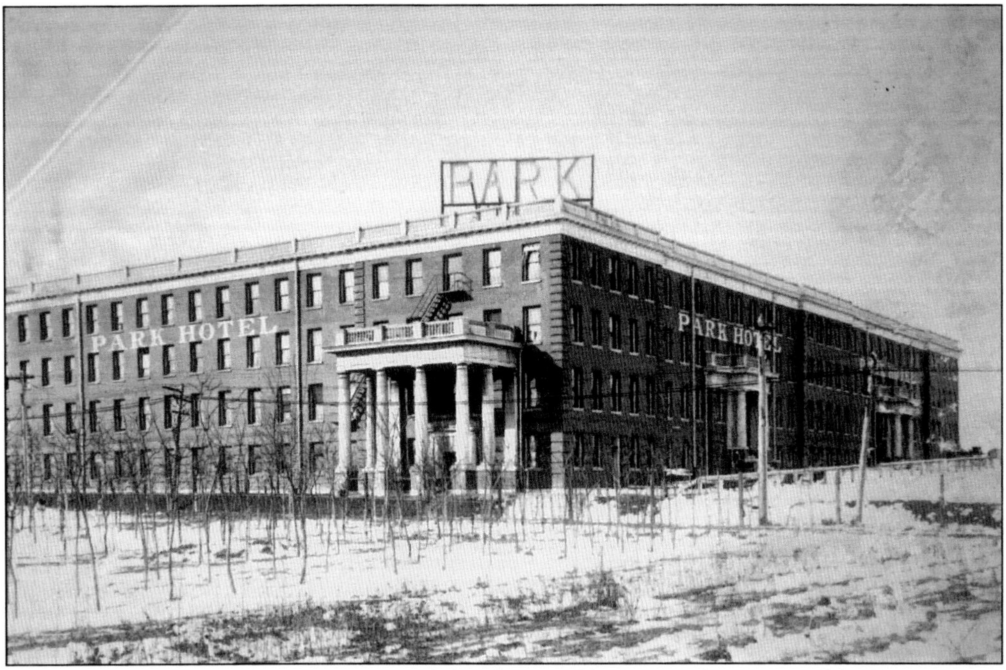

The nearby Park Hotel was constructed for the World's Fair and patronized by Fair visitors. After the Fair, the building became a residential hotel and after 1914, it was purchased by the Christian Old People's Home. In 1977, the building was converted to the Greenway Apartments for Washington University students. (Photo Courtesy of the Archives of the University City Public Library.)

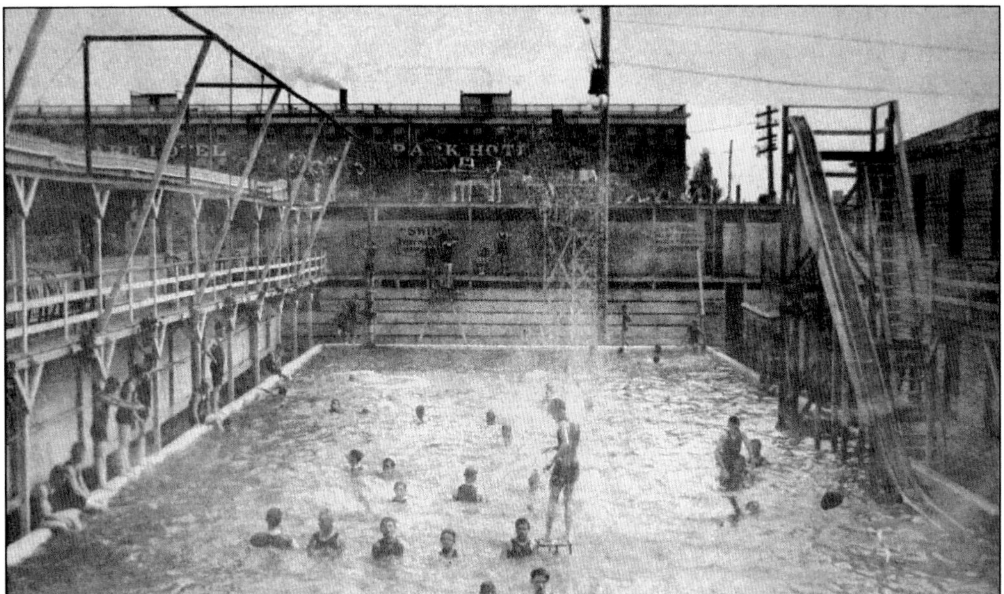

The area swimming pool on Delmar near Commerce Bank, in the early 1900s, served as a refreshing place for area residents and visitors to enjoy during the hot summer days. (Photo Courtesy of the Archives of the Historical Society of University City.)

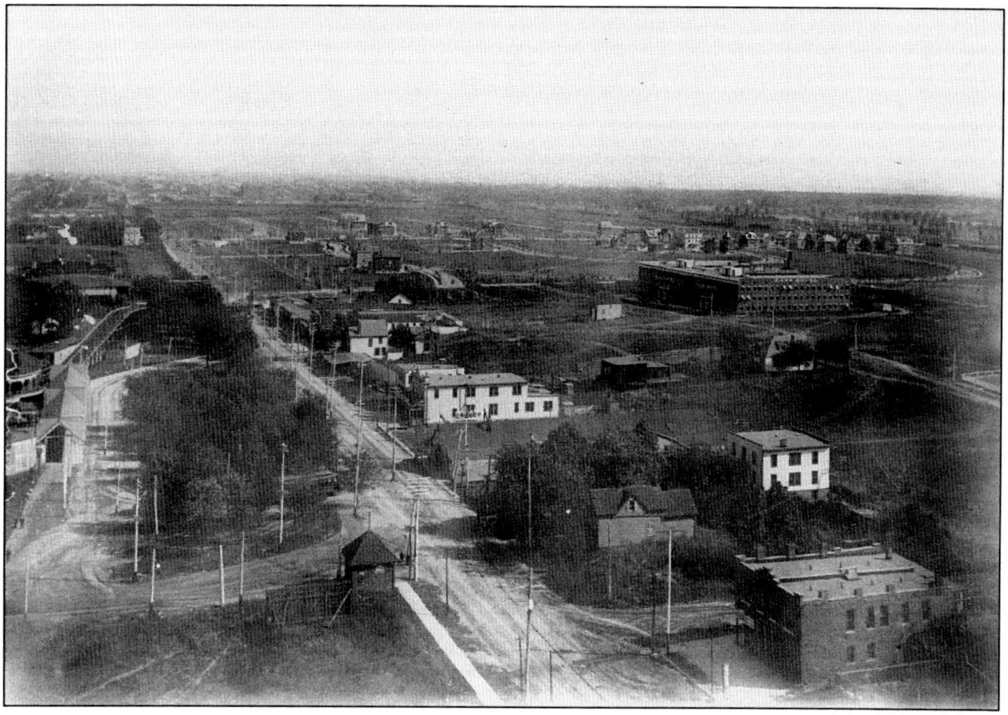

Area residents and visitors used the streetcar to take them to the Race Track, Delmar Gardens, and the Lewis Publishing Company. When the car reached Heman Avenue it turned north to Enright Avenue, then south on Kingsland Avenue and back to Delmar Boulevard. This area became known as "the Loop," and although the streetcar and the tracks were taken away long ago, the area still retains the name. (Top Photo Courtesy of the Mercantile Library. Bottom Photo Courtesy of the Archives of the University City Public Library.)

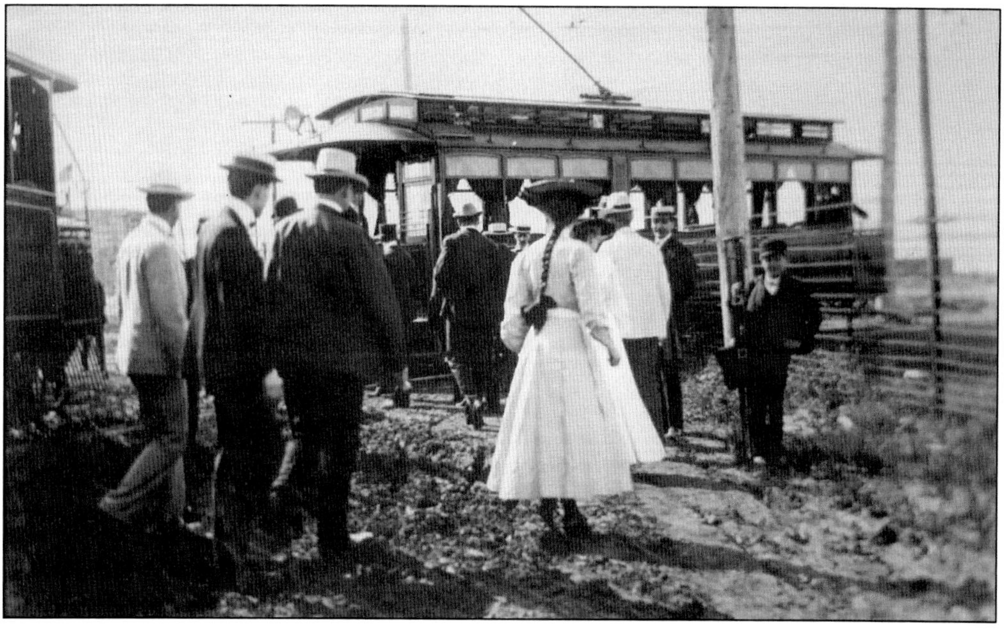

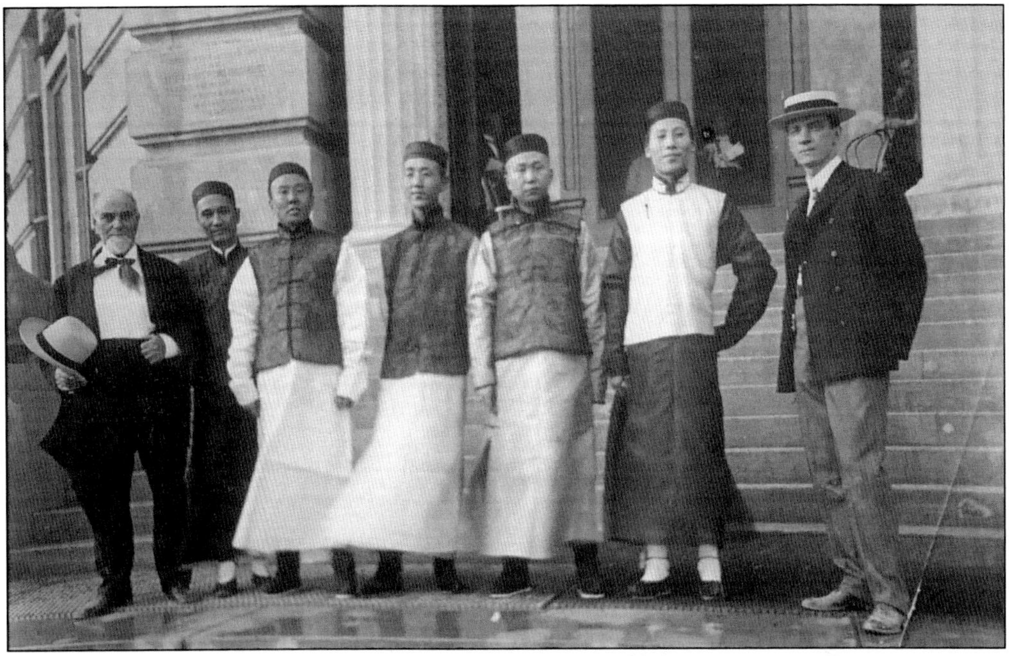

The World's Fair was closed on Sundays—but not Lewis' Publishing Company. Fair visitors came to the plant for tours and at the same time had their pictures taken, subscribed to magazines, and entered contests. Pictured here are Chinese World's Fair Commissioners in front of the headquarters with Lewis. (Photo Courtesy of the Archives of the University City Public Library.)

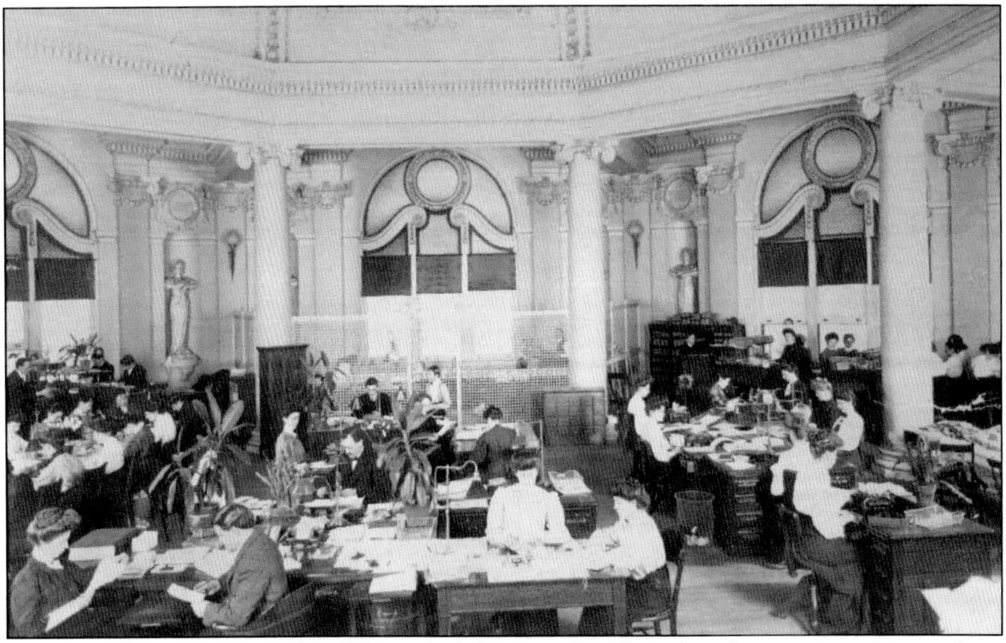

Once inside, visitors to the Woman's Magazine Building found an impressive working staff handling the company's mail from its million plus subscribers. These workers were photographed on the top floor of the office building, which is now the City Council Chambers. (Photo Courtesy of the Archives of the University City Public Library.)

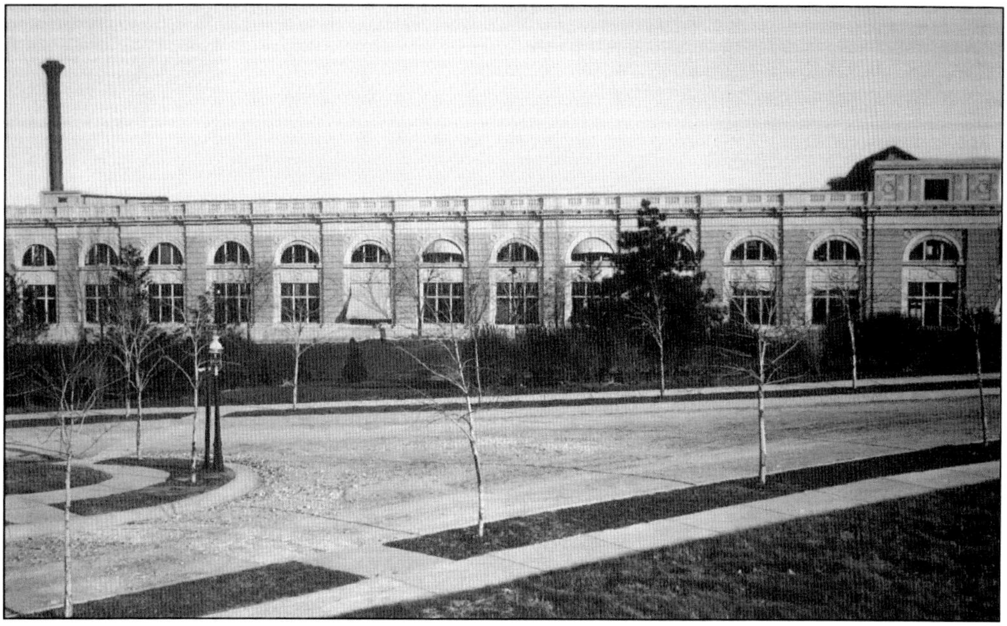

This plant housed the printing press for the *Woman's Magazine*. The magazine held claim to the greatest circulation of any publication in the world—1,600,000 copies each issue. The magazine's nearest competitor, the *Ladies' Home Journal*, at the time, could claim less than half that number. Part of this building now serves as the headquarters for University City's Fire and Police Departments. (Photo Courtesy of the Archives of the University City Public Library.)

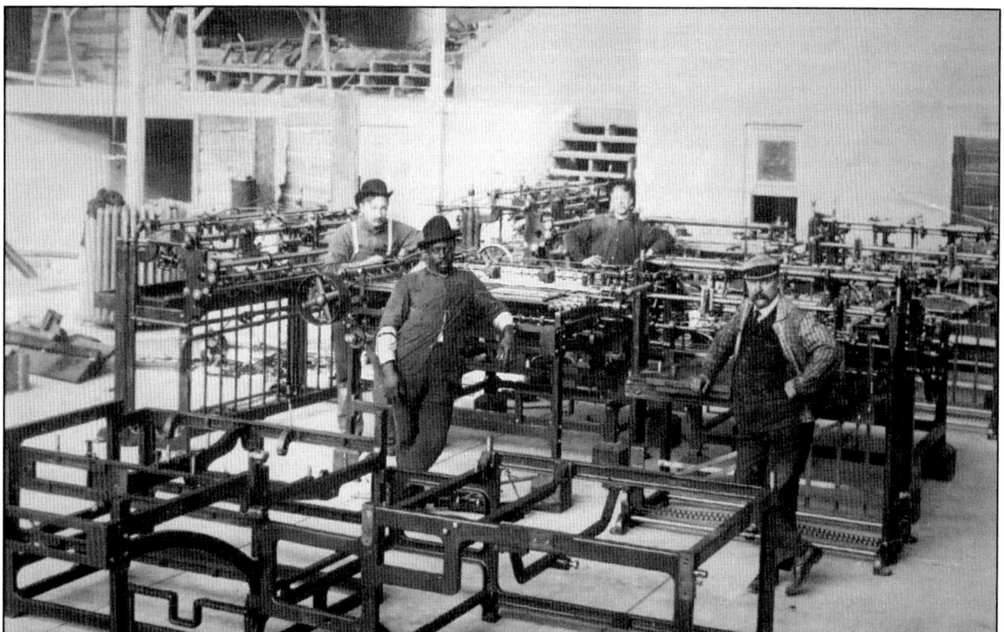

Although Lewis' community was restricted to "those of the Caucasian race," African Americans were allowed to work in homes and in his plant, as can be seen in this photo. (Photo Courtesy of the Archives of the University City Public Library.)

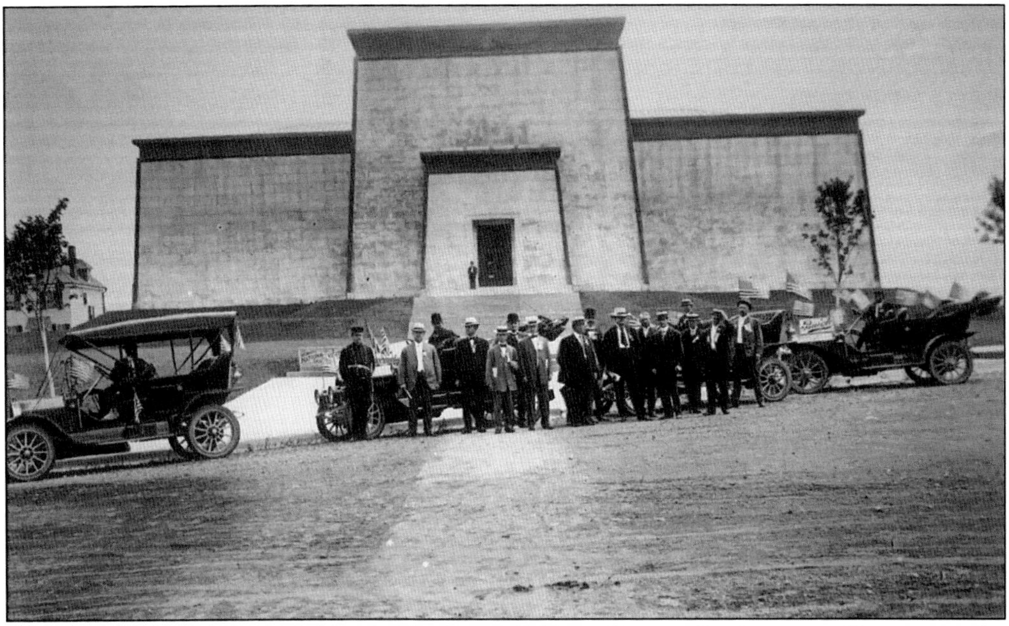

Early in 1904, Lewis began plans for the People's United States Bank, reportedly to serve the many rural people unable to have access to the normal banking services. Lewis' goal was to use the bank's assets to further his real estate development. To house his bank Lewis designed the Egyptian-style building pictured here. It is reported that the building was a likeness of the temple at Karnak on the Nile River. (Photo Courtesy of the Archives of the University City Public Library.)

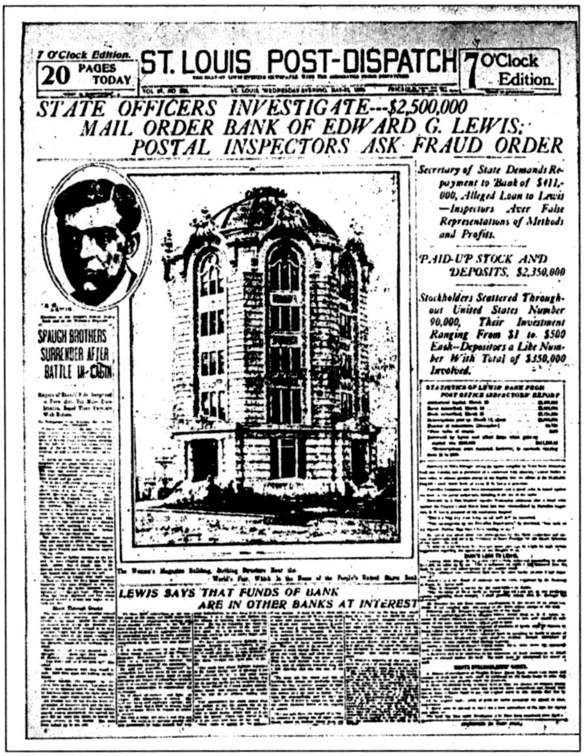

7 O'Clock Edition.

20 PAGES TODAY

ST. LOUIS POST-DISPATCH

7 O'Clock Edition.

STATE OFFICERS INVESTIGATE---$2,500,000 MAIL ORDER BANK OF EDWARD G. LEWIS; POSTAL INSPECTORS ASK FRAUD ORDER

Secretary of State Demands Repayment to 'Bank of $411,000, Alleged Loan to Lewis—Inspectors Aver False Representations of Methods and Profits.

PAID-UP STOCK AND DEPOSITS, $2,350,000

Stockholders Scattered Throughout United States Number 90,000, Their Investment Ranging From $1 to $500 Each—Depositors a Like Number With Total of $350,000 Involved.

SPAUGH BROTHERS SURRENDER AFTER BATTLE IN CABIN

LEWIS SAYS THAT FUNDS OF BANK ARE IN OTHER BANKS AT INTEREST

In 1905 , Missouri's secretary of state ordered the restrictions on the People's United States Bank's Board and a reduction of its investments in Lewis' real estate. In less than a month, the institution was placed in receivership after the postmaster general found what he believed was some fraudulent practices occurring. Lewis then redesigned the building to house the publishing plant of the *Woman's National Daily*. (Article Courtesy of the Archives of the University City Public Library, from *The Siege of University City*.)

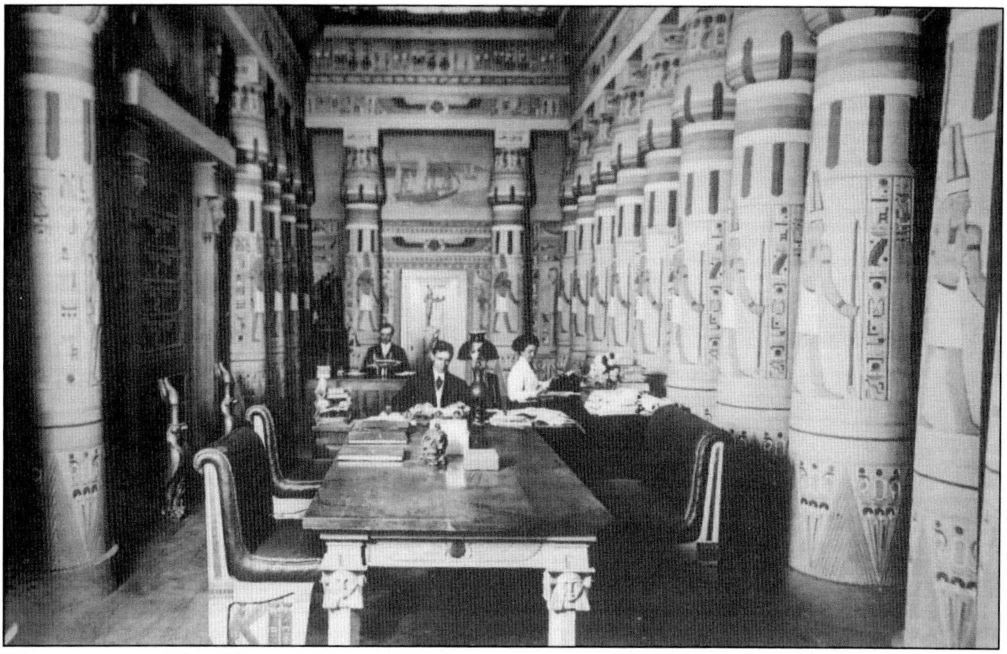

The sanctum of the *Woman's National Daily*, north pylon of the Egyptian Building, is pictured here with George W. Stearns, managing editor-in-charge. The staff traveled from the Egyptian Building to the Octagon Building through a tunnel under Delmar. (Photo Courtesy of the Archives of the University City Public Library.)

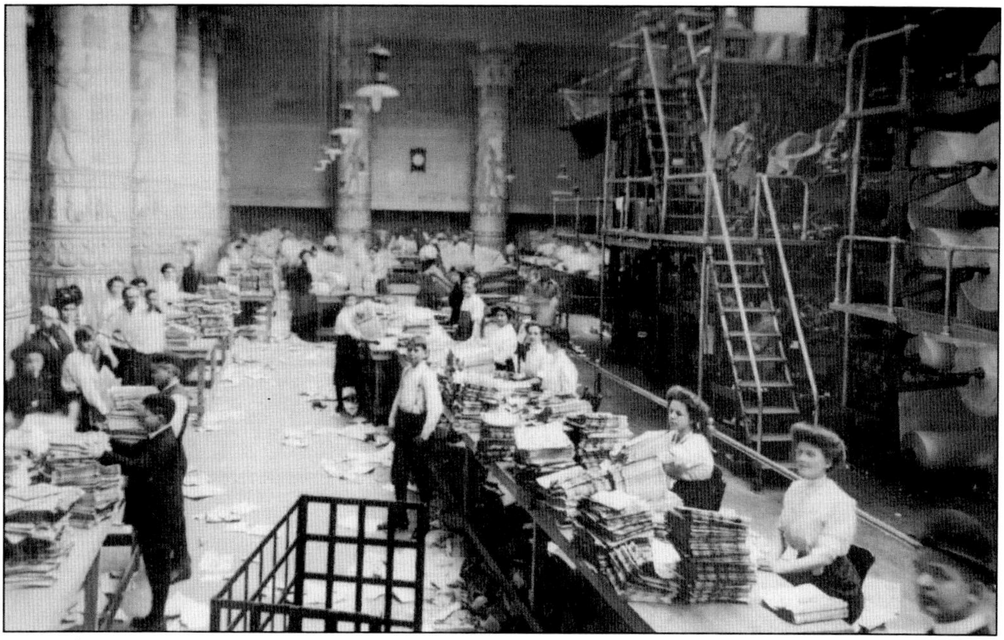

Lewis' $100,000 printing press, reported to have been the largest in the world, is pictured in the background. The press reputedly printed papers at the rate of 83 plus per second, or 5,000 per minute. The first issue of Lewis' *Woman's National Daily* had over 600,000 subscribers. (Photo Courtesy of the Archives of the University City Public Library.)

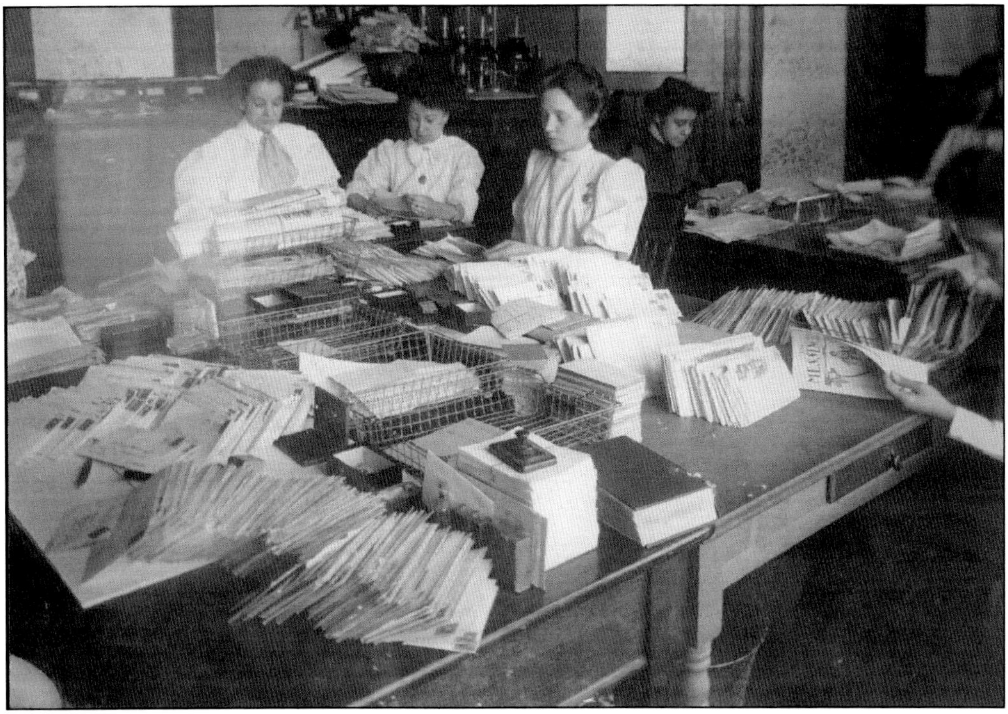

Lewis' Publishing Company received large quantities of mail daily. According to Lewis, for a long period of time, one-sixth of the total mail of the City of St. Louis originated from his buildings. (Photo Courtesy of the Archives of the University City Public Library.)

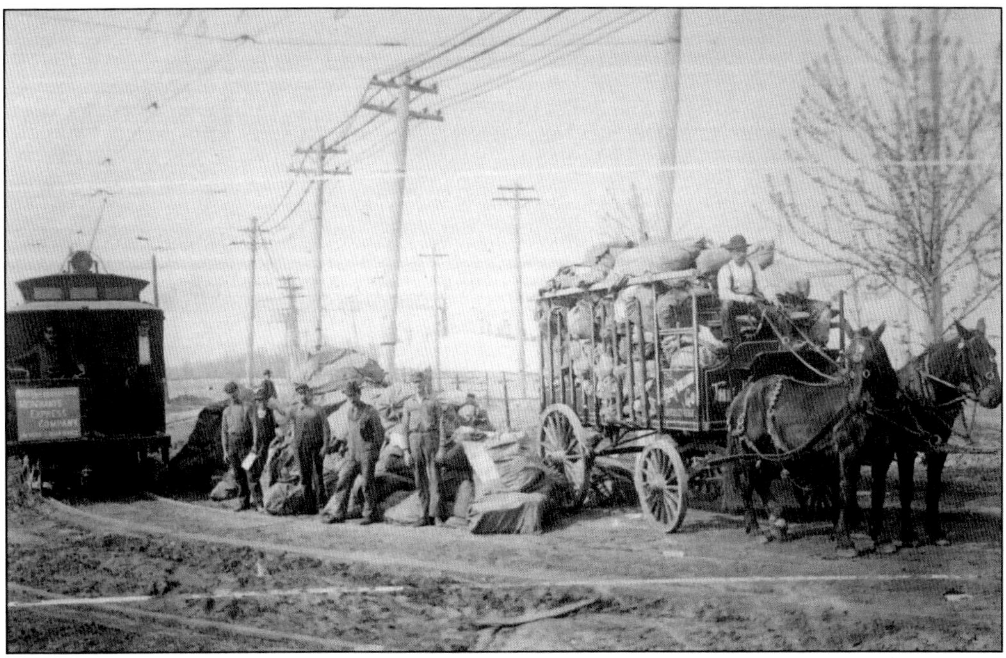

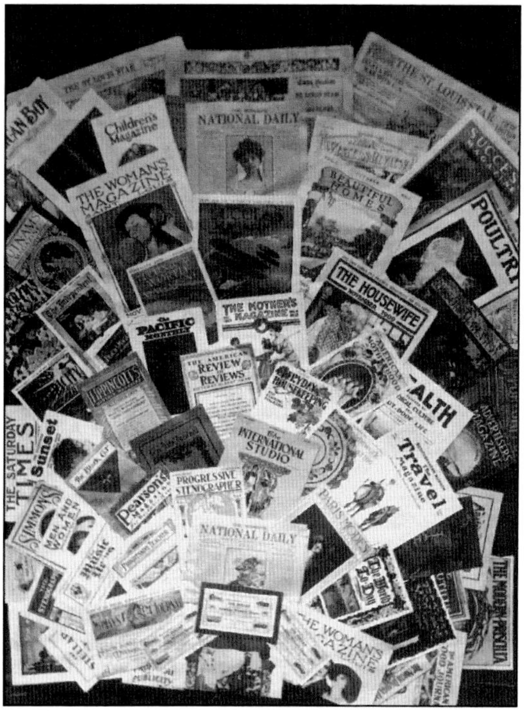

For many years daily, weekly, and monthly journals were published from Lewis' company and were reported to be in one of every five homes in the United States and Canada. For several years a standing offer of $100 was available to any person in the United States or Canada who could find a post office where 50 or more persons received their mail, which did not include at least one bona fide subscriber to one of Lewis' journals. (Photo Courtesy of the Archives of the University City Public Library.)

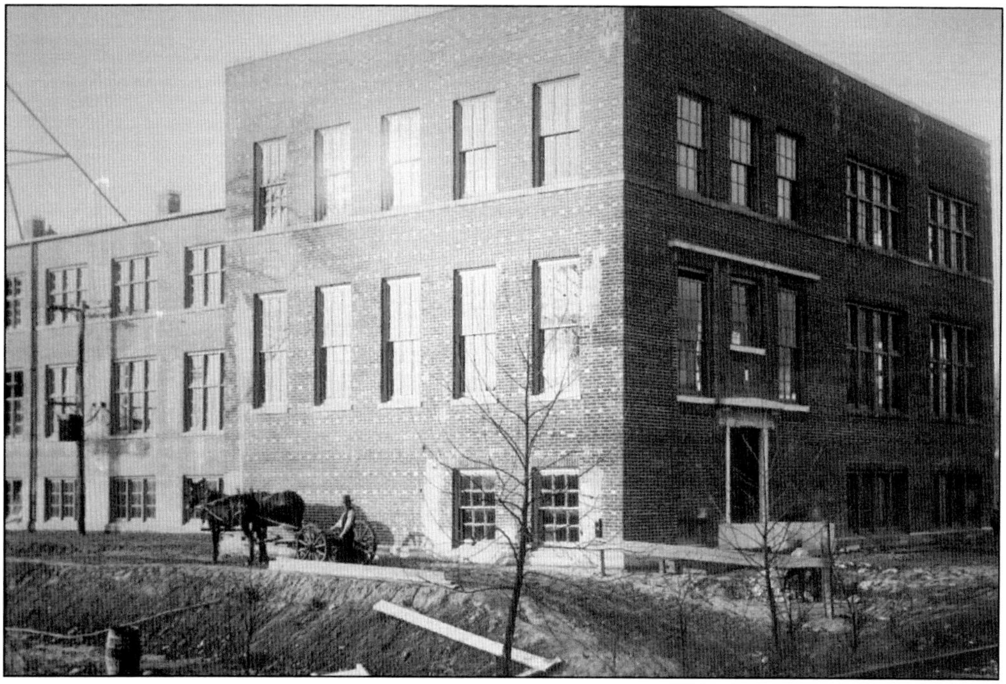

Because of the large amount of paper generated by Lewis' Publishing Company, he organized the United States Fiber Stopper Company at Kingsland and Vernon Avenues. He used a trolley line to transport the waste paper from his publishing plant to the Fiber Stopper building shown here. A flaw was found in the product and Lewis was forced to cancel contracts and buy back stock. (Photo Courtesy of the Archives of the University City Public Library.)

E.G. Lewis is pictured here with his wife, Mabel Gertrude Wellington Lewis, whom he married in 1892 in Baltimore, Maryland. She was his partner and closest companion, and very active in feminist causes such as the Women's Suffrage Movement. (Photo Courtesy of the Archives of the University City Public Library)

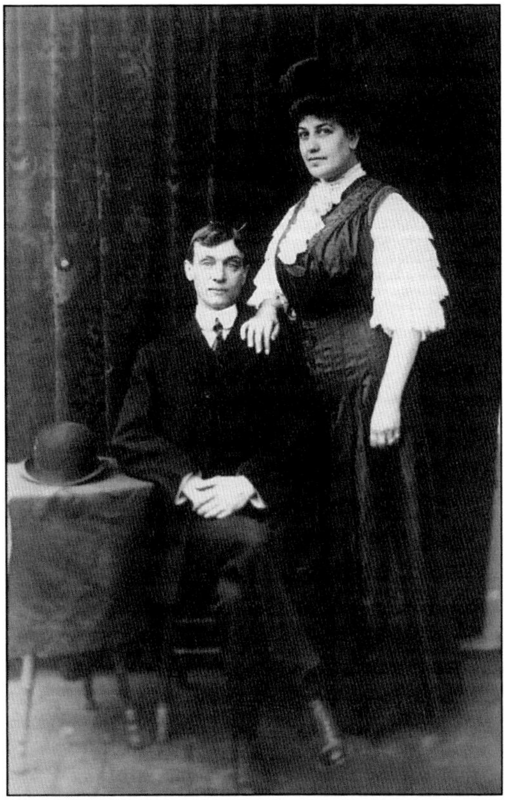

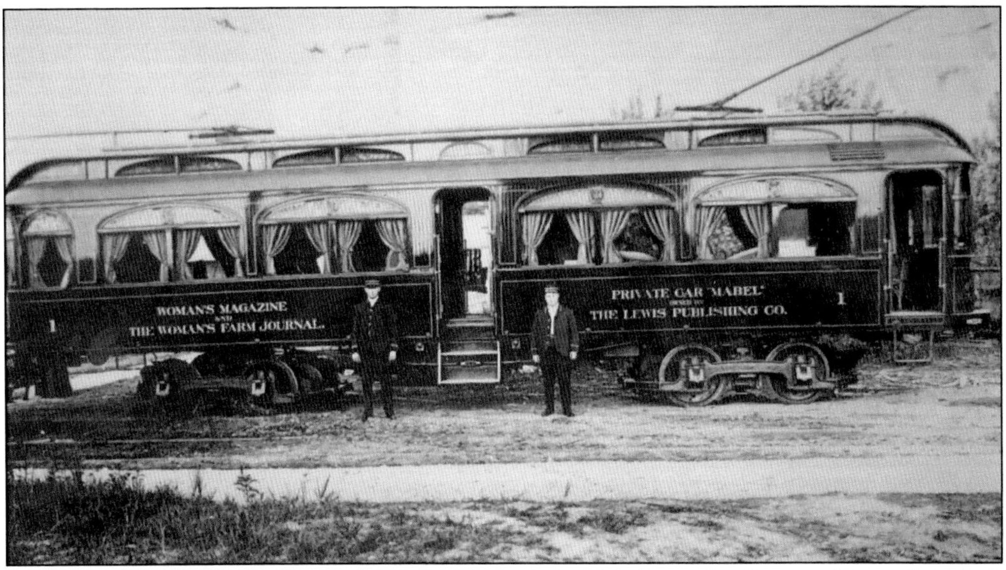

"Private Car Mabel," pictured here, was constructed by E.G. Lewis for the use of his wife Mabel. It had two sections—a buffet and a parlor. A pea-green Empire ceiling with carved and inlaid woods that stretched the length of the car. The carpets of both sections matched the ceiling, and in the center of the parlor compartment was a handsomely-carved and upholstered settee. The upholstery was of a light yellow fabric. (Photo Courtesy of the Archives of the University City Public Library.)

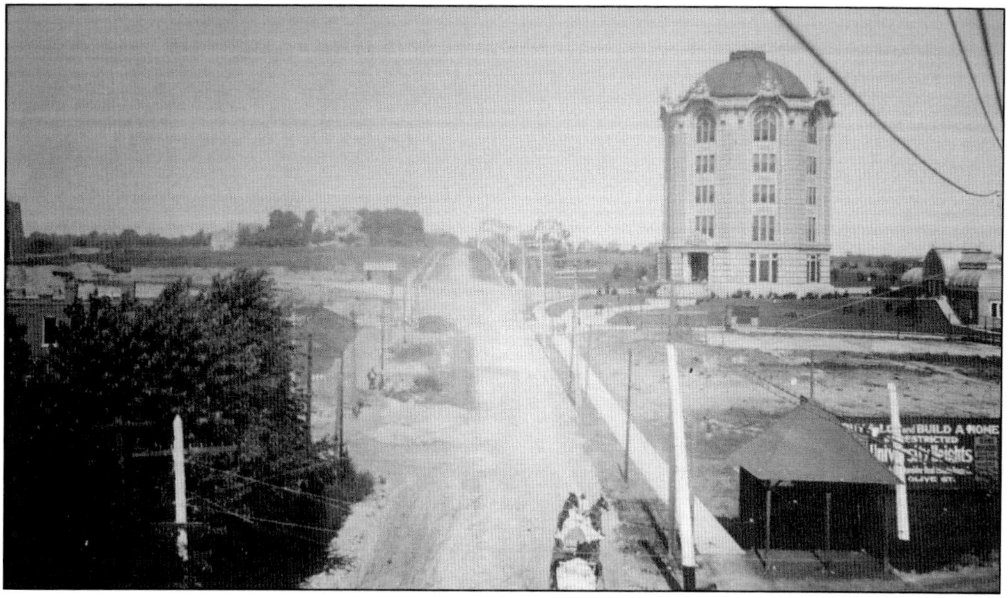

Lewis planned seven different subdivisions along Delmar—University Heights One through Seven—each with a distinctive street layout. Because of his business difficulties and early departure in 1912, he only brought University Heights into being. This picture of Delmar looking west was taken around 1904. (Photo Courtesy of the Archives of the University City Public Library.)

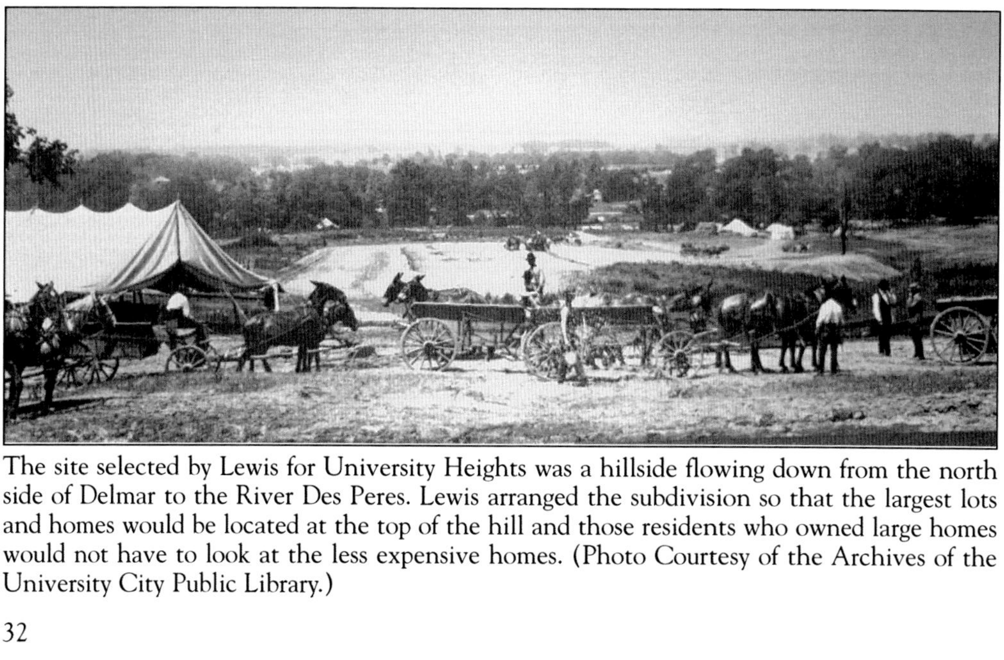

The site selected by Lewis for University Heights was a hillside flowing down from the north side of Delmar to the River Des Peres. Lewis arranged the subdivision so that the largest lots and homes would be located at the top of the hill and those residents who owned large homes would not have to look at the less expensive homes. (Photo Courtesy of the Archives of the University City Public Library.)

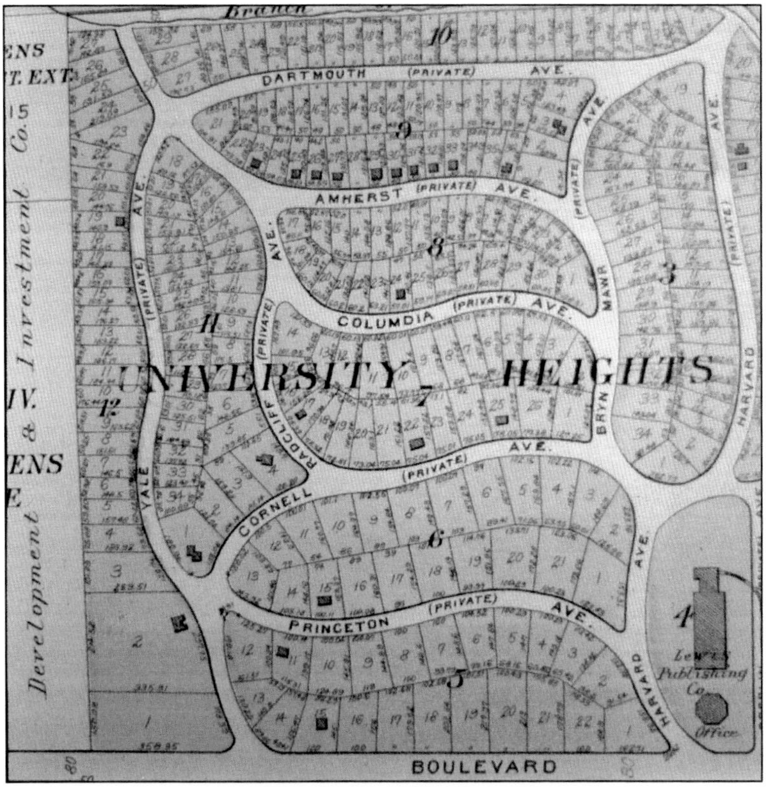

Residential planner Julius Pitzman, who designed University Heights for Lewis, avoided the rectangular grid pattern by adjusting the streets to the topography. Lewis provided for a variety of incomes in University Heights, though street design and deed restrictions were placed on cost. A minimum cost of $6,000 was required on homes located at the top of the hill; $1,500 for those at the bottom. (Photo Courtesy of the Archives of the University City Public Library.)

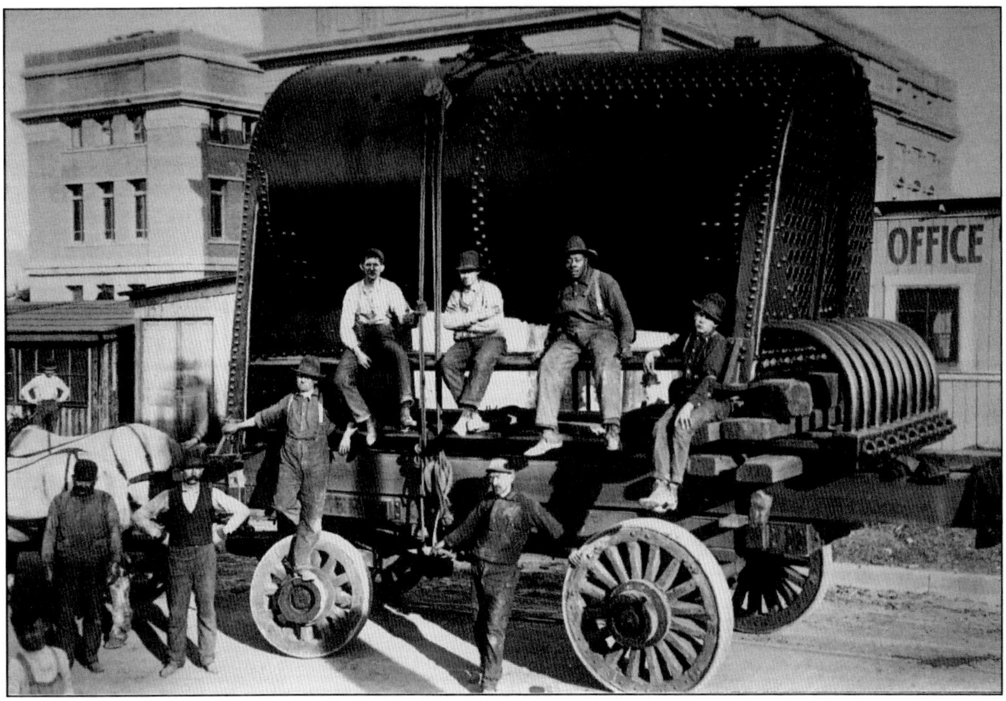

Workers pose outside the University Heights sales office. (Photo Courtesy of the Archives of the University City Public Library.)

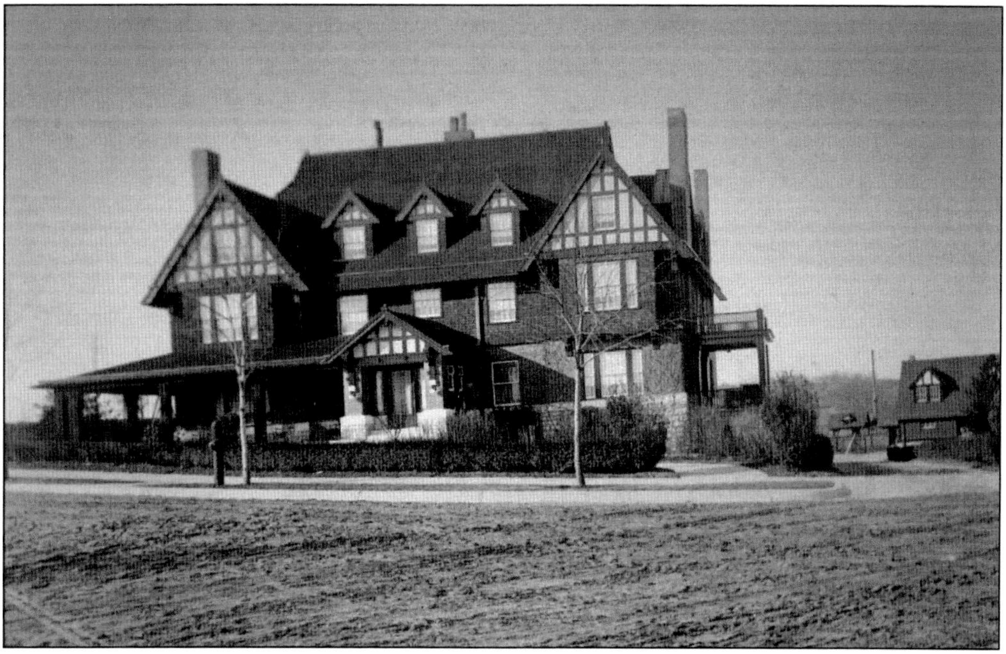

Lewis built this elegant, 28-room Tudor Revival house on Yale Avenue where it intersects with Delmar. Reportedly, the house, once completed, was said to have cost $26,000. The site included a greenhouse, stable, and a chicken shed on the west side of the lot. A large part of this site is now known as Lewis Park. (Photo Courtesy of the Archives of the University City Public Library.)

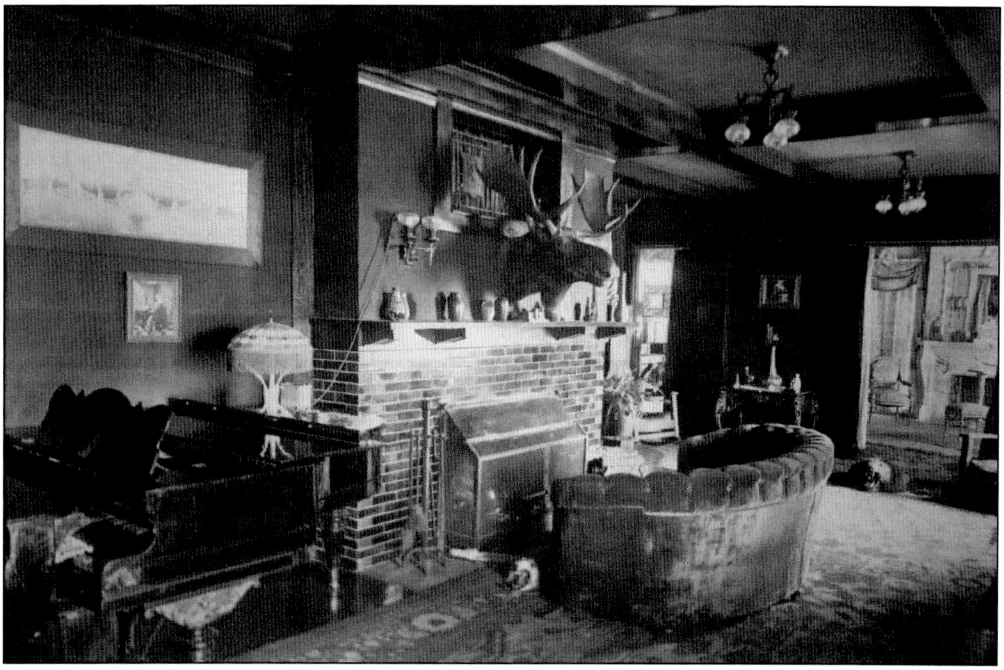

The entrance hall and living room of the Lewis' home was just as impressive as the exterior. A glimpse of the drawing room can be seen adjacent to the living room on the right. (Photo Courtesy of the Archives of the University City Public Library.)

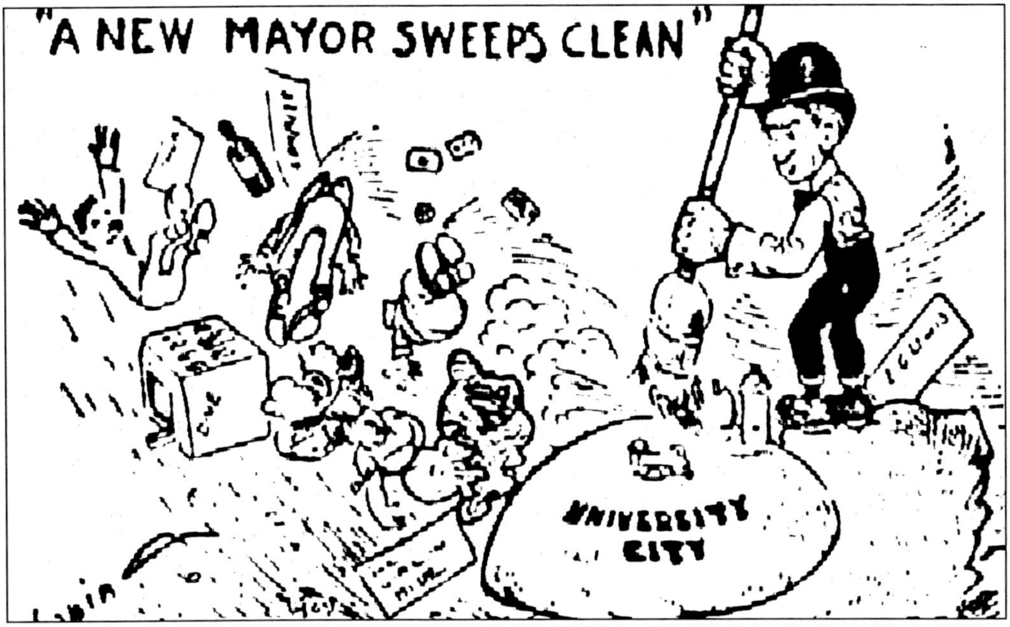

On September 4, 1906, Lewis took steps to help fulfill his dream: He presented a petition to the County Court signed by residents of the area for the incorporation of University City. The petition was granted and Lewis became the city's first mayor. The city's name was inspired by the area's proximity to Washington University. It was Lewis' hope that the city would become a center of learning and culture. Lewis felt incorporation would give him the influence he wanted over the undesirables in the community. (Document Courtesy of the Archives of the University City Public Library.)

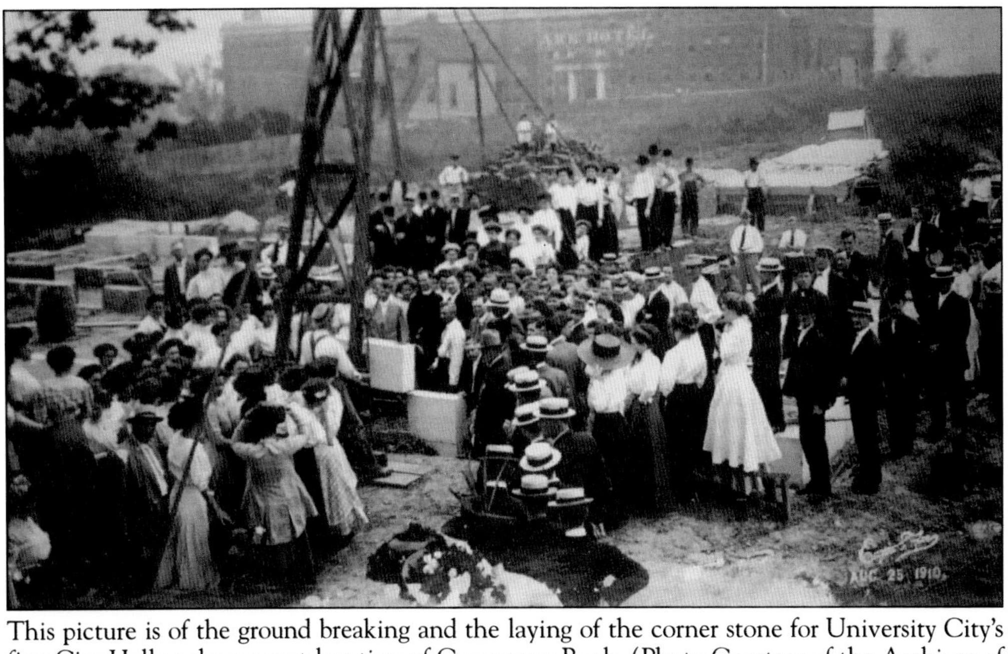

This picture is of the ground breaking and the laying of the corner stone for University City's first City Hall at the present location of Commerce Bank. (Photo Courtesy of the Archives of the University City Public Library.)

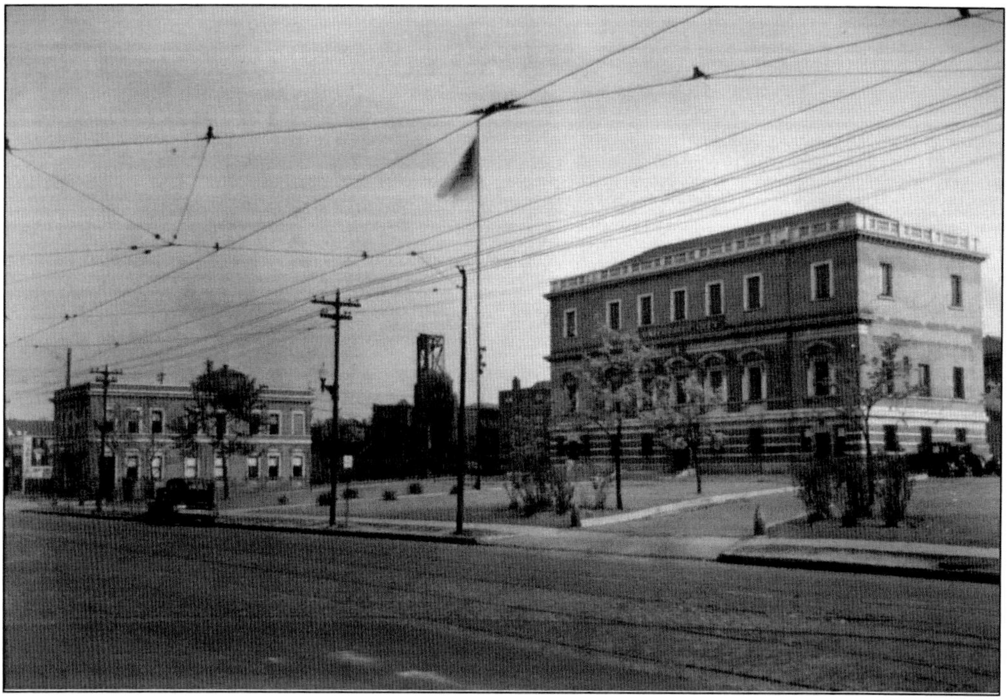

The city's first City Hall, pictured here, was used until 1930. One of the city's first ordinances was a heavy licensing fee of $600 per month for dance halls. Lewis wanted some control over the unwanted business in the community around Delmar Gardens Amusement Park and Delmar Race Track. (Photo Courtesy of the Mercantile Library.)

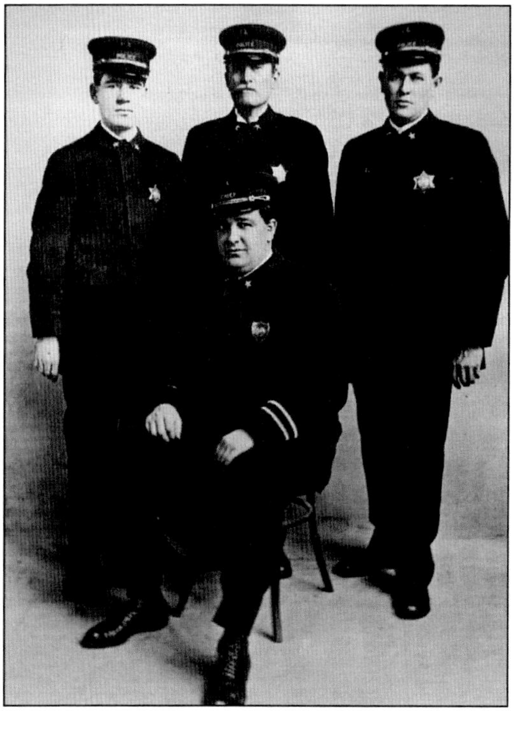

Pictured here are members of University City's first police force. (Photo Courtesy of the Archives of the University City Public Library.)

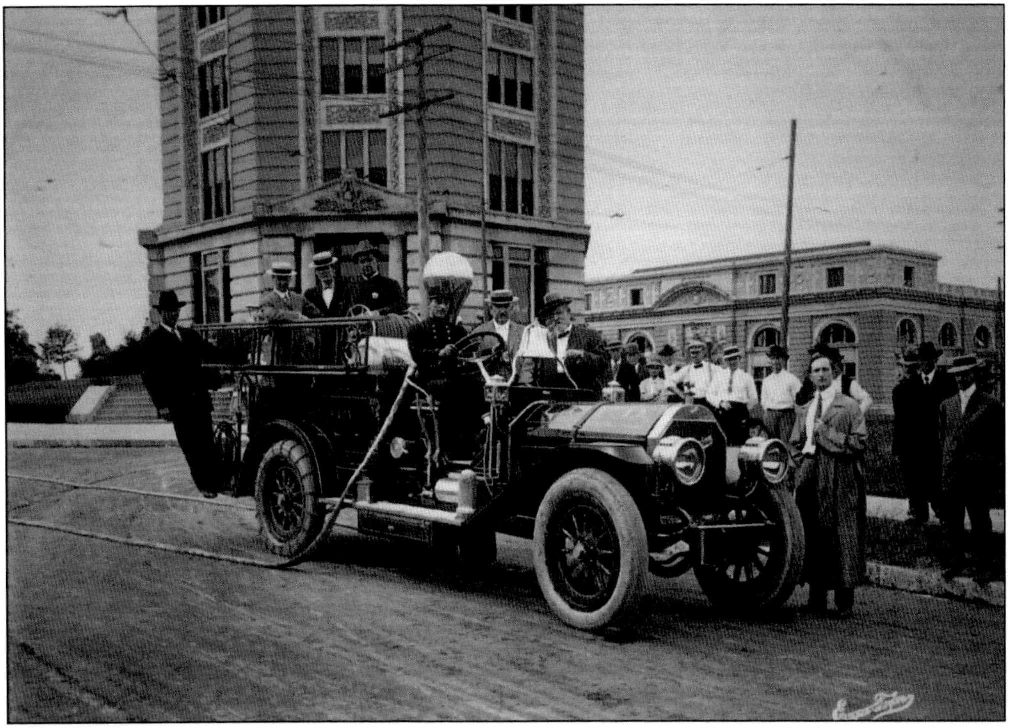

Members of the University City Fire Department pose with the city's second fire engine, *c*.1909. (Photo Courtesy of the Archives of the University City Public Library.)

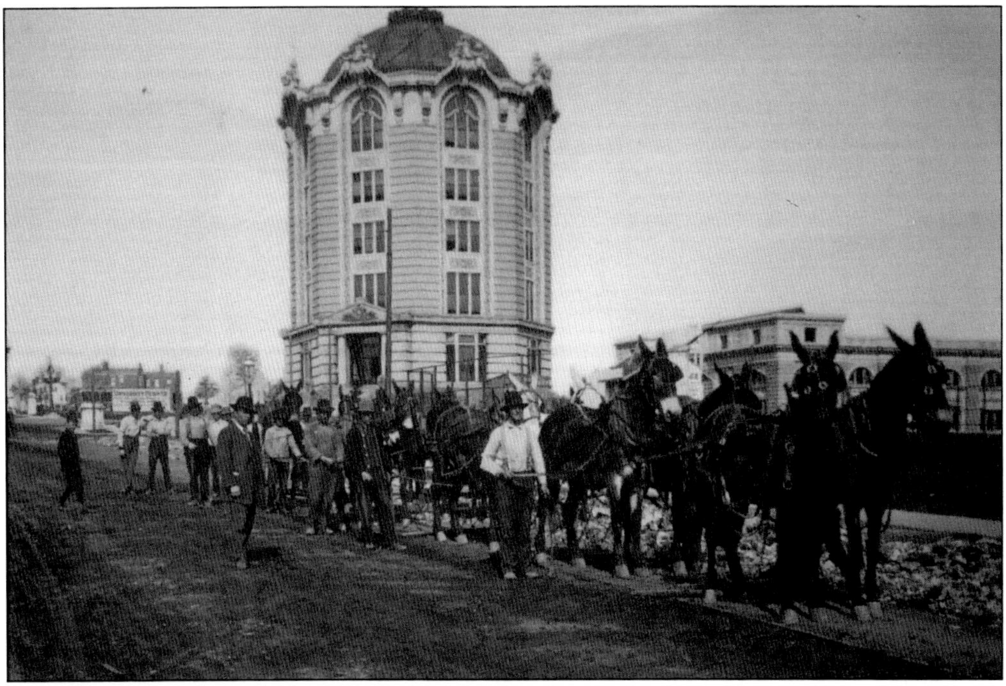

In 1910, these men and horses were preparing the ground for the trolley tracks on Delmar near City Hall. (Photo Courtesy of the Archives of University City Public Library.)

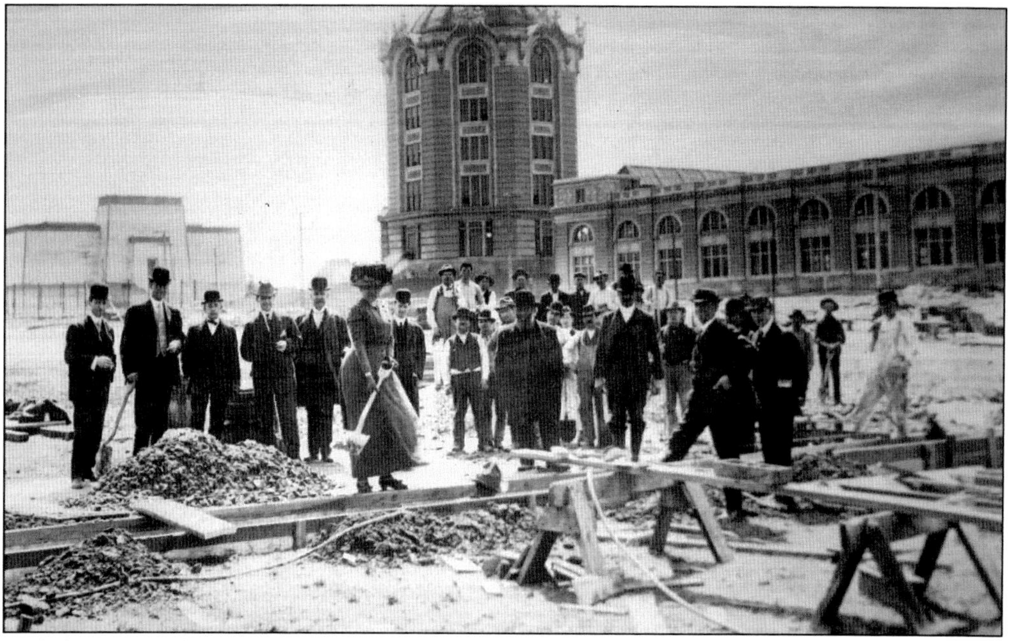

Mabel Lewis is shown here during the ground breaking for the Art Institute of the People's University. E.G. Lewis had planned a large campus with six buildings modeled on the Palace of Versailles, but only the Art Institute was completed. (Photo Courtesy of the Archives of the University City Public Library.)

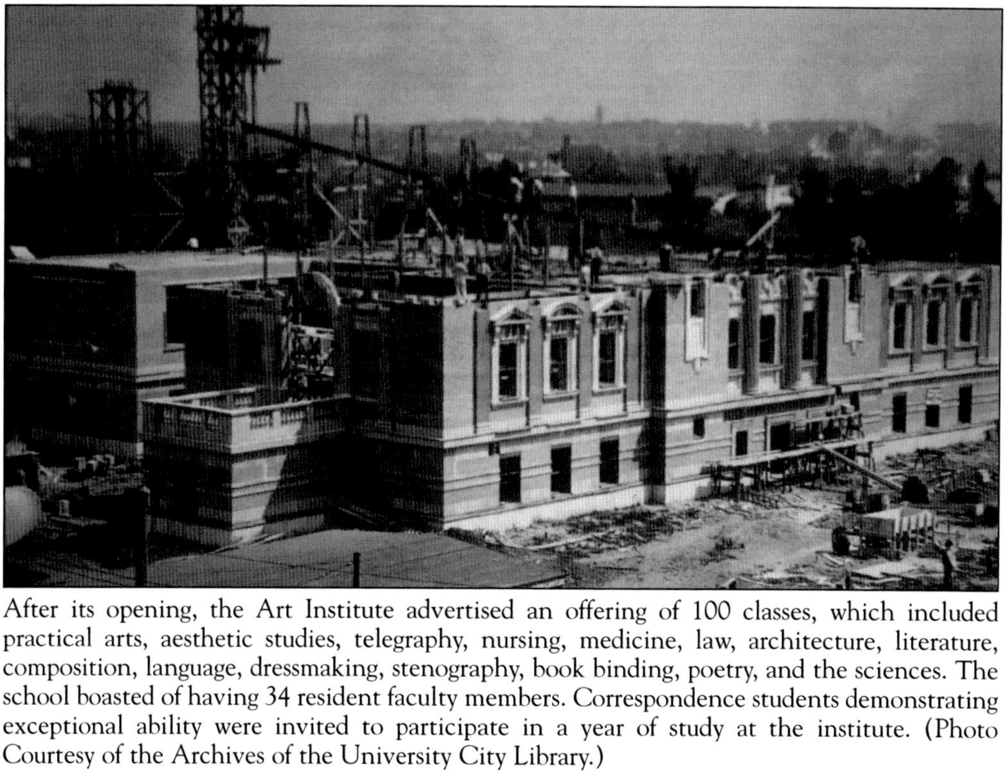

After its opening, the Art Institute advertised an offering of 100 classes, which included practical arts, aesthetic studies, telegraphy, nursing, medicine, law, architecture, literature, composition, language, dressmaking, stenography, book binding, poetry, and the sciences. The school boasted of having 34 resident faculty members. Correspondence students demonstrating exceptional ability were invited to participate in a year of study at the institute. (Photo Courtesy of the Archives of the University City Library.)

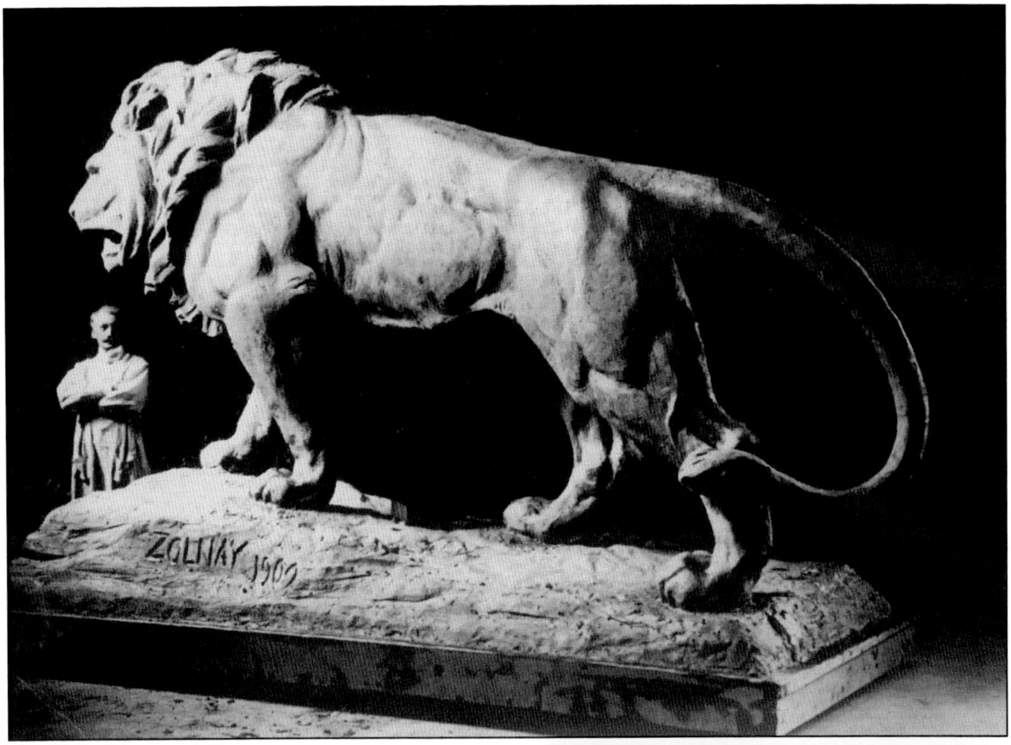

Sculptor George Julian Zolnay, an honor graduate of the Imperial Academy of Fine Arts in Vienna and the Royal Academy of Bucharest, was hired as the director of the Art Institute. Zolnay is pictured above next to one of his two lion sculptures placed on pylons on Delmar. Lewis called them the "Gates of Opportunity." Because of these sculptures, the lion has become the symbol of University City. (Photo Courtesy of the Archives of the University City Public Library.)

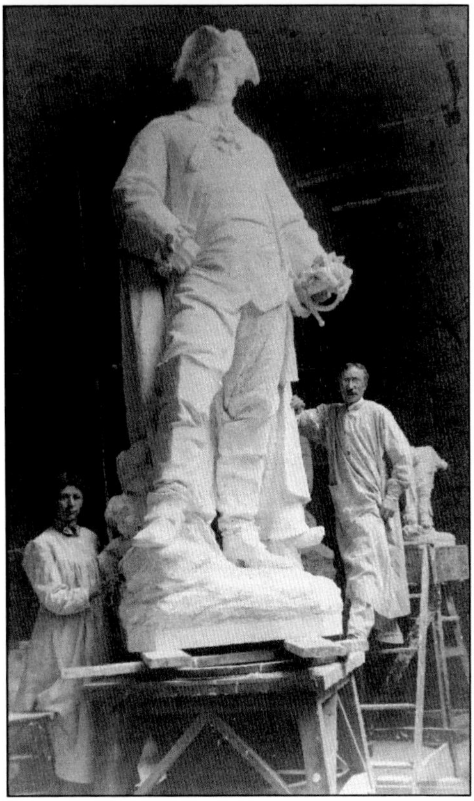

Julian Zolnay is shown on the right next to his statue of Pierre Laclede. This statue is now next to the St. Louis City Hall. Other works by Zolnay include the *Naked Truth* on Grand Boulevard and Russell Avenue near the Compton Heights reservoir and the *Confederate Memo*rial in Forest Park. Zolnay, a Hungarian by birth, came to St. Louis to direct the Art Department of the Louisiana Purchase Exposition. After winning the commission for the development of Lewis' Lion Gate he was appointed director of the Art Institute. (Photo Courtesy of the Archives of the University City Public Library.)

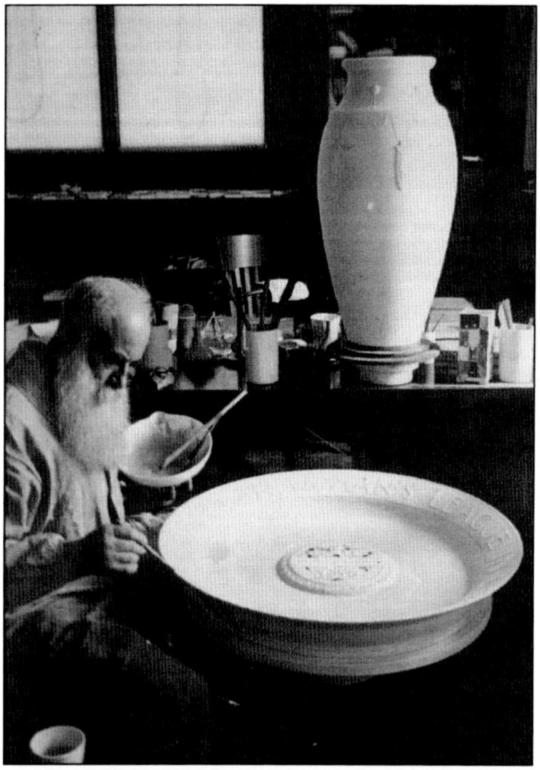

Taxile Doat, one of the art world's leading authorities on ceramics, was chosen by Lewis to head the Ceramics Department of the Academy of Fine Art. Lewis became interested in ceramics in 1903 after reading Doat's textbook, *Grand Feu Ceramics*. Lewis used Doat's book as a guide for doing his work in ceramics. (Photo Courtesy of the Archives of the University City Public Library.)

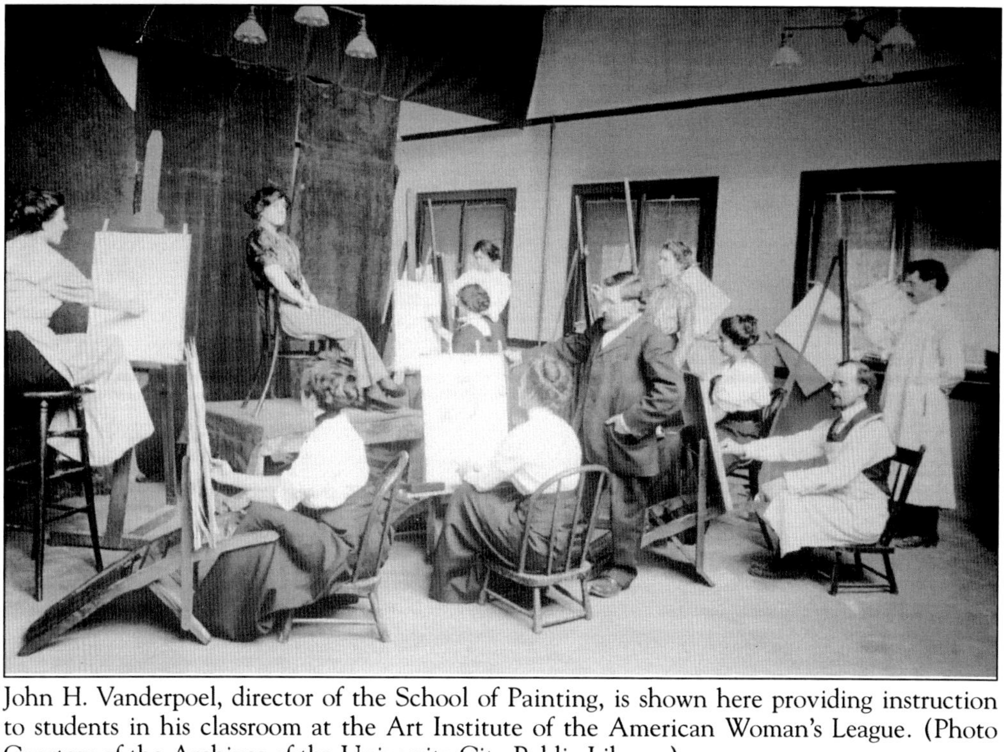

John H. Vanderpoel, director of the School of Painting, is shown here providing instruction to students in his classroom at the Art Institute of the American Woman's League. (Photo Courtesy of the Archives of the University City Public Library.)

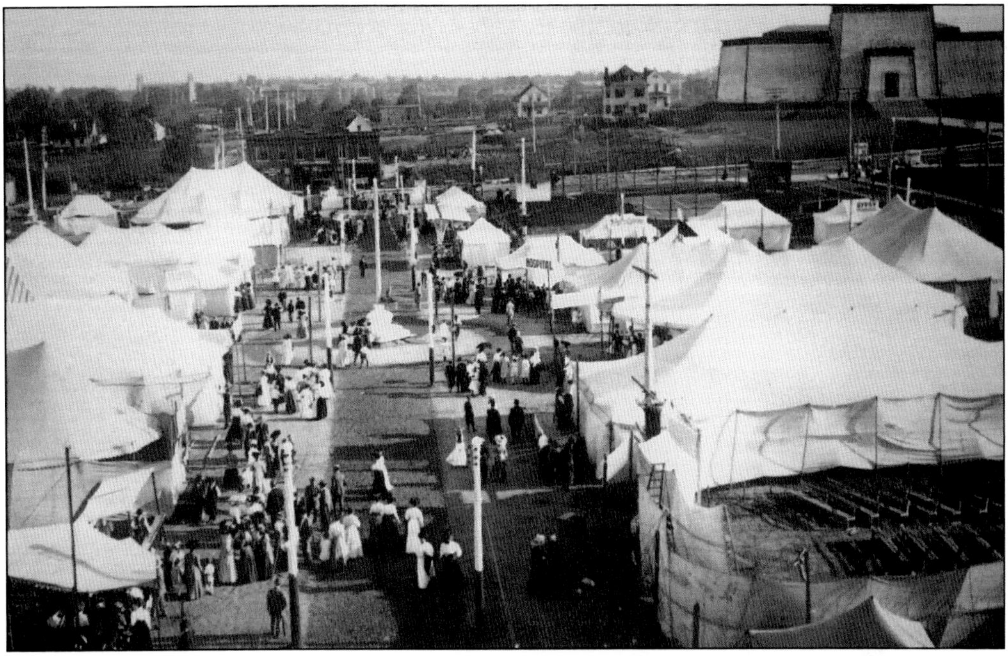

In 1910, University City was the site of the American Woman's League Convention. One goal of the convention was to declare a woman's republic. Some said since American men had Washington, D.C. as their capital, women needed their own—University City. (Photo Courtesy of the Archives of the University City Public Library.)

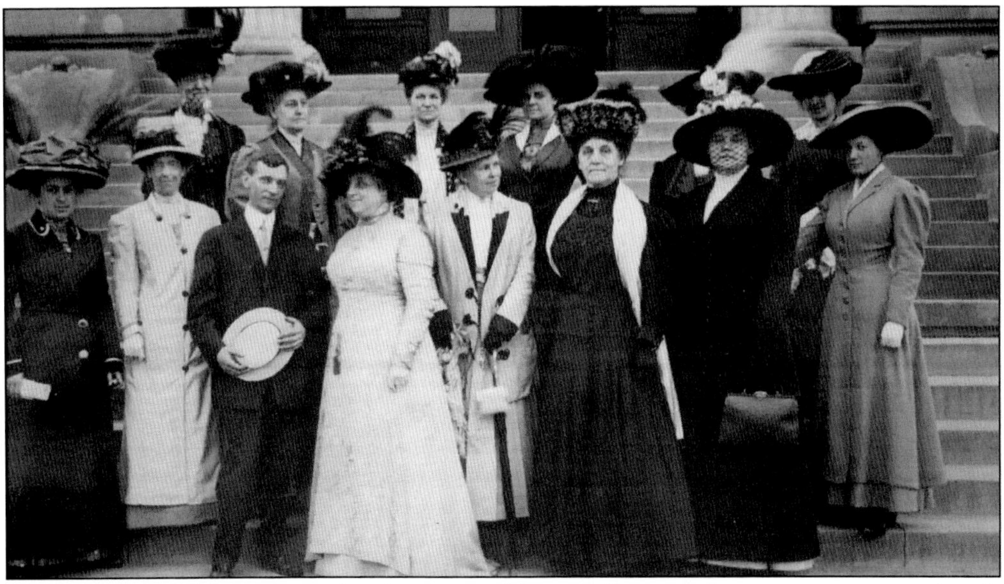

Several women delegates to the American Woman's League Convention are posed with E.G. Lewis outside the Woman's Magazine Building. Lewis wanted to use the league to sell his publications and to provide capital for his University City ventures. The League's revenue grew from $75,000 in 1908 to $1,250,000 in 1910. Lewis promised that if an individual obtained $52 in magazine sales in a single year, that individual would receive a life membership in the League. (Photo Courtesy of the Archives of the University City Public Library.)

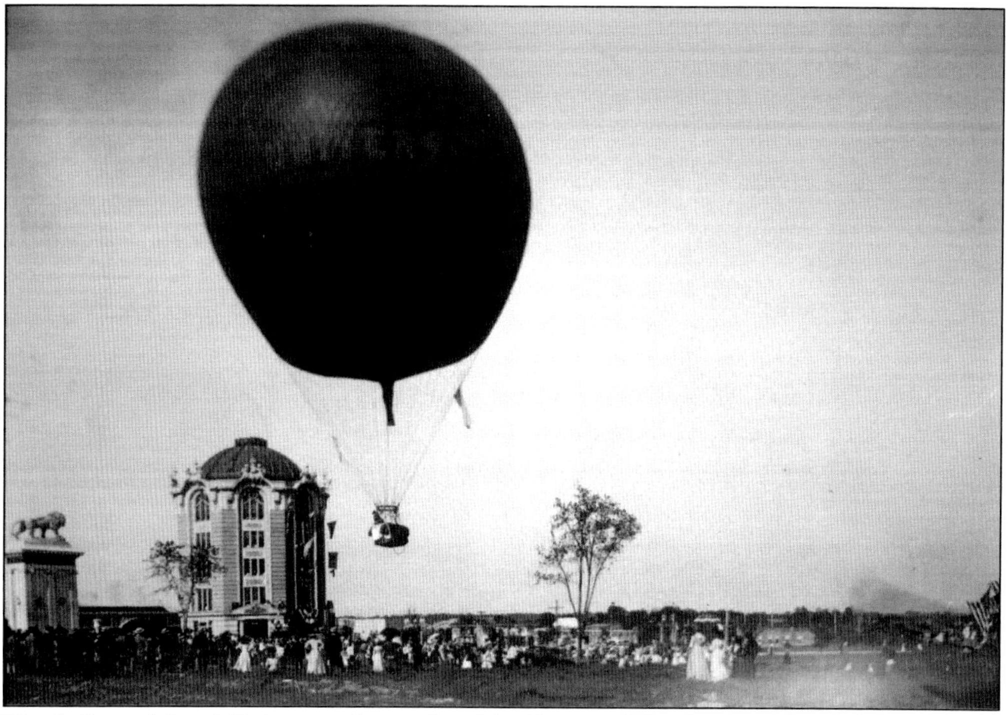

The balloon dubbed University City, piloted by Captain John Berry, is shown here in flight during the American Woman's League Convention in University City. The balloon won a trophy at the first national balloon race in Indianapolis, Indiana, on June 3, 1909. (Photo Courtesy of the Archives of the University City Public Library.)

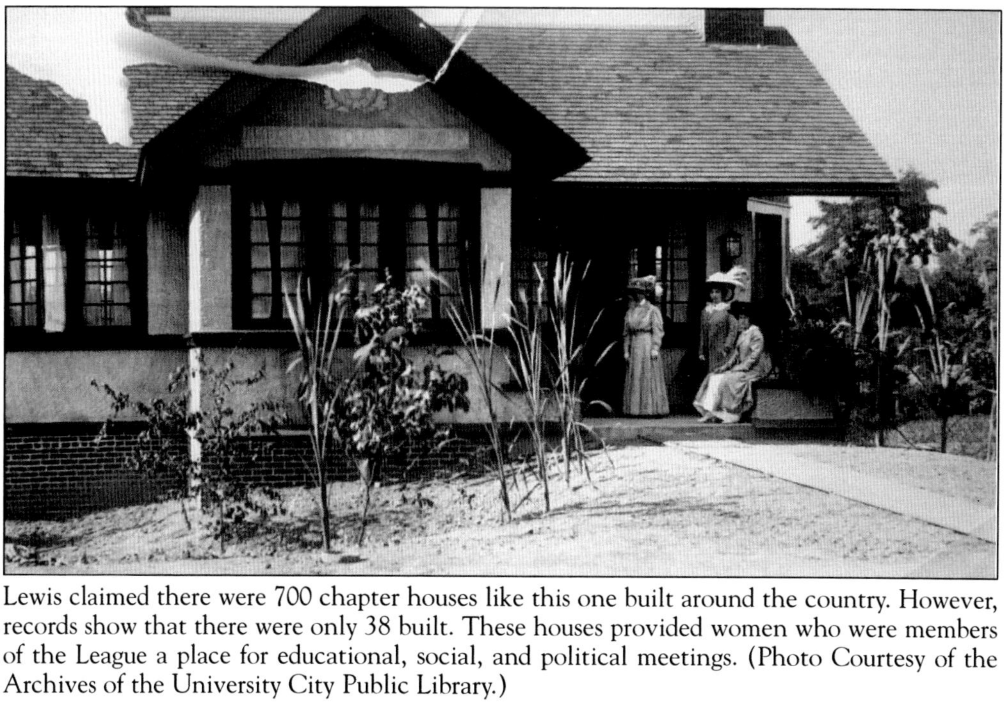

Lewis claimed there were 700 chapter houses like this one built around the country. However, records show that there were only 38 built. These houses provided women who were members of the League a place for educational, social, and political meetings. (Photo Courtesy of the Archives of the University City Public Library.)

On February 21, 1911, 75 residents of the community voted to establish the University City School District. The school population had out grown the Ferguson School. During the February meeting, the first school board was chosen with two members elected for three-year terms, two for two-year terms, and two for one-year terms. (Photo Courtesyof the Archives of the University City Public Library.)

NOTICE OF ORGANIZATION

OF

UNIVERSITY CITY SCHOOL DISTRICT

Notice is hereby given by the Undersigned Freeholders, residents of the City of University City, St. Louis County, Missouri, of a meeting of the QUALIFIED VOTERS, who are resident Tax Payers within the corporate limits of the City of University City, to be held on the 21st Day of FEBRUARY, 1911, at the National Daily Building, Delmar Avenue, University City, at the hour of eight (8) o'clock, p. m., for the purpose of organizing a City School District, to be known as the "UNIVERSITY CITY SCHOOL DISTRICT," within and bounded by the corporate limits of the City of University City and including also all that portion of School District No. 33, Ferguson School (Formerly District No. 2, Township 45, Range 6) lying without the corporate limits of the City of University City.

Freeholders	Residence
E. G. LEWIS	2 Yale Ave.
D. S. RALSTON	6965 Delmar Ave.
ALLAN J. SHOWERS	6700 Washington Ave.
NICHOLAS LAMB, JR	875 66th St.
EDW. GREUNINGER	6851 Olive St. Road.
JAMES F. COYLE	4 Yale Ave.
JOHN W. LEWIS	1 Yale Ave.
F. W. SHIPLEY	539 Hanley Road.
LUTHER T. WARD	8 Princeton Ave.
H. J. HOPKINS	16 Yale Ave.
F. L. HARRIS	8 Radcliffe Ave.
PINCKNEY FRENCH	6925 Delmar Ave.
F. V. PUTNAM	15 Princeton Ave.

Original Notice of Organization of University City School District

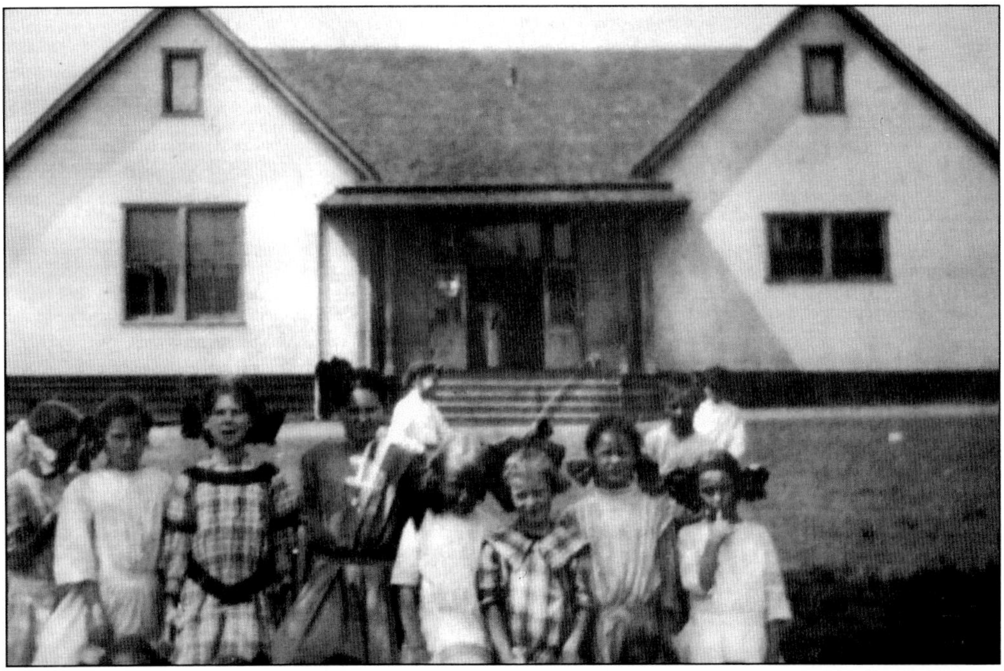

Immediately after the University School District was organized, the Board of Education opened two temporary schools. Students are shown here outside the two-room building at 6600 Bartmer Avenue. This building was used until 1920 when Pershing School opened. The other building was located in the Frazier Flat at 6702 Delmar Boulevard. It went out of existence in 1913, when the Delmar School opened. (Photo Courtesy of the Archives of the University City Public Library.)

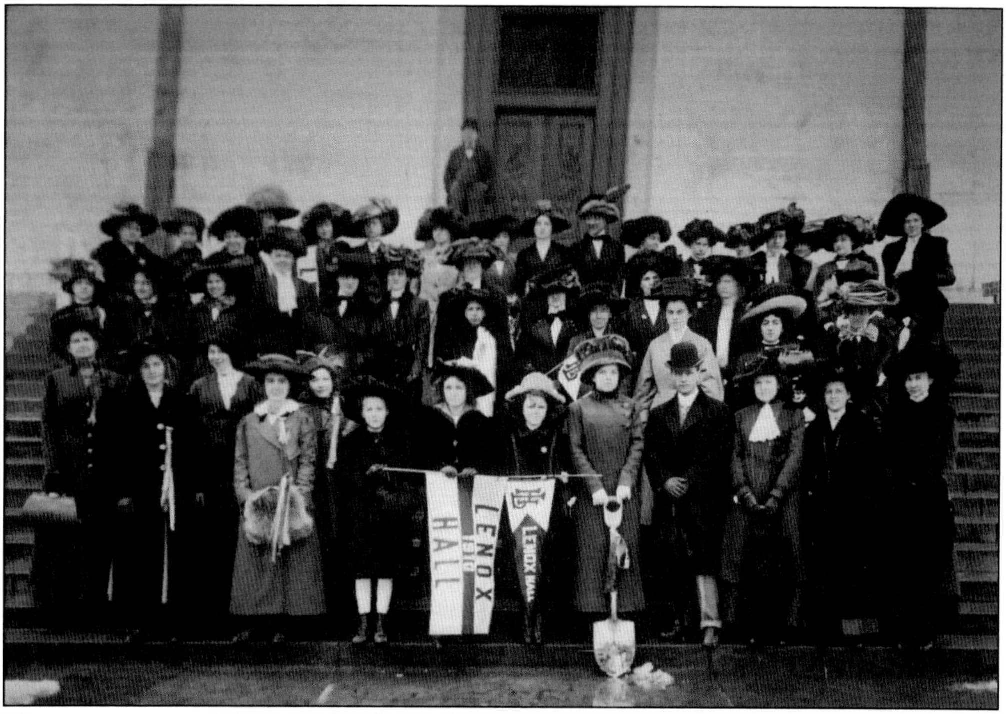

These supporters of Lenox School are shown in front of the Egyptian Building after the ground breaking for Lenox Hall on Delmar Boulevard. (Photo Courtesy of the Archives of the University City Library.)

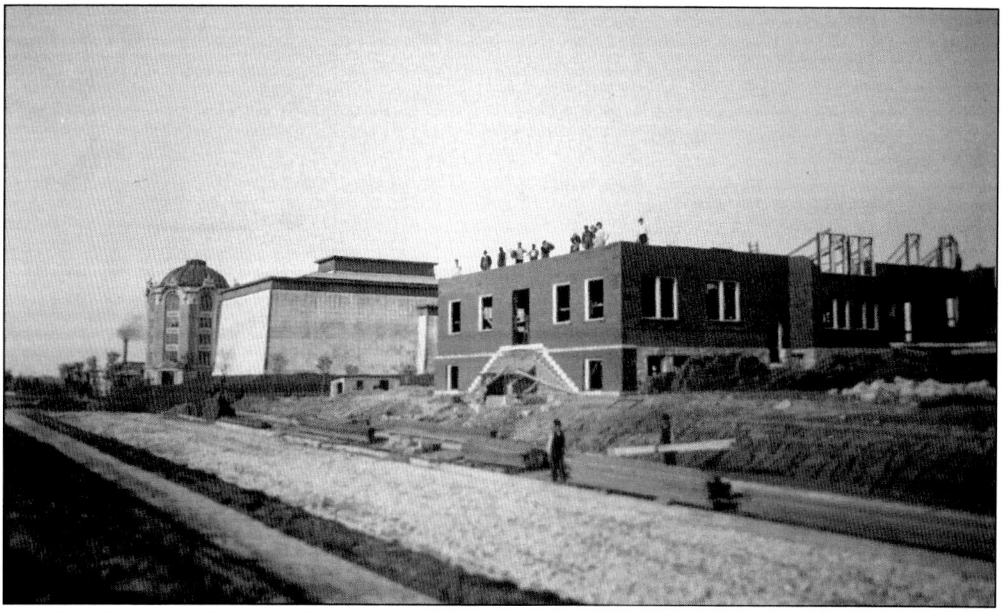

In 1911, Lenox Hall, an exclusive school for girls, moved to University City from its St. Louis site. The school, shown during construction at Washington and Trinity Avenues, was later used as a Presbyterian Seminary and afterwards torn down for the construction of B'Nai Amoona Synagogue. (Photo Courtesy of the Archives of the University City Public Library.)

Three

The City Moves On

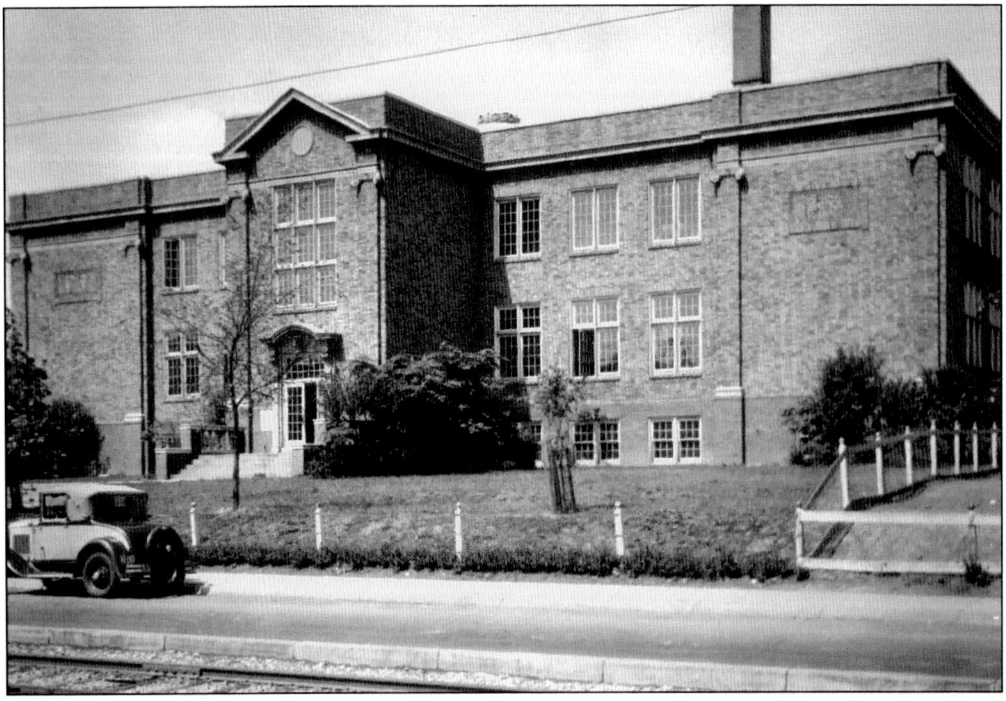

In 1911, the Lewis empire began to collapse after rumors started to spread that the educational courses advertised by the American Woman's League were not available. With this news the League began to falter, along with other parts of Lewis' kingdom. In 1912, Lewis' enterprises went on the auction block and he resigned as mayor and moved to California with his possessions. Although Lewis left the city with debts and with plunging property values, August Heman, who succeeded Lewis as mayor, got the city on sound footing and its growth and development continued. Between 1910 and 1920, the city grew faster than any other city in Missouri.

The Delmar School, pictured here, was constructed in 1913 to meet the needs of a growing student population. This was University City School District's first new school. (Photo Courtesy of the Archives of the University City Public Library.)

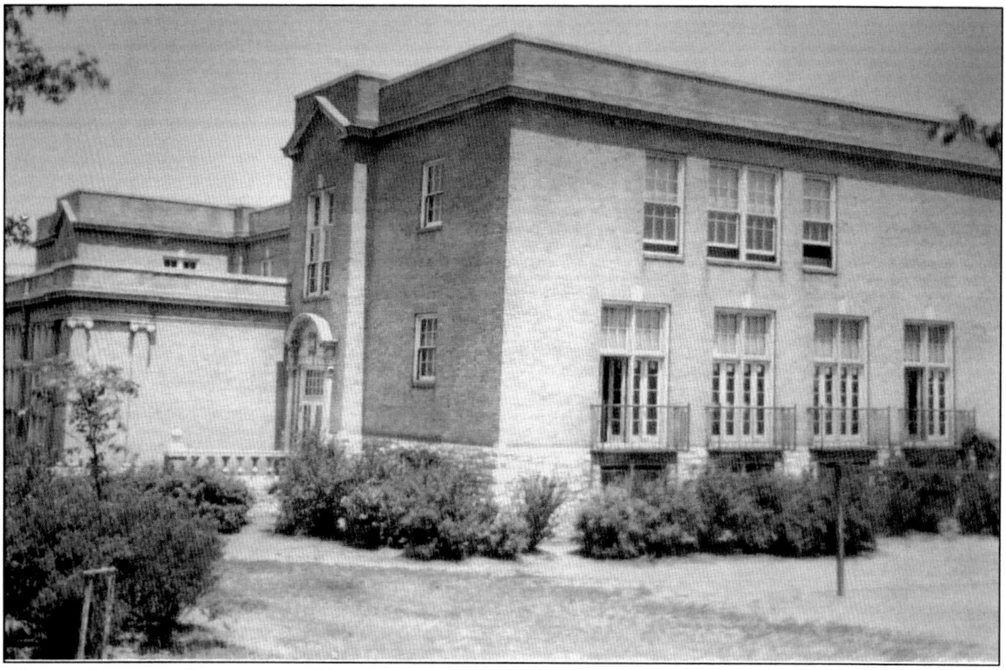

The student population served by the Delmar School continued to grow at a rapid pace, making it necessary to erect the Harvard building west of the Delmar building, facing Harvard Avenue. The Harvard building added ten classrooms to the eight in the Delmar Building, along with a room for kindergarten and a gymnasium. (Photo Courtesy of the Archives of the University City Public Library.)

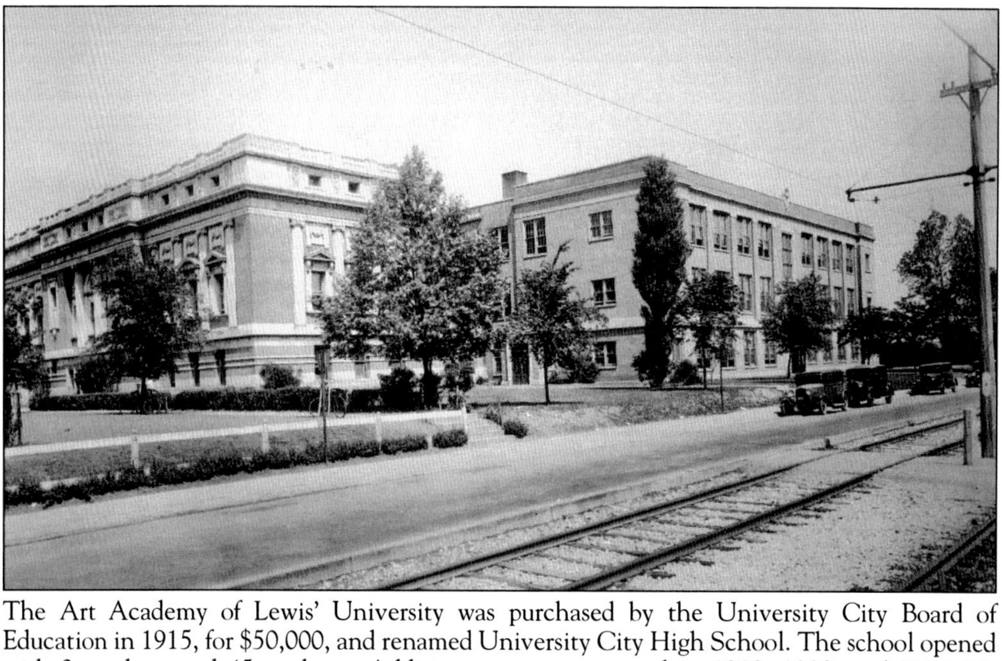

The Art Academy of Lewis' University was purchased by the University City Board of Education in 1915, for $50,000, and renamed University City High School. The school opened with 3 teachers and 45 students. Additions were constructed in 1919, 1923, and 1926–27. (Photo Courtesy of the Archives of the University City Public Library.)

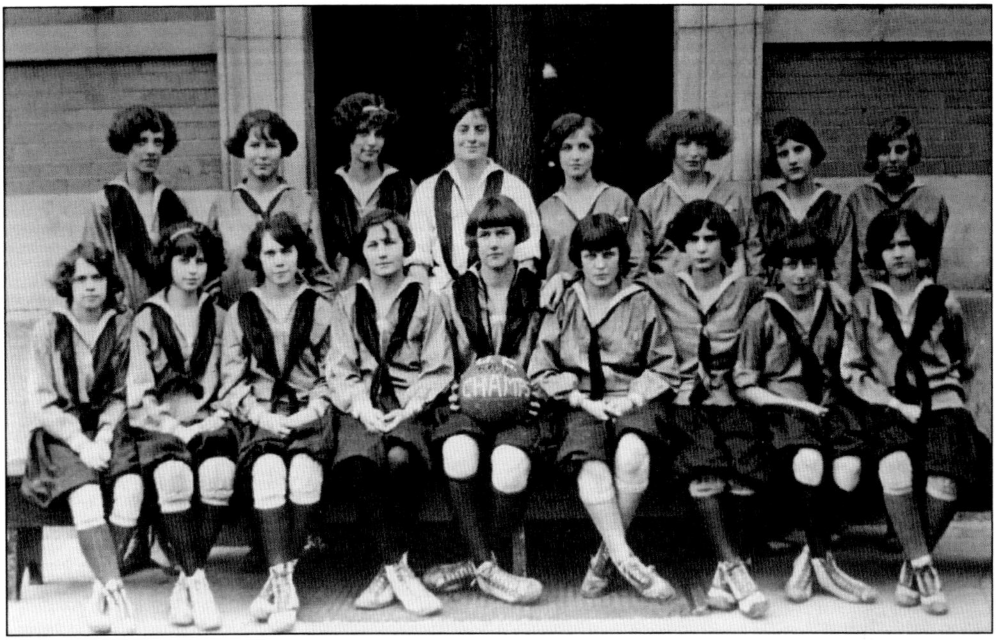

These girls posing in front of the old high school are part of a string of champions who have attended University City High School. (Photo Courtesy of the Archives of the Historical Society of University City.)

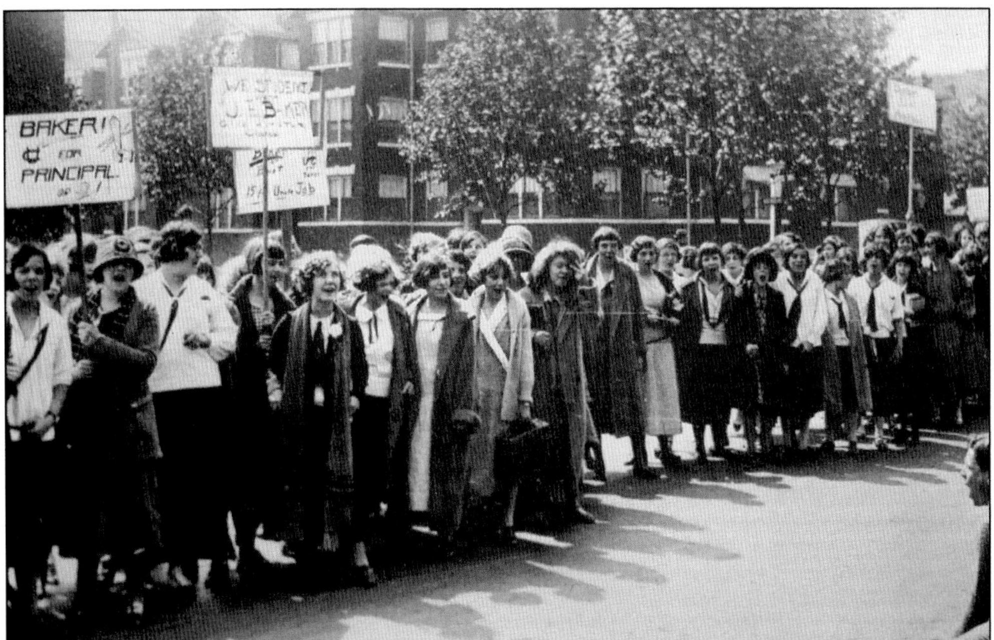

Protests and involvement by citizens of all ages have never been lacking in University City. These students are protesting on behalf of University City High School Principal James E. Baker, regarding a dispute between Baker and the Board of Education. Baker continued as principal of the high school until 1953, when he retired after spending almost 50 years as an educator. (Photo Courtesy of the Archives of the University City Historical Society.)

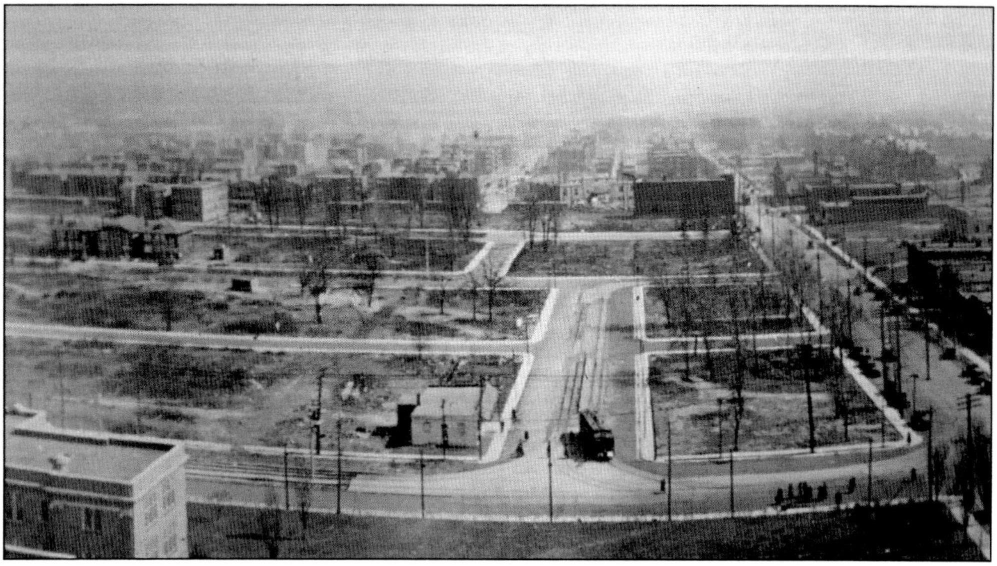

These two photographs of the Loop, the top taken in 1922 and the bottom in 1928, show the development of the area during the 1920s. The streetcar making its "loop" gave the area its name and can be seen in both pictures. During the 1920s, nearly 20,000 new residents moved into University City, increasing its population by 280 percent. (Photos Courtesy of the Archives of the University City Public Library.)

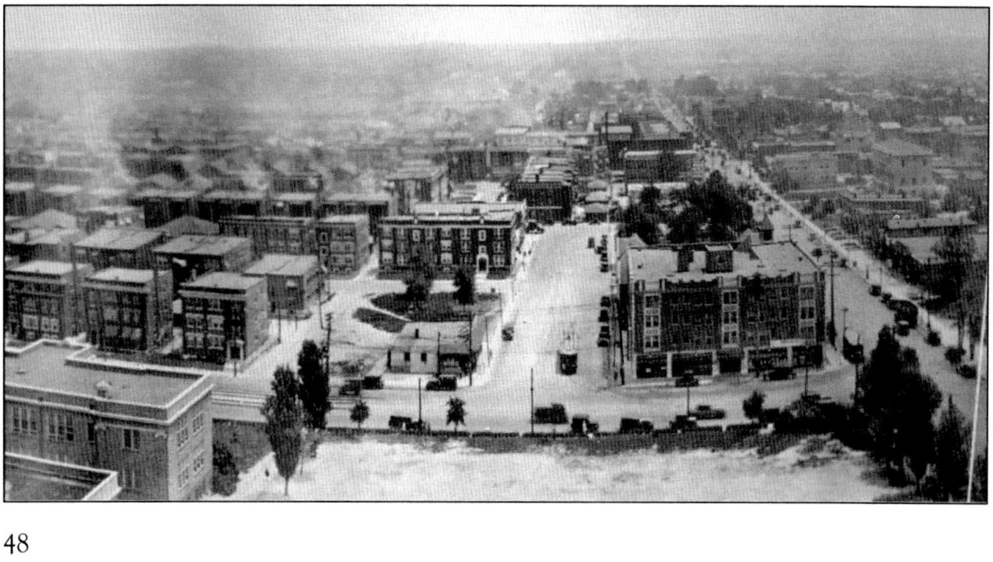

In the spring of 1914, the United Methodist Church added its presence to the University City scene when its congregation broke ground for a new chapel. The chapel was completed in 1915. Prior to its construction, services were held in the lecture hall of the Lewis Fine Arts Building and the chapel of Lenox Hall, on the present site of the Center of Contemporary Arts (COCA). (Photo by John A. Wright.)

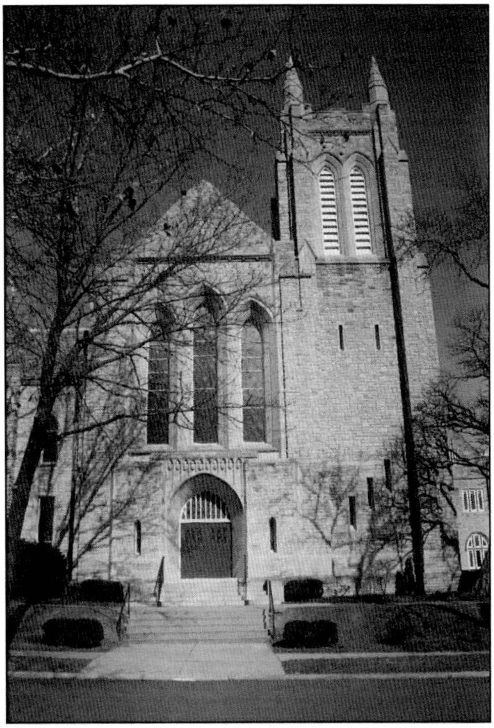

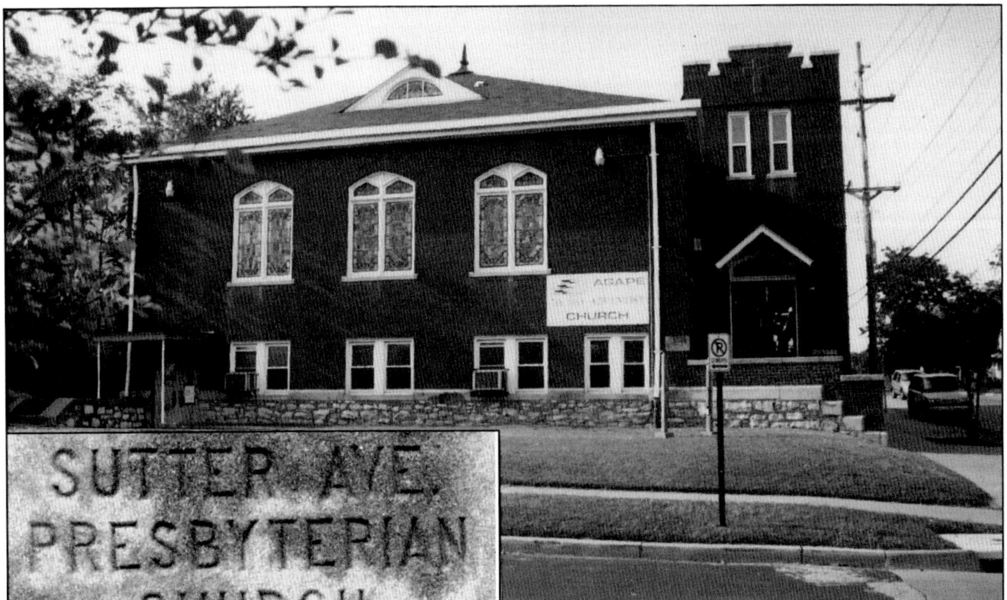

In 1914, on the north side of the community, the Sutter Avenue Presbyterian Church at 6502 Bartmer Avenue built this Craftman-Gothic Revival building. The church was organized as North Cabanne Church in 1898, just east of University City. In 1987, the congregation moved to West County and the church is now the AGAPE Seventh Day Adventist Church. (Photo by John A. Wright.)

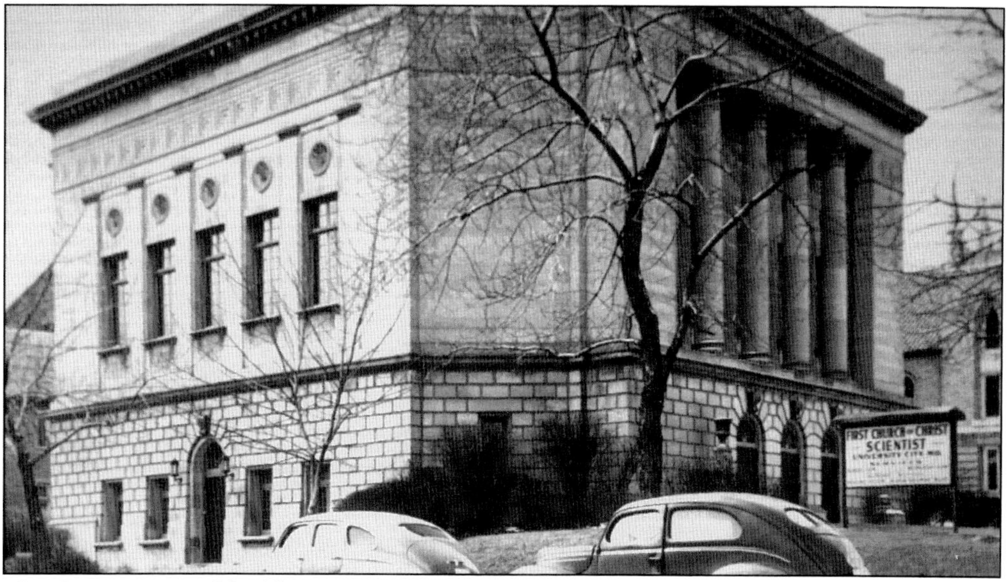

This Roman-inspired building at 6900 Delmar Boulevard was constructed for the First Church of Christ Scientists in 1924. The building was used by the Assumption Greek Orthodox Church between 1958 and 1982. It presently serves as the office of Mary Engelbreith, a nationally-known artist. The large auditorium, which has a coffered dome ceiling, was preserved when the building was converted to office space. (Photo Courtesy of the Mercantile Library.)

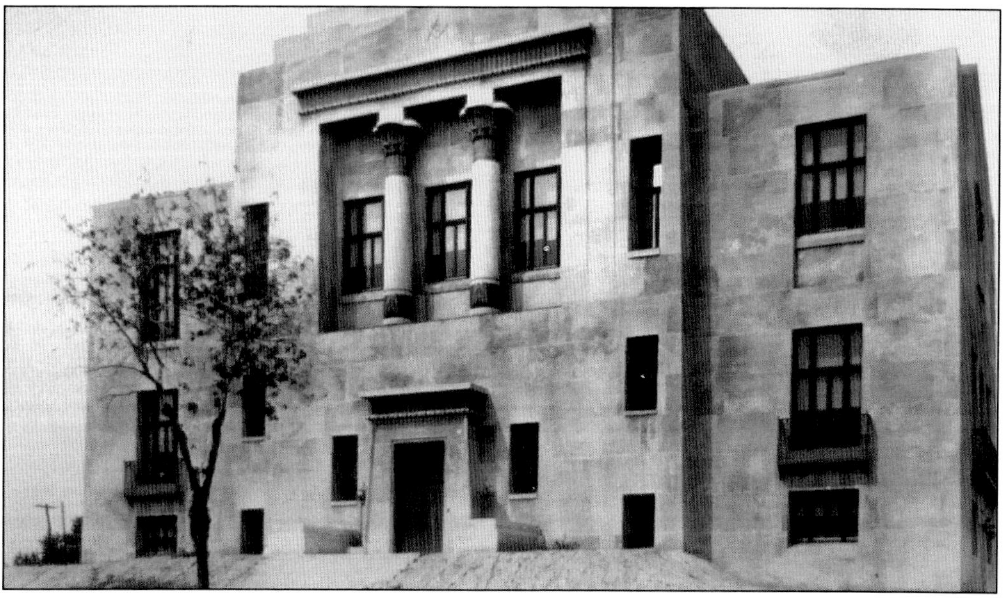

The University Temple Association, a Masonic organization, had this building constructed at 6901 Delmar Boulevard between 1925 and 1926. It was the second Egyptian-style building on the plaza. It and the Roman-inspired building on the opposite side of Delmar Boulevard, pictured above, completed the major buildings on the plaza. Anchor Temple, another Masonic organization, operated the building from 1935 to 1977, until it was purchased by Childgrove School. The building is now the home of the Church of Scientology. (Photo Courtesy of Archives of the University City Public Library.)

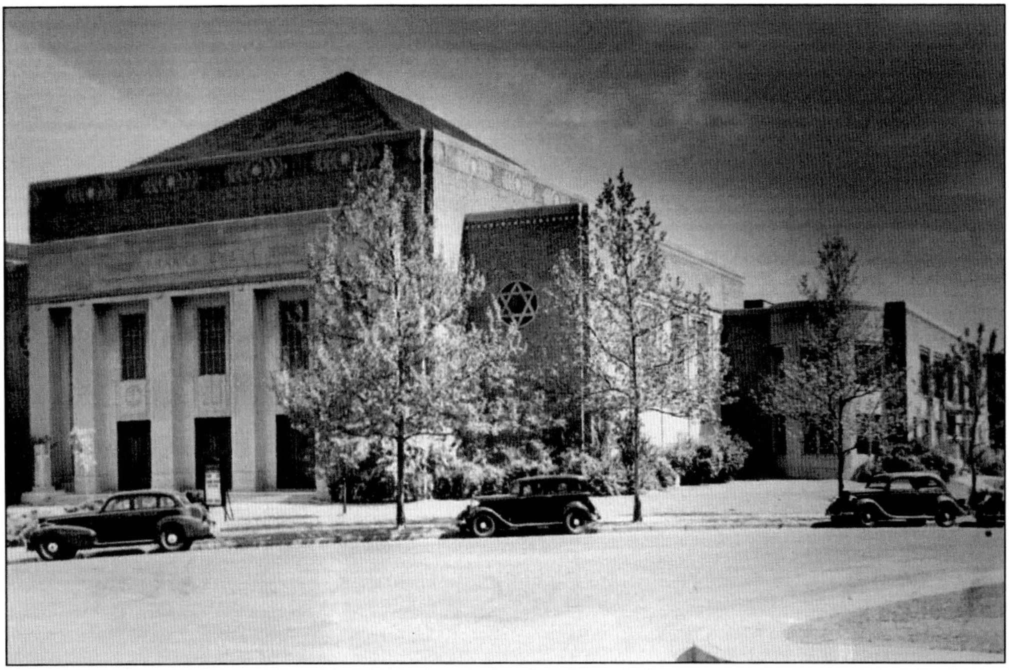

Shaare Emeth at 6848 Delmar Boulevard was the first Jewish Synagogue constructed in St. Louis County. The Synagogue was moved to University City in 1931; the congregation had planned to use the Egyptian-style building previously erected by E.G. Lewis, which was already on the site. However, after this idea was found impractical, that building was torn down for the construction of the Synagogue. St. Louis Conservatory and School for the Arts occupied the building after the congregation moved from University City in 1978. It is now owned by Webster University. (Photo Courtesy of the Archives of the University City Public Library.)

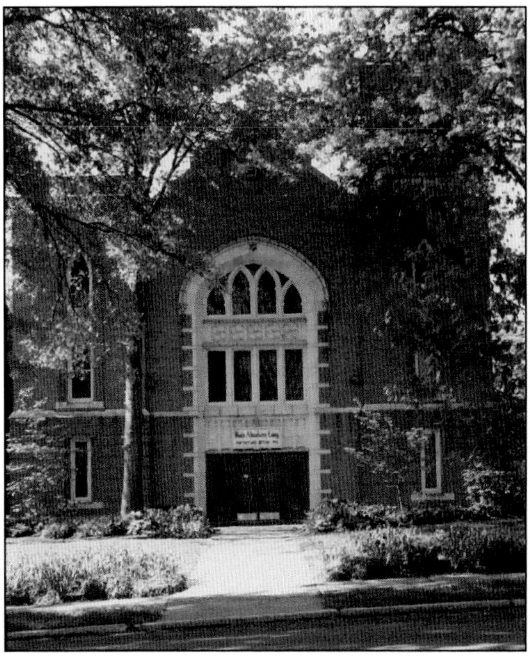

This building at 6910 Delmar Boulevard is home of Bais Abraham Synagogue, founded in 1894. It was constructed by the University Church of Christ in 1927. The building was sold to the Tpheris Israel Congregation, who in turn sold it to Bais Abraham after they merged with Chevra Kadish in 1960 and moved from University City. Prior to moving into the building, Tpheris Israel worshiped in the Loop above Talisnicks Market. (Photo by John A. Wright.)

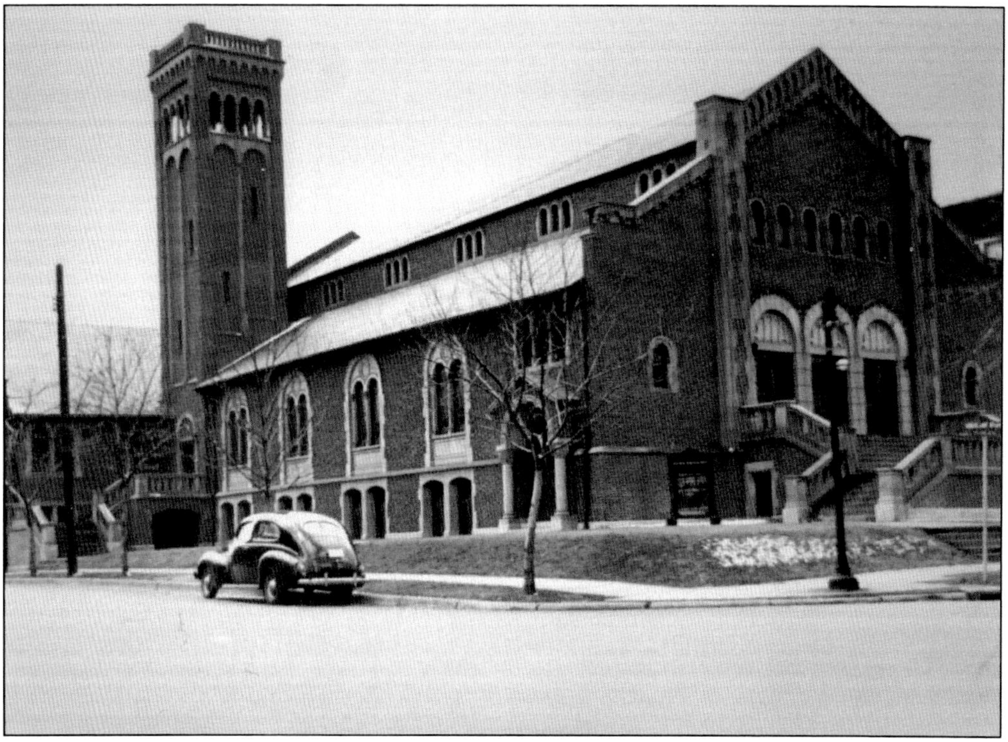

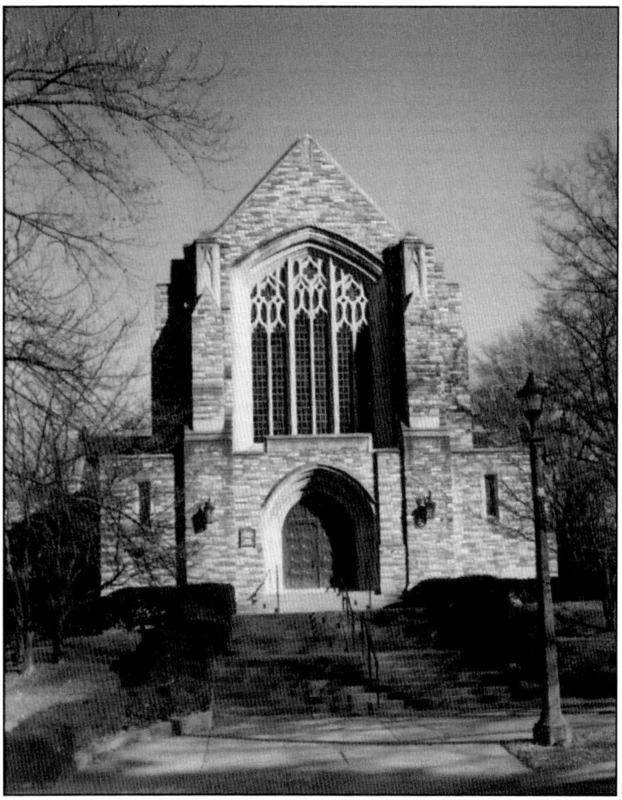

Trinity Presbyterian Church at 6800 Washington Avenue is outside of the Civic Plaza Historic District, but is considered a part of the cultural area. The church was constructed by the First United Presbyterian Church between 1922 and 1926, in two stages. The church became Trinity Presbyterian Church in 1953, when it merged with Kingshighway Presbyterian Church. (Photo Courtesy of the Archives of the University City Public Library.)

The First Presbyterian Church moved to its third home, at 7200 Delmar Boulevard in the University Hills subdivision, in 1927. The church can tract its origin to 1817. (Photo by John A. Wright.)

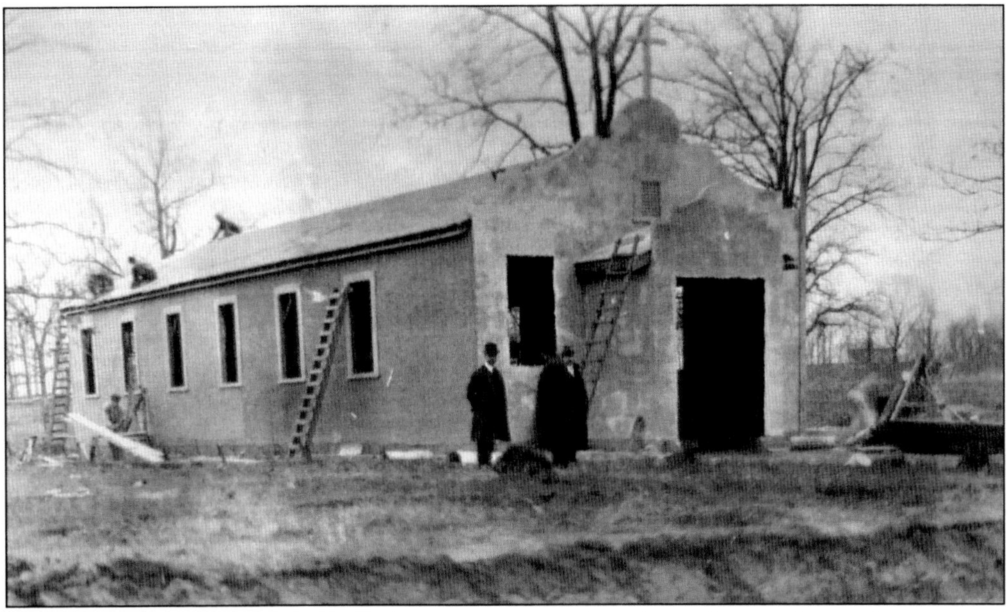

While growth was occurring in the Loop area, it was also taking place in the southeast part of the city. In 1916, Our Lady of Lourdes built its first church. This little, Spanish-style chapel at Forsyth Boulevard and Asbury Avenue was hailed as "a bit of old Madrid" and reported to be the first permanent stucco building in the area. Father Francis J. O'Connor celebrated the first parish mass here on May 7, 1916. (Photo Courtesy of the Sisters of St. Joseph of Carondelet.)

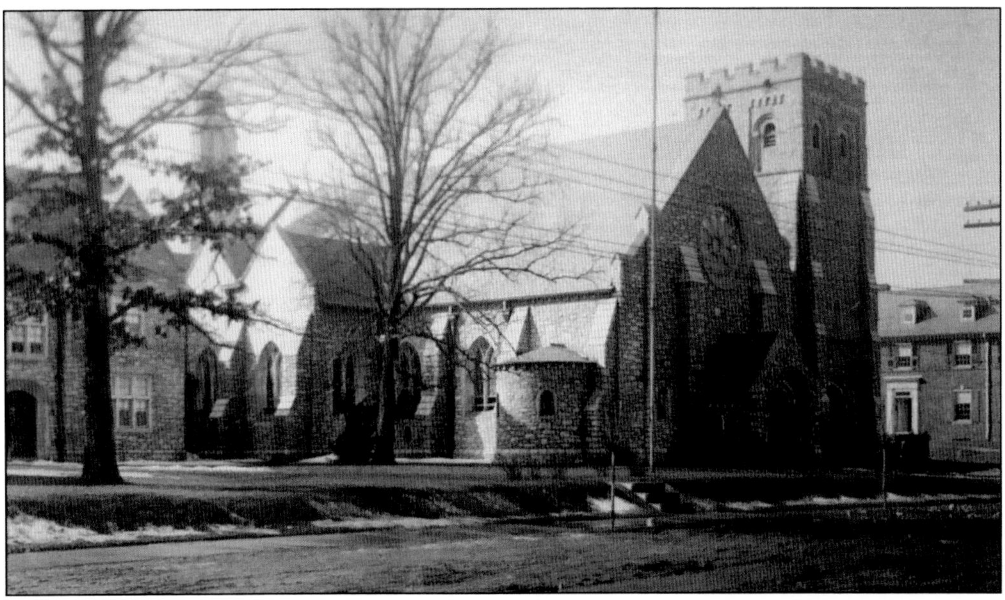

The members of Our Lady of Lourdes Parish soon outgrew their small chapel on Forsyth Boulevard and on May 21, 1917, ground was broken for this new Chapel at 7252 Forsyth Boulevard. World War I caused delays, but the building was completed in September of 1919. The building has no woodwork on the outside; even the leaded "silver glass" windows, characteristic of Norman churches, are set directly into the stone work without wooden frames. (Photo Courtesy of the Sisters of St. Joseph of Carondelet.)

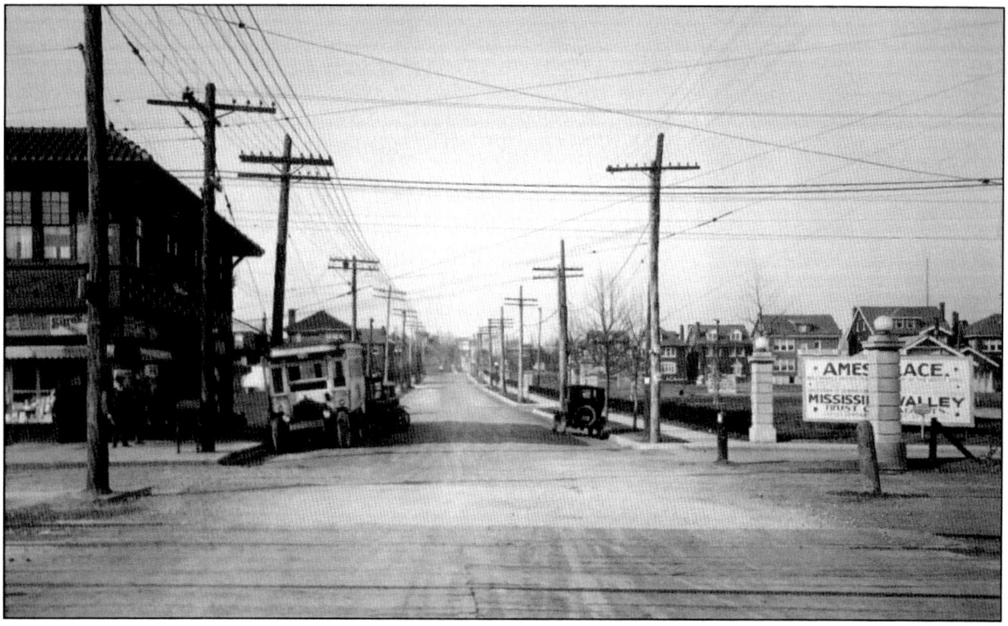

During the 1920s, the population of University City increased over 300 percent. It was reported that during this era the state building inspector issued more building permits for University City than any other municipality in the state. To meet the ever-growing demand, subdivisions such as Ames Place began to be developed. Ames Place was subdivided in 1914 by Lucy Semple Ames, a wealthy widow and businesswoman. The homes were developed in Tudor, Colonial. and Renaissance Revival style. (Photo Courtesy of the Archives of the University City Public Library.)

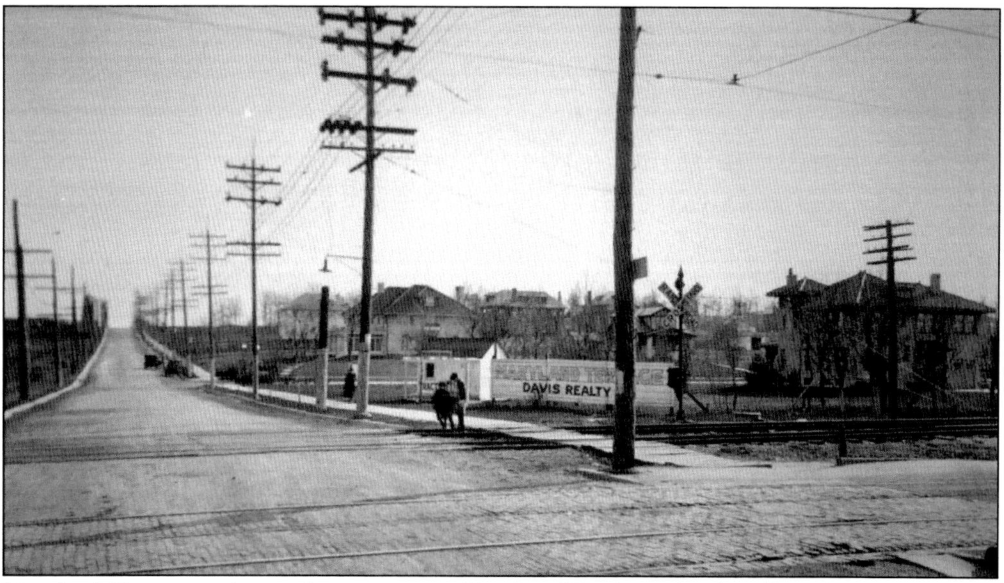

Maryland Terrace on the southwest corner of Big Bend Boulevard and Millbrook was subdivided and platted in 1911. This long and narrow subdivision stretches westward from Big Bend Boulevard to Jackson Avenue, and includes the streets of Maryland Avenue and Westmoreland Avenue. Between 1922 and 1924, the Board of Aldermen approved plats for 19 subdivisions. (Photo Courtesy of the Archives of the University City Public Library.)

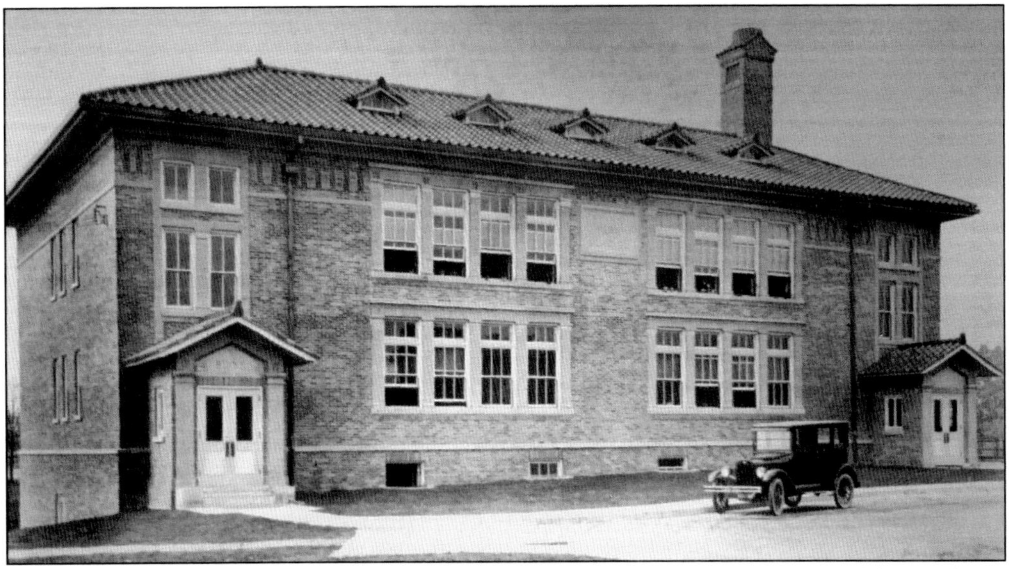

In 1917, Mr. J.W. Creveling leased the University City Board of Education part of the southeast corner of his farm at 7200 Pershing Avenue, on which a portable building known as the Creveling School was erected. There were between 32 and 38 pupils enrolled for the four years the school was open. The pupils went to Delmar-Harvard School for sixth grade. In 1924, the University City School District constructed the main building of Flynn Park Elementary School, shown here. The building was named for University City's Mayor Warren C. Flynn. (Photo Courtesy of the Archives of the University City Public Library.)

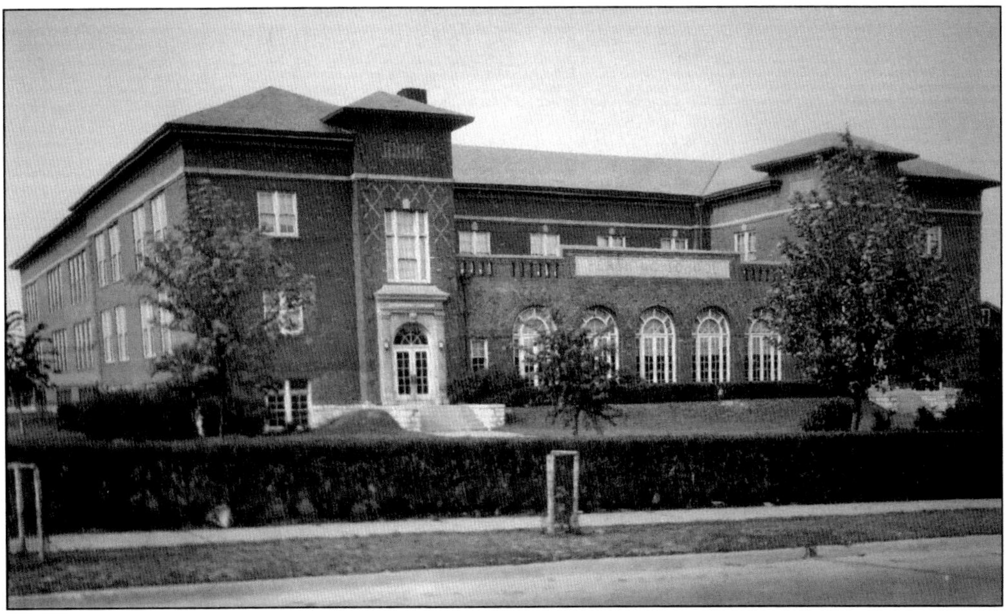

After Pershing School opened in 1920, Bartmer School at 6605-07 Bartmer Avenue, which had served the students, was closed. General Pershing, for whom the school is named, came to University City to take part in the dedication ceremony. In 1925, six classrooms, a cafeteria and a gymnasium were added in the large wing at the west side of the school. (Photo Courtesy of the Archives of the University City Public Library.)

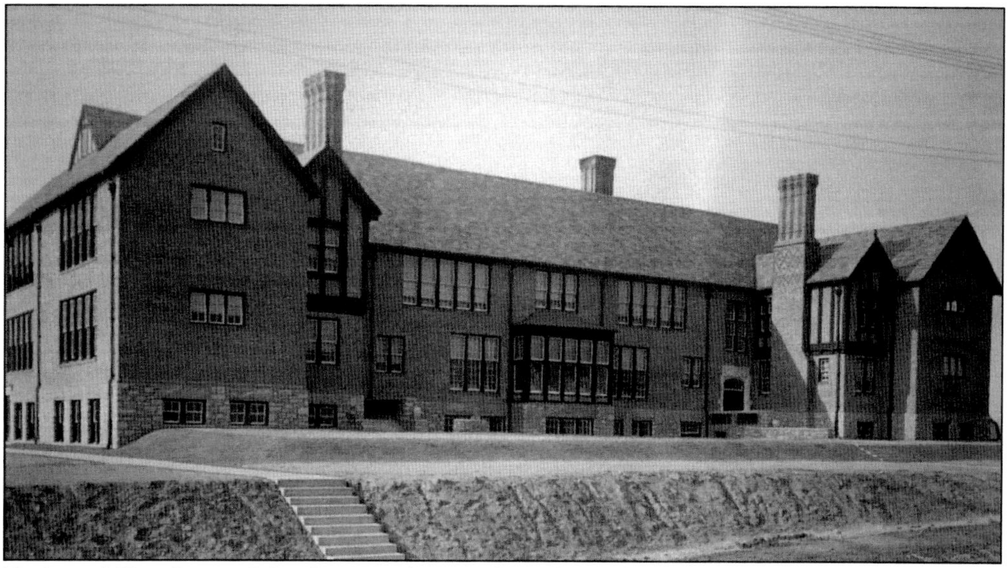

Nathaniel Hawthorne School on Hanley Road was built during the summer and fall of 1930, and was opened for students on January 26, 1931. The students, who were attending Boone Elementary School after the old Mount Olive School closed, were transferred to the new school. When the school opened it had only ten rooms. At the time it opened, it was the only school in the district that had its name chosen by the students. (Photo Courtesy of the Archives of the University City Public Library.)

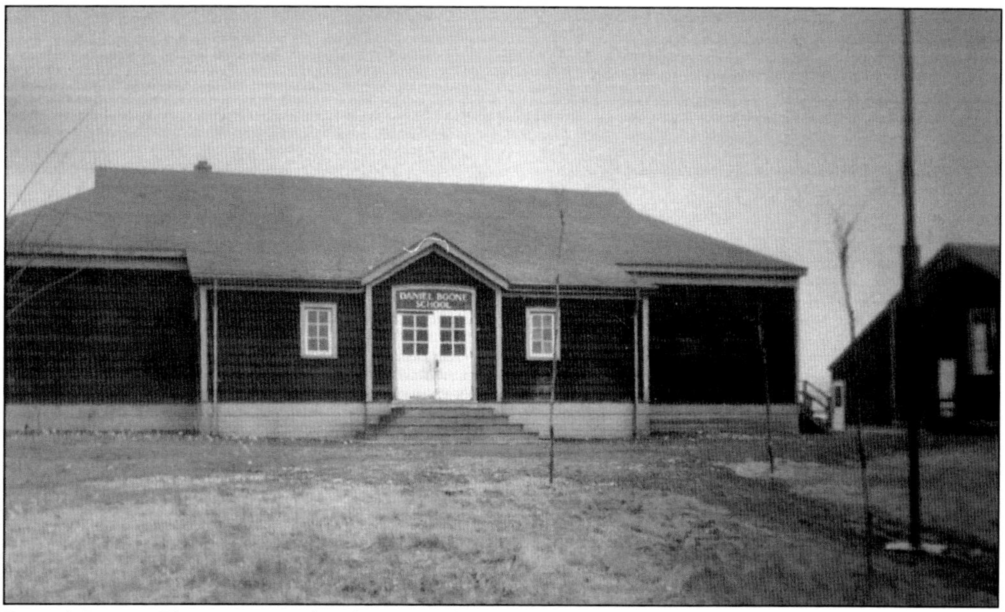

Daniel Boone Elementary School on 82nd Street north of Olive Street Road, in the region known as Darsdale, opened in this temporary building in September of 1930 to house the students who could not be accommodated in the old Mount Olive School, and later those students who lived too far from the new Hawthorne Elementary School. When the school opened it was staffed by two teachers and had an enrollment of 65 students. (Photo Courtesy of the Archives of the University City Public Library.)

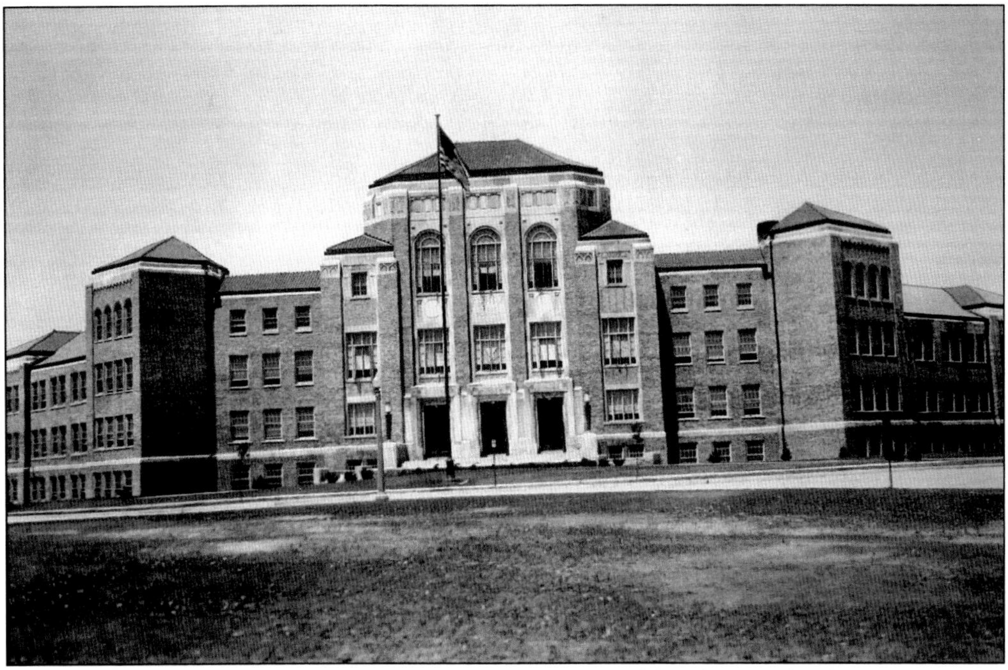

On January 27, 1930, University City High School opened for classes. The first occupants of the new building were 29 teachers and 500 students. In 1936, an auditorium with a seating capacity of 1,600 was added along with several classrooms. (Photo Courtesy of the Archives of the University City Public Library.)

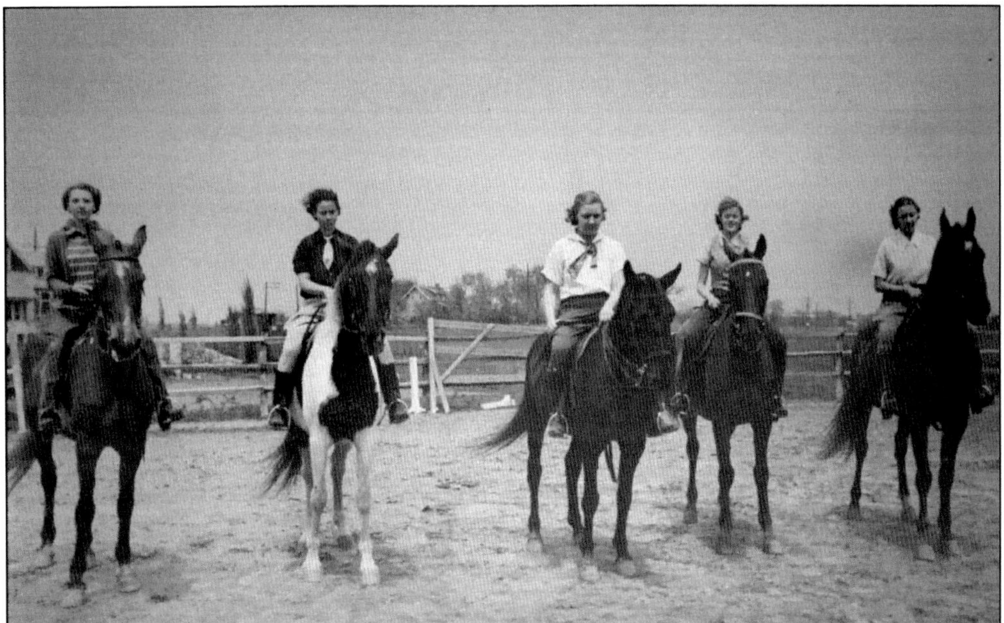

Since its inception, University City High School has offered its students a wide range of curricular offerings. These students, pictured in 1937, are involved in an equestrian class. (Photo Courtesy of the Archives of the University City Public Library.)

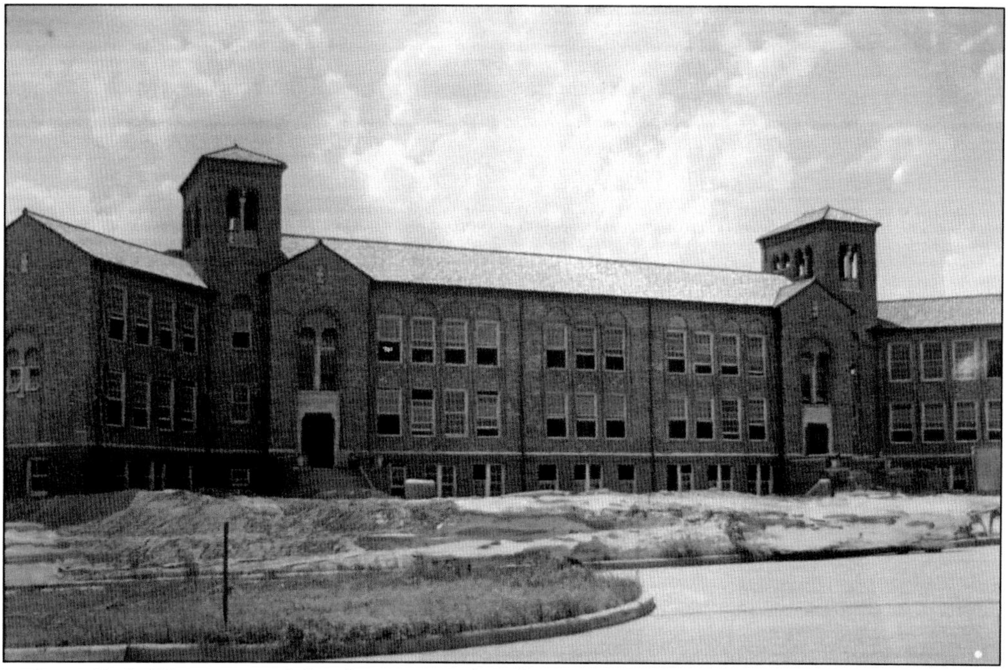

Jackson Park Elementary School was completed on January 27, 1930, and opened in 1933 with 322 students and 10 teachers. Mrs. Helen Rossai served as part-time principal the first year. The school was part of a plan for an educational center to be developed in the area from Jackson Avenue to Hanley Road and from Shaftesbury Avenue to Tulane Avenue. (Photo Courtesy of the Archives of University City Public Library.)

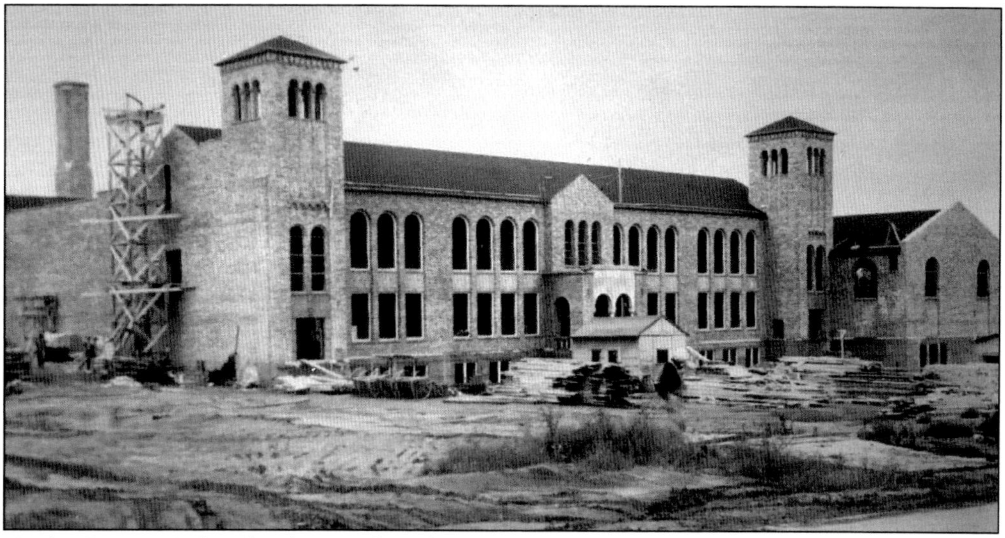

Hanley Junior High School opened its doors in September of 1937, with 25 teachers and an enrollment of 559 pupils. Only 50 of the students were new to University City schools. Later additions were added to Hanley Junior High, Jackson Park Elementary School, and the Senior High School with funds from the federal government's Work Projects Administration (WPA). Hanley was later demolished to make way for the University Place subdivision. (Photo Courtesy of the Archives of University City Public Library.)

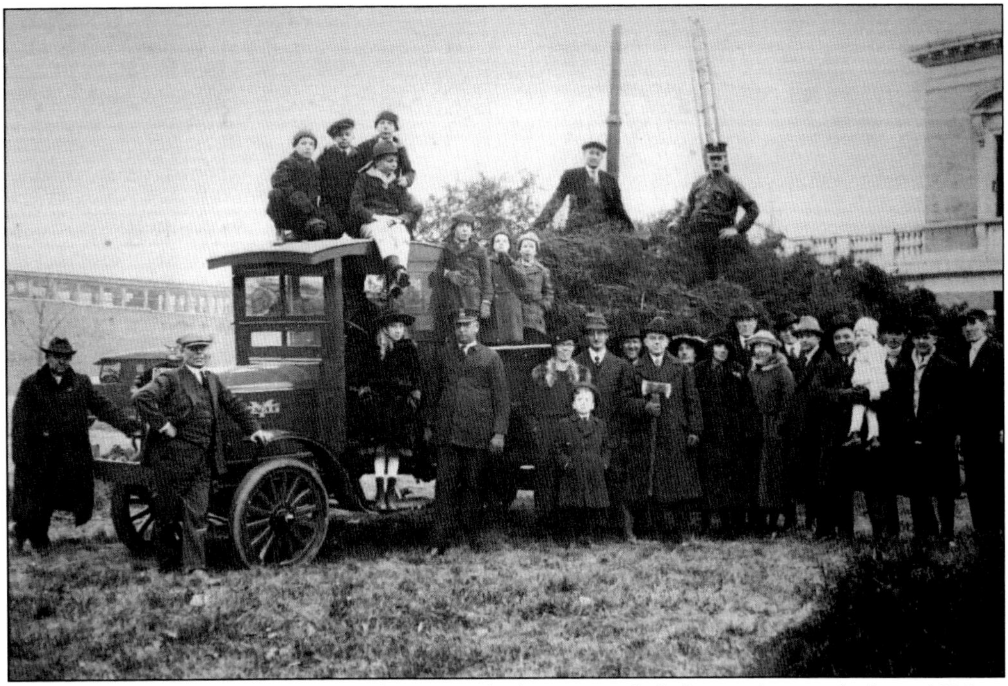

Mayor Warren C. Flynn, the gentleman with the ax, guided the city's growth from 1920 to 1929. When he took office the city was healthy and had stable property values. During Flynn's administration, the city extended its boundaries to the northwest and created a Department of Parks and Recreation in 1922. Prior to that time the city had designated no land for a park. (Photo Courtesy of the Archives of the University City Public Library.)

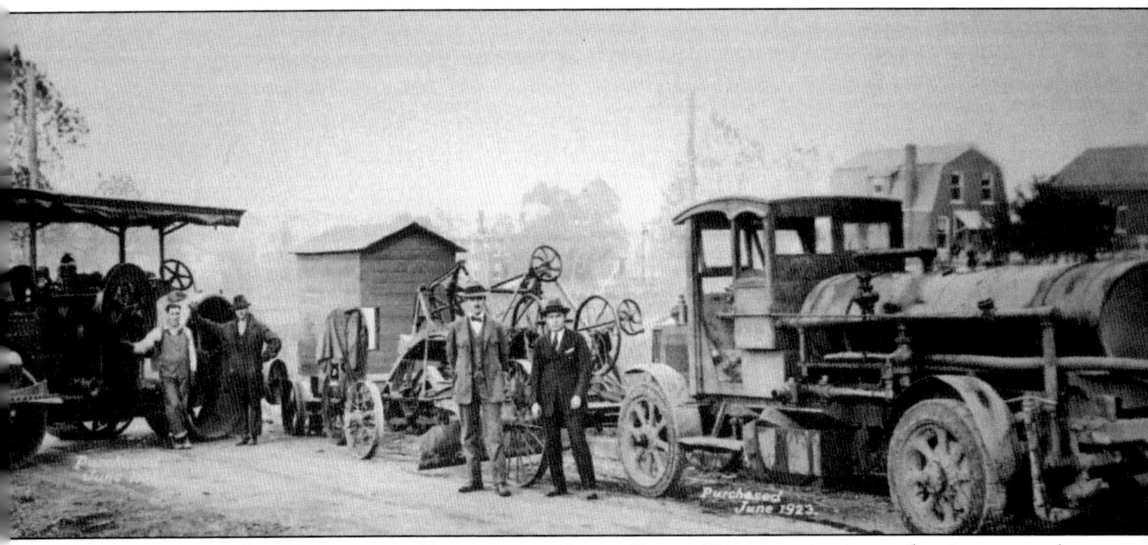

The University City Engineering Department, Street Repair Division, is pictured as it appeared in 1924 under Walter Heimbuecher, the city engineer. (Photo Courtesy of the Archives of the University City Public Library.)

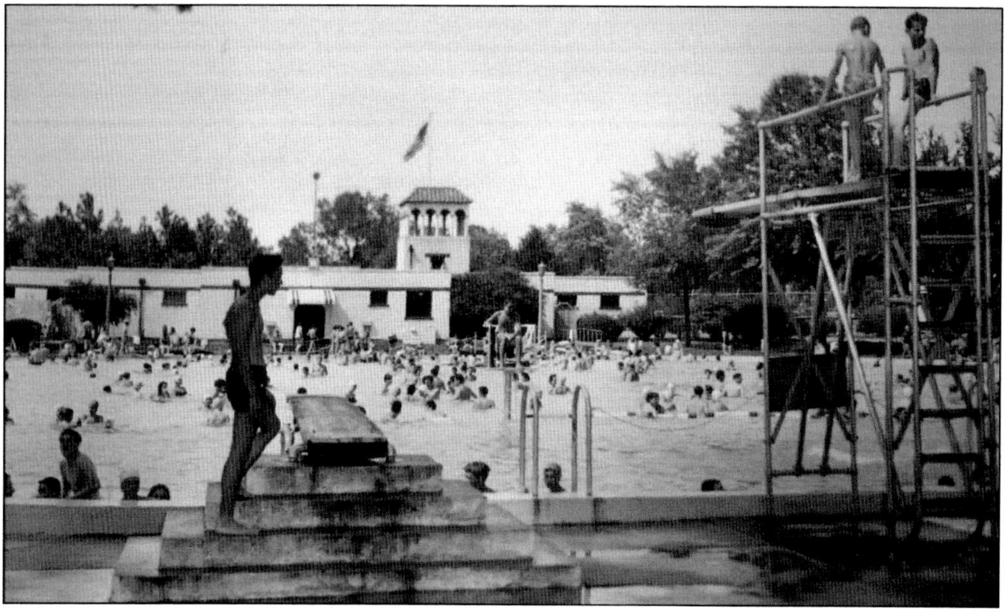

Under the Flynn Administration, University City opened Heman Park. In order to provide work, the pool, completed in the 1930s, was done entirely by hand. The park was named for August Heman, the city's second mayor. City residents, young and old, still enjoy a swim at the pool during the summer. The park also offers picnic grounds, baseball diamonds, play area, basketball stands, community center, and tennis courts. (Photo Courtesy of the Archives of the University City Public Library.)

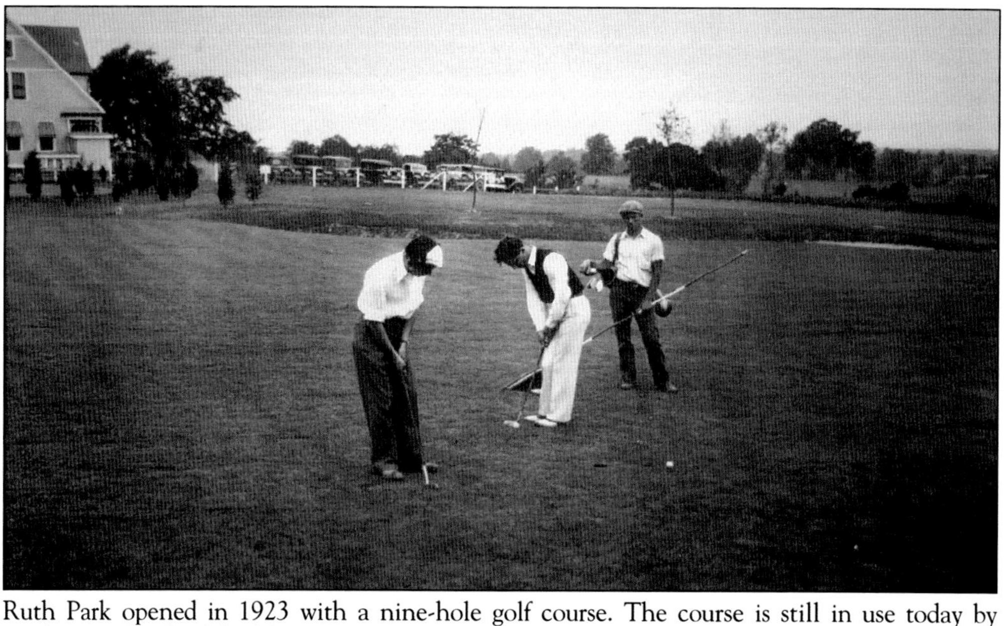

Ruth Park opened in 1923 with a nine-hole golf course. The course is still in use today by residents. The land had been owned by Jacob Klein and was used as a farm on which he harvested the last wheat crop grown in University City. A 26-acre, wooded tract on the north side of the park off McKnight, known as Ruth Park Woods, had been set aside as a forest preserve and nature study area. (Photo Courtesy of the Archives of the University City Public Library.)

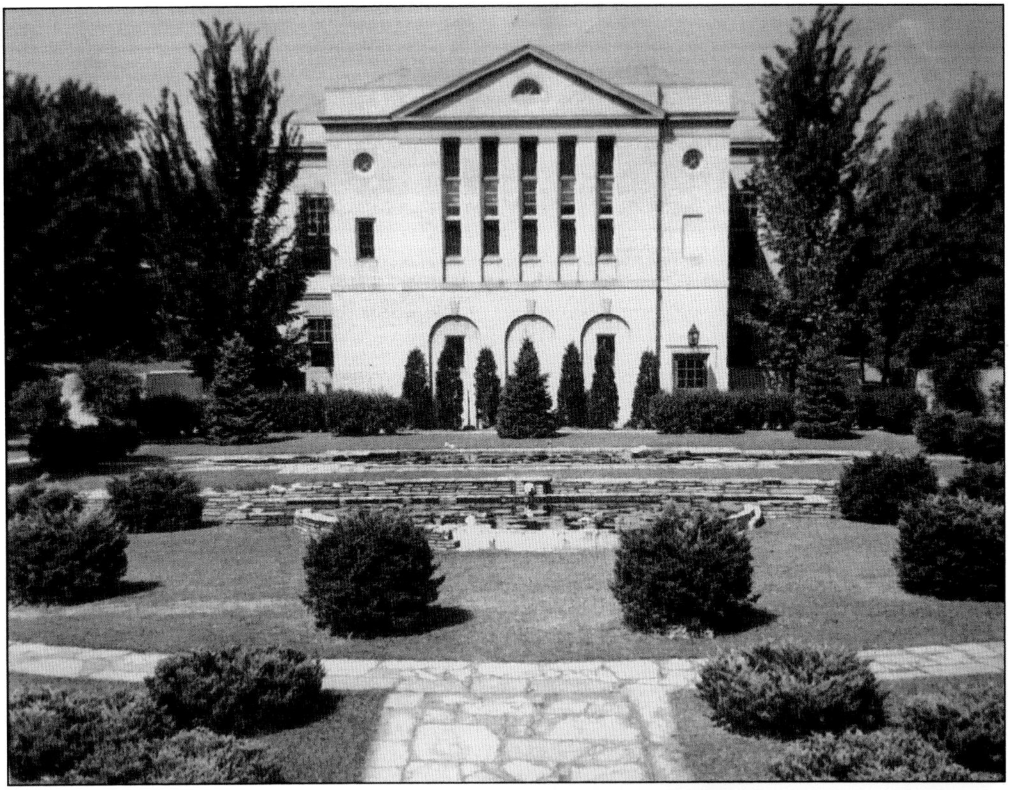

University City did not feel the problems of many communities during the 1930s, and was able to take advantage of the grants-in-aid funds available through the Work Projects Administration (WPA), which enabled it to build the library, pictured above, and the River Des Peres channel, pictured below. All employees working on the projects were paid the prevailing wage of 87.5¢ per hour. The library served the community until 1969. The pond has long since disappeared. The River Des Peres hand-laid stonework can still be seen in several parts of the city. (Top Photo Courtesy of the Archives of the University City Public Library, Bottom Photo by John A. Wright.)

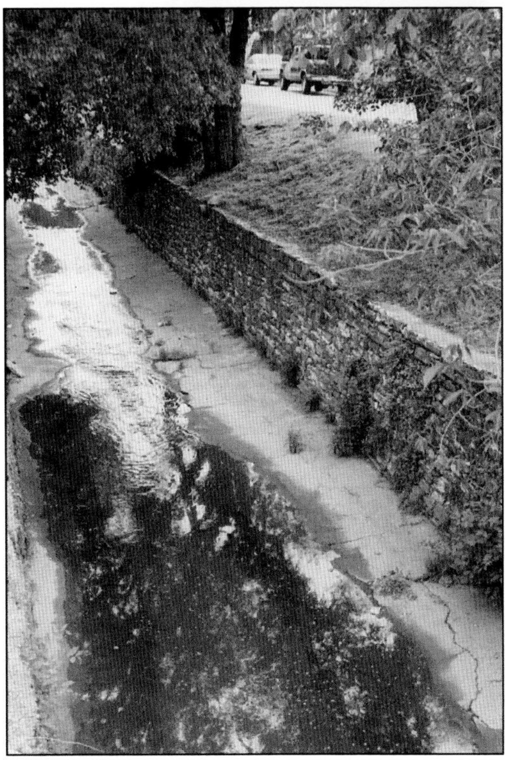

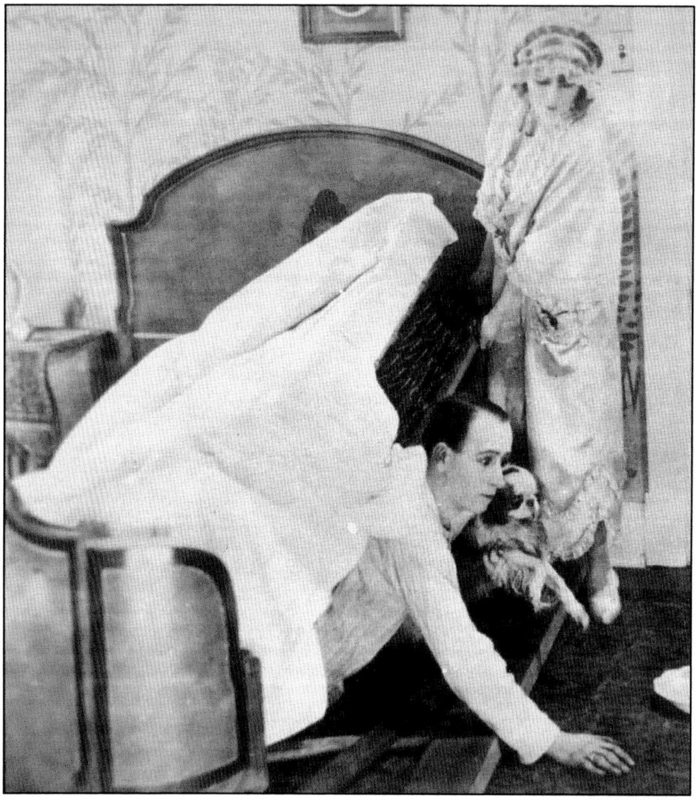

After E.G. Lewis departed University City, the General Film Corporation used the Egyptian Building to produce silent pictures. According to E.G. Lewis in a news article, the first moving picture house showing French moving pictures, mostly a series of pen and ink cartoons, was located on Delmar a block west of the suburban tracks. He stated, "The Lewis Publishing Company had on lease, one of the three first moving picture cameras sent to this country." (Photo Courtesy of the Archives of the University City Public Library.)

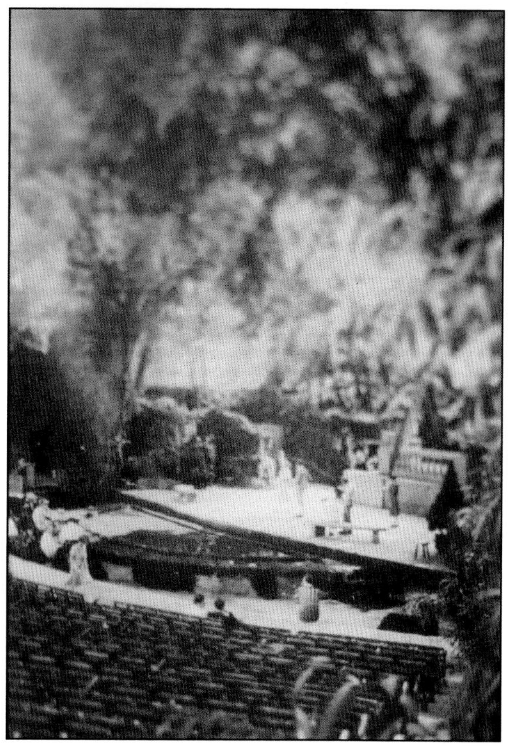

A short-lived spot of entertainment was the open-air Garden Theatre on Olive Street Road near Midland Avenue, which opened in 1925. It was an impressive place with fountains, gardens, and walkways on terraces surrounding an amphitheater. The theater boasted of its Shakespearean plays and productions of the *Queen of Sheba* and *Don Juan* on its stage. Unfortunately, it was forced to close after its third season due to labor and financial problems. (Photo Courtesy of the Archives of the University City Public Library.)

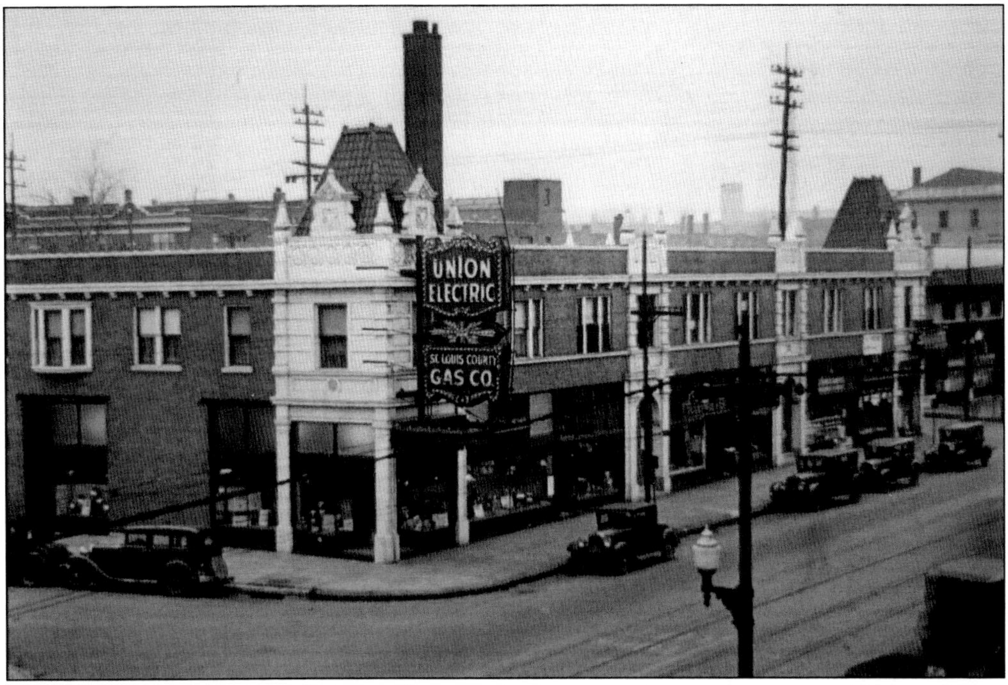

As the city developed, so did the Loop. Within a few blocks residents and visitors could have all their needs met. In the 1920s, the Loop was predominately Catholic; however, by the 1930s, it became known as a middle-class Jewish neighborhood. (Photo Courtesy of the Mercantile Library.)

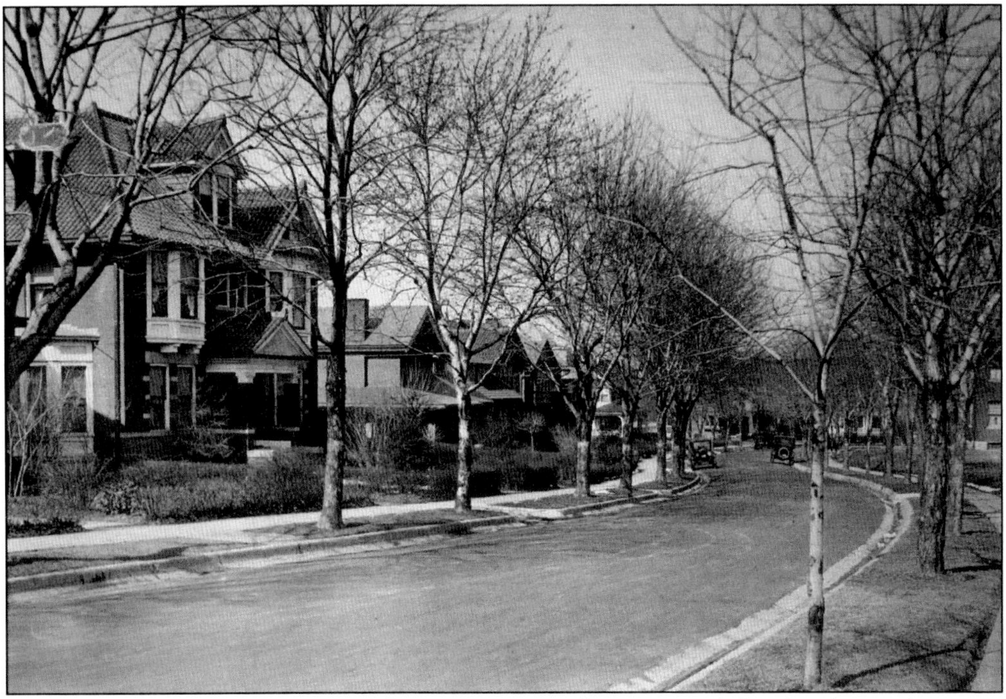

University Heights, Lewis' first subdivision, continued to grow and develop during the 1920s and 1930s. (Photo Courtesy of the Archives of the University City Public Library.)

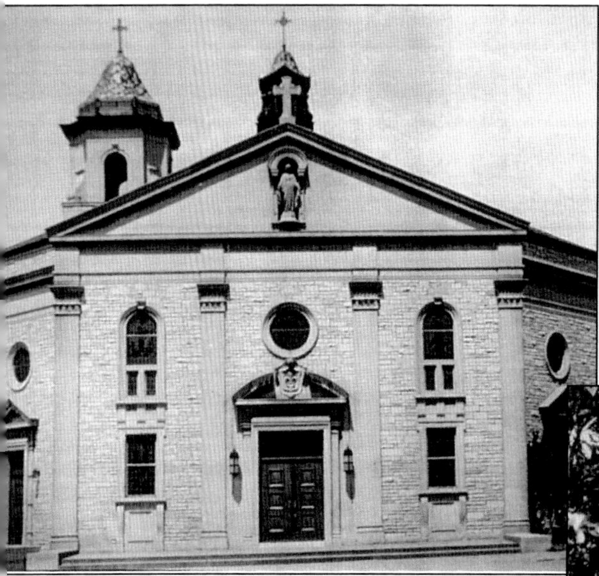

When the Delmar Race Track was razed, All Saints Catholic Parish bought a section of the land the track once occupied at Westgate and Clemens Avenues. In 1917, a fire destroyed the old All Saints Church and School at Maple Avenue and Third Street. The following year the parish built a three-story school building from stone found in University City, on its new site. The third floor of the school was used for religious services until this church was built in 1936. This octagon-shaped edifice was made to symbolize the Eight Beatitudes and contains no interior pillars. (Photo Courtesy of the St. Louis Archdiocesan Archives.)

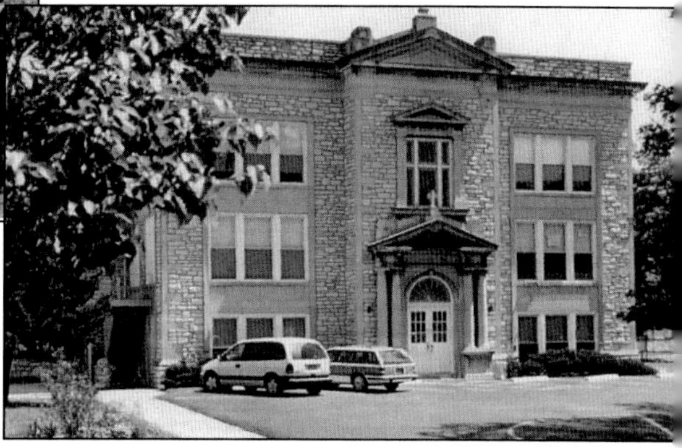

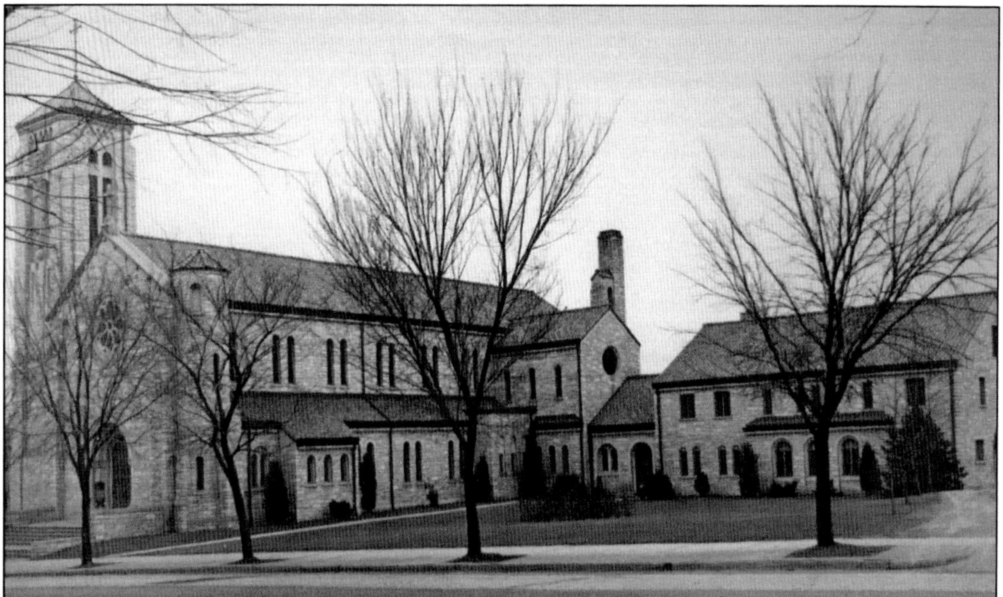

Christ the King Catholic Church was founded in 1927. The site, located at 7300 Balson at that time, was the western limit of University City. The parishioners were of various national backgrounds, the largest group being Irish. The cornerstone of the church was laid in 1940. The church presently operates an elementary school with grades kindergarten through eighth. (Photo Courtesy of the Archives of the St. Louis Archdiocesan Archives.)

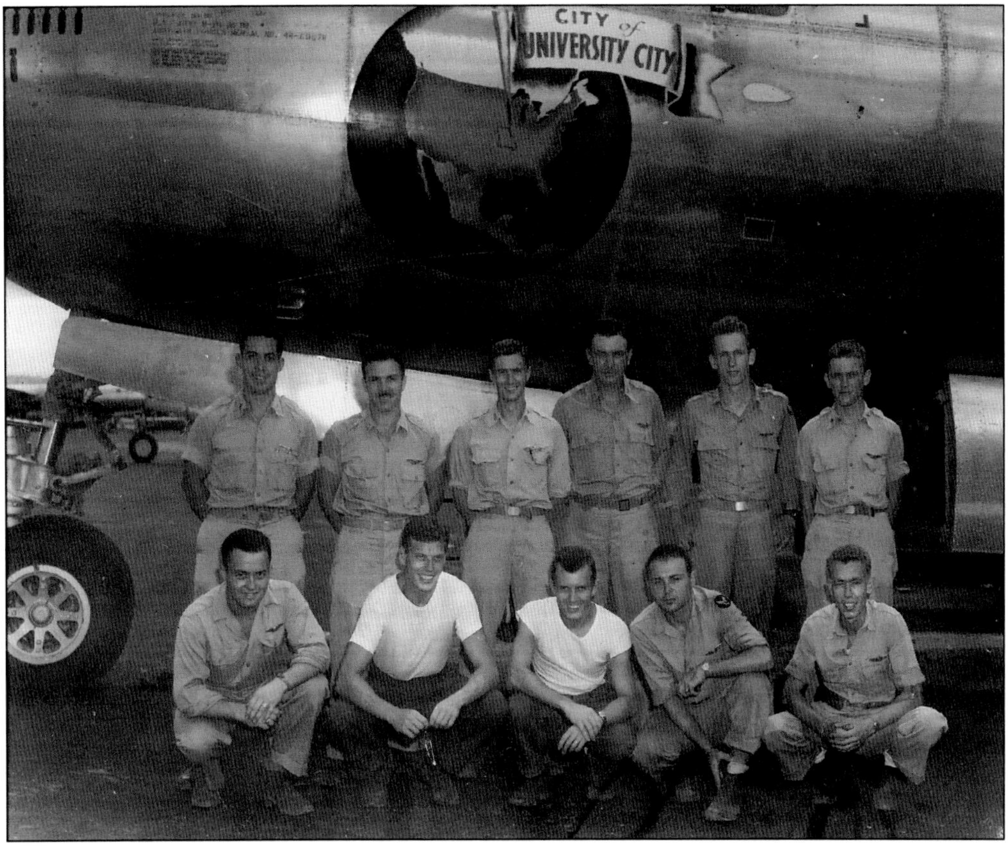

During World War II, a number of University City's young men joined the efforts to secure freedom. This is the Superfortress *City of University City* and her crew, which were acting as University City's representatives in carrying the war to the Japanese homeland. An insignia can be seen on the plane showing University City's location on a map of the United States. Kneeling on the left is Sergeant Marcus C. Saphian, a radio operator, from 731 Inter-drive Avenue. (Photo Courtesy of the Mercantile Library.)

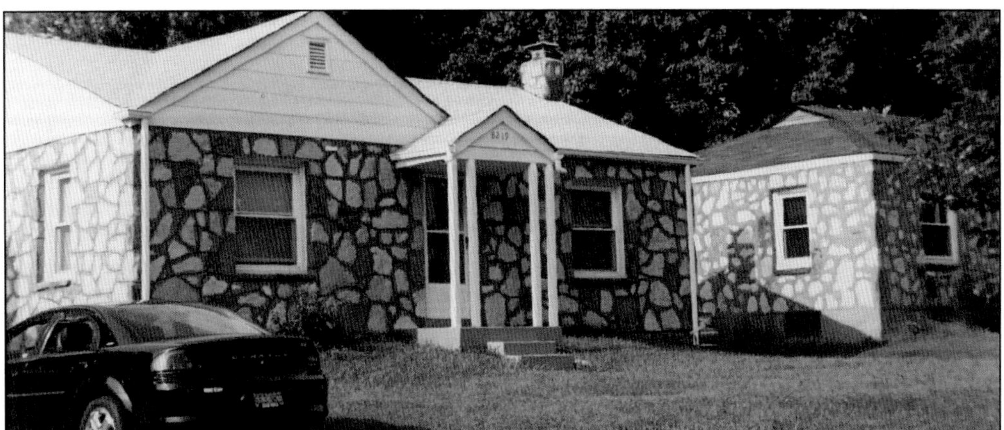

After World War II, University City experienced its greatest housing construction. The new homes, however, were much smaller and one story. (Photo by John A. Wright.)

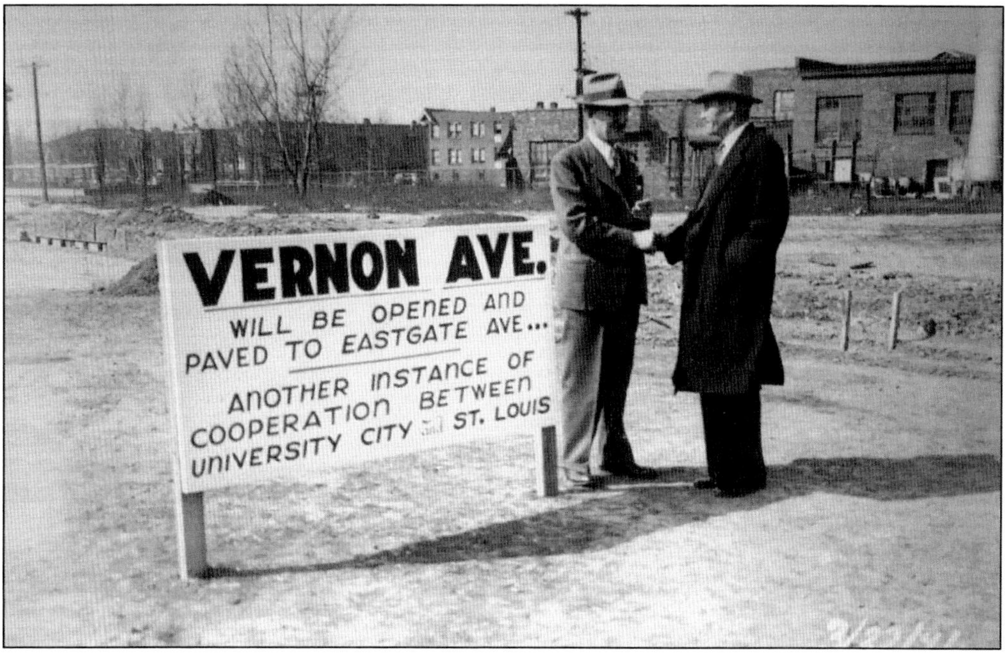

In 1941, an agreement was worked out between the City of St. Louis and University City to open Vernon Avenue to Eastgate to help the movement of traffic. However, when the decision was made to open the street further into University City in 1955, it was met with a brief protest. (Photo Courtesy of the Archives of the University City Public Library.)

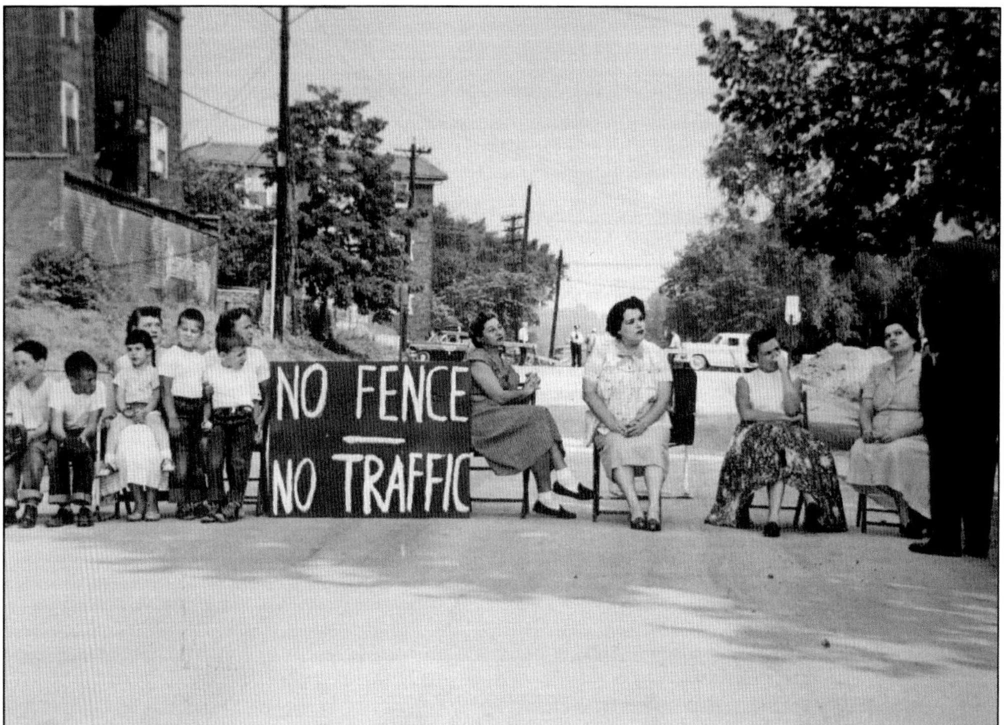

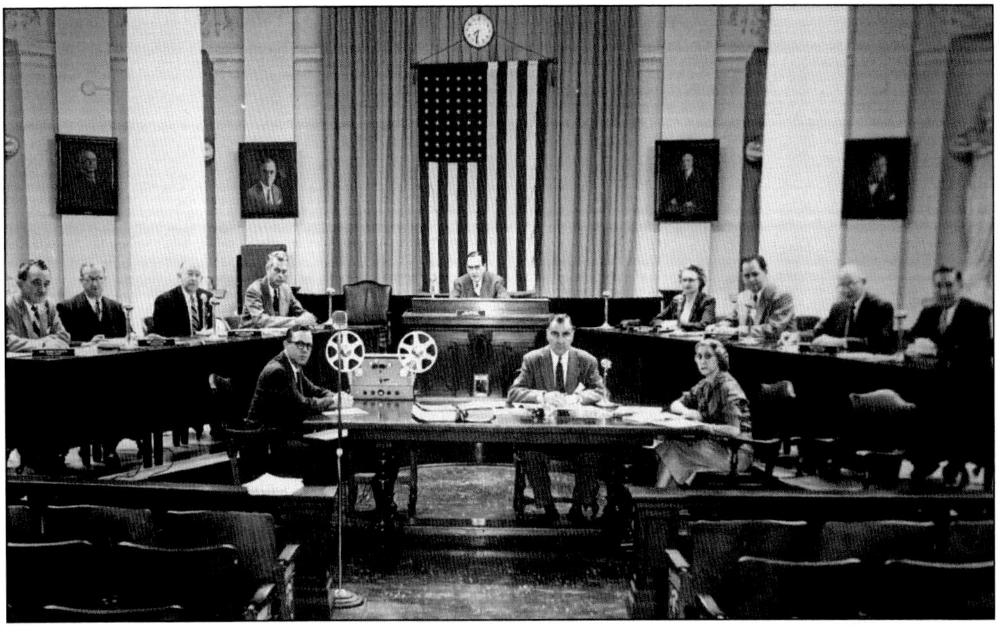

This is a 1955 photo of Mayor Harold Ackert and the council, taken while they were holding a monthly meeting in the council chambers on the top floor of City Hall. Mayor Ackert was followed by Mayor Walter L. Metcalfe in 1954. Under Ackert's Administration, the city continued to improve and expand its facilities; developments included Greensfelder Park and Lamb's Quarry into Metcalfe Park, and construction began on Heman Park Community Center. (Photo Courtesy of the Archives of the University City Public Library.)

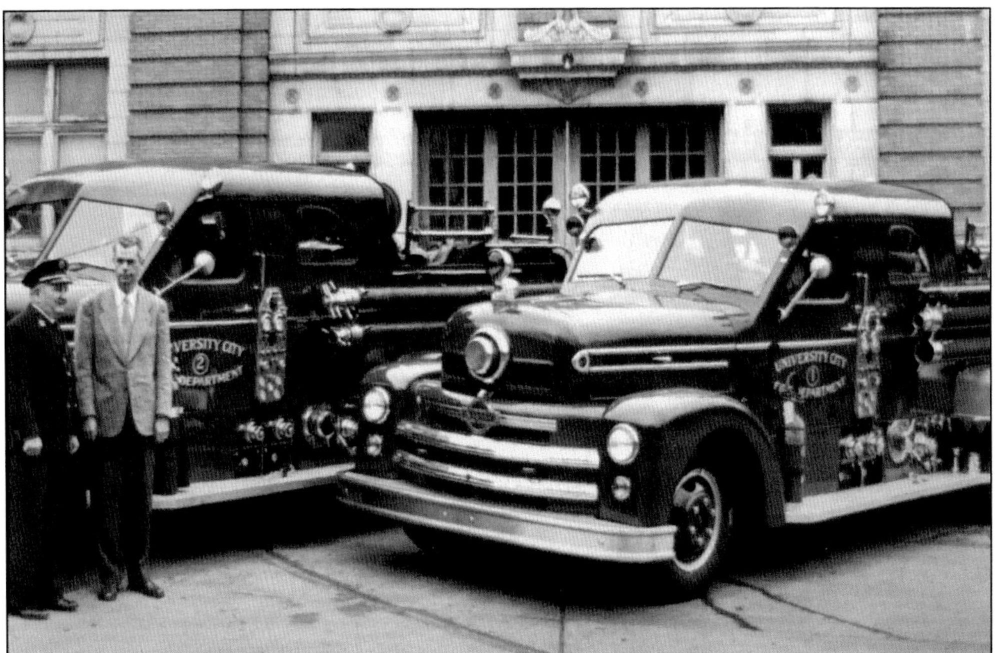

City Manager Elder Guntes and Fire Chief Ernest Byrone stand outside the Fire Department in front of the city's new fire engine in 1953. (Photo Courtesy of Mercantile Library.)

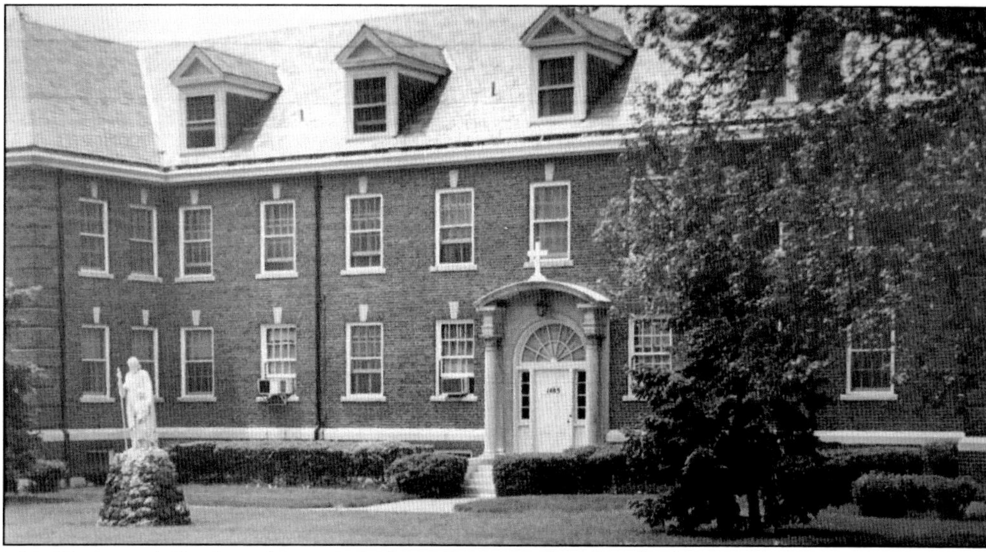

The Sisters of St. Joseph moved their Institute for the deaf to University City in 1935 and constructed it on four acres of land donated by Joseph A. Matter. Matter, a retired landscape gardener, with donations from St. Louis nurserymen, transformed the bare, clay grounds of the Institute into charmingly-landscaped gardens. (Photo Courtesy of the St. Louis Archdiocesan Archives.)

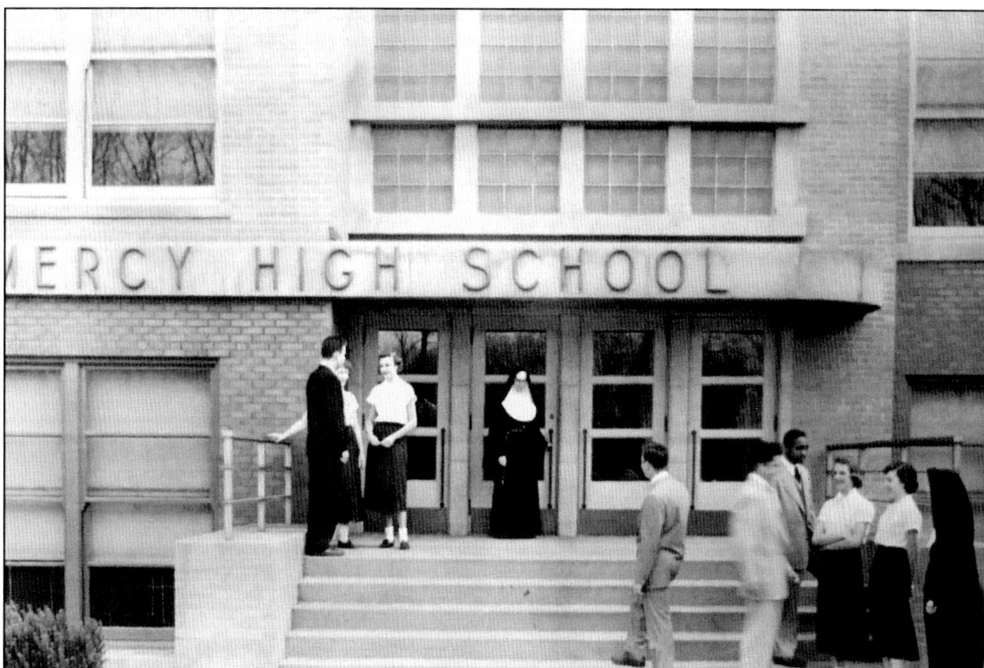

In 1958, the St. Louis Archdiocese opened Mercy High School at Olive Street Road and Pennsylvania Avenue. With a wing added in the 1950s, the school could accommodate 1,200 students. It closed in 1985, and students were transferred to St. Thomas Aquinas High School. The school site is now occupied by a Schnucks Supermarket Shopping Center. (Photo Courtesy of the Sisters of Mercy Archives.)

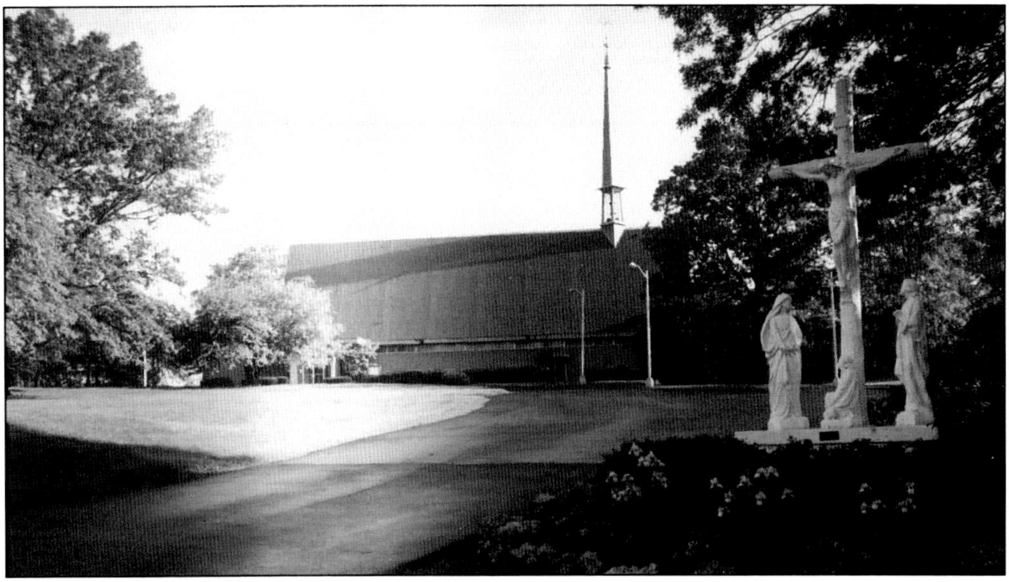

St. Patrick's Parish was established in 1940 in the northwest section of the city on Olive, near the Olivette border. The first building served both as a school and a chapel. The new church was dedicated by the Cardinal at the time, Joseph E. Ritter, on March 16, 1958, and it was closed in 2001 due to dwindling membership. To mark the closing of the church, the parishioners held an Irish wake. The school ceased to operate in 1968 due to its merger with All Saints in the Loop. The church is presently the home of St. Andrew Kim Korean Catholic Church. (Photo by John A. Wright.)

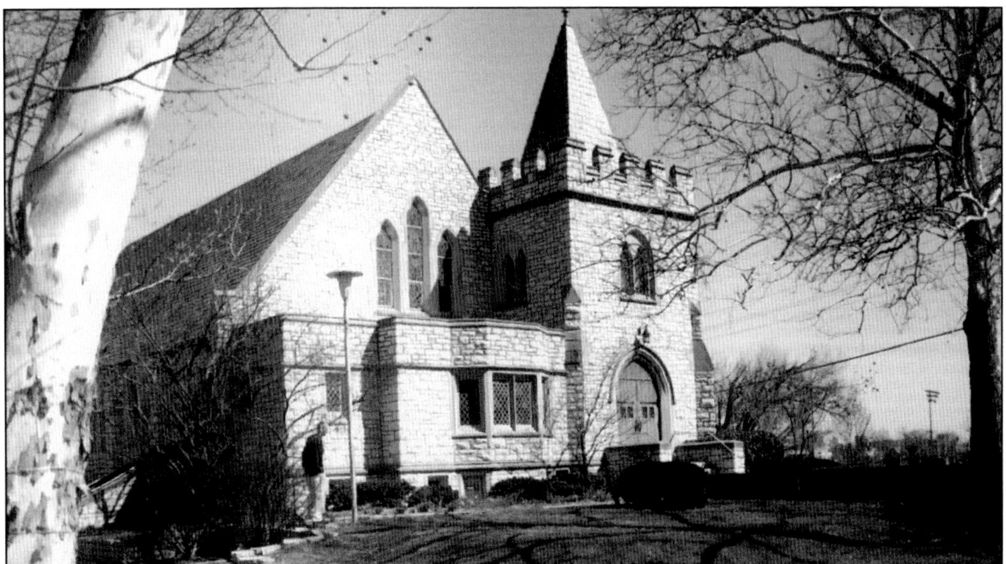

In 1923, Bethel Lutheran Church moved it services to this building at 7001 Forsyth Boulevard. The church was founded in Clayton, Missouri, in 1913. Services were held in the new church's basement for several years, until the completion and dedication of the building took place in 1934. Bethel Lutheran presently operates a school which serves students in grades pre-school through eighth. (Photo By John A. Wright.)

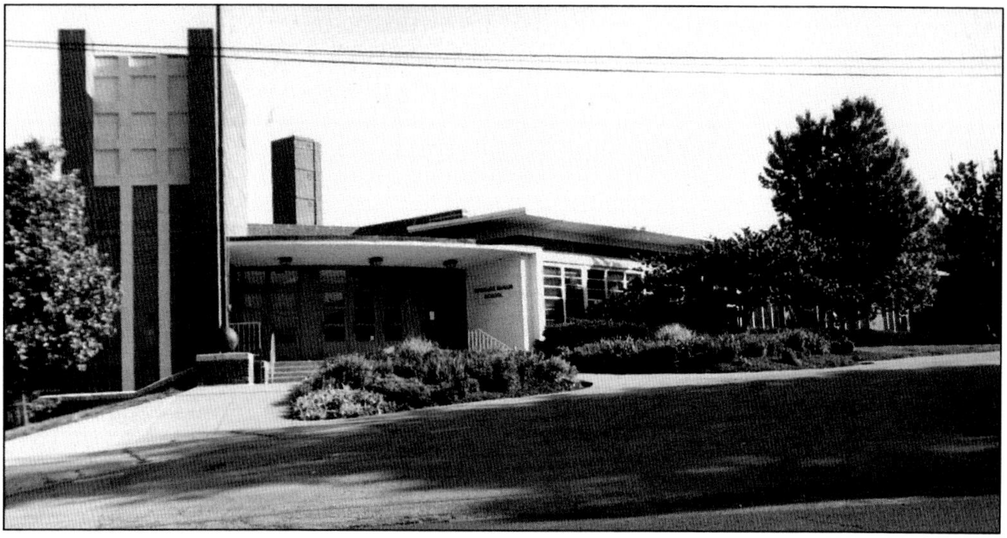

Blackberry Lane Elementary School opened in 1949 to serve the west-central section of the city around Ruth Park. The following year the enrollment was too large for the building, and 150 students were bussed to Flynn Park and Delmar-Harvard. Six more rooms and a playroom were added the following year.

The school is now part of the Brittany Woods complex and was renamed for Ronald McNair, the African-American astronaut who lost his life when the space shuttle *Challenger* exploded. (Photo by John A. Wright.)

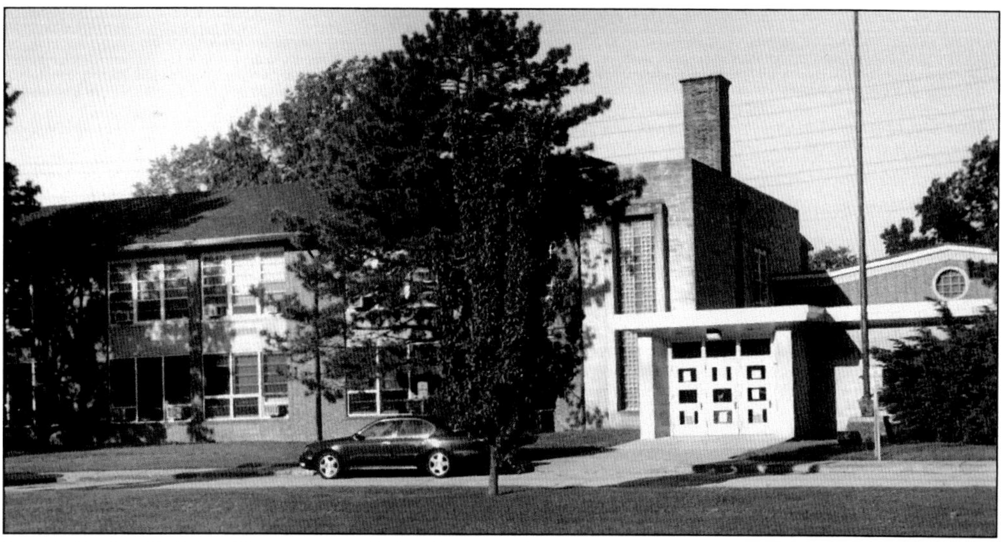

In 1953, McKnight Elementary School opened to serve the growing population in the southwestern part of University City. The site was selected for its convenient and congenial location. The school was closed when its enrollment dwindled. The district's central office was moved to the building.

Two other school buildings—Canterbury and Greensfelder Park—were constructed during the 1950s to meet the growing needs of the district. The buildings were later sold and are now used for other purposes. (Photo by John A. Wright.)

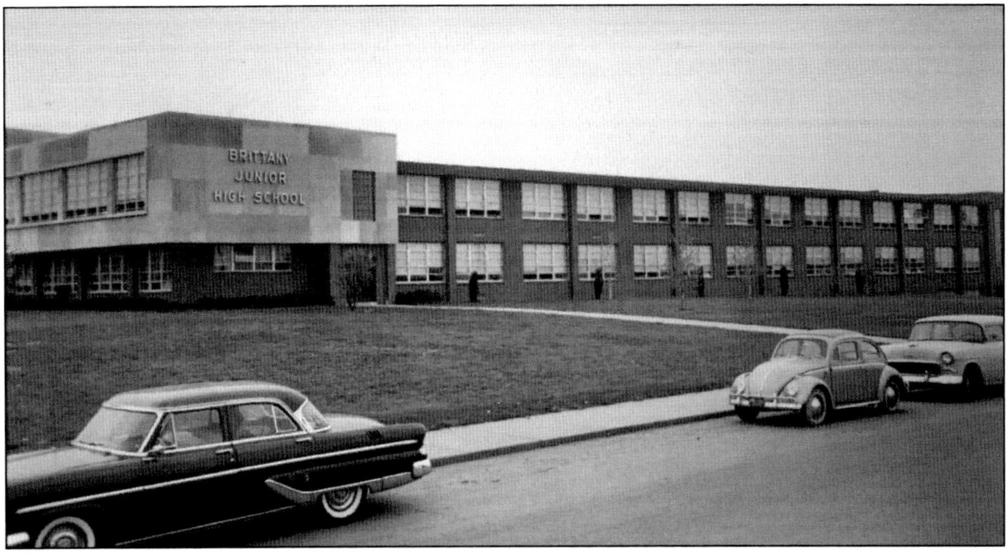

Soon after the end of World War II, when Hanley Junior High's enrollment reached 1,335, it became evident that it had outgrown its 900-student capacity. Numerous subdivisions had been built in the area west of North and South Road which created a need for a junior high school program. Brittany Junior High School opened in 1955, with 591students. While the building was being planned, a junior high program was conducted in the Ward Building. (Photo Courtesy of the Archives of the University City Public Library.)

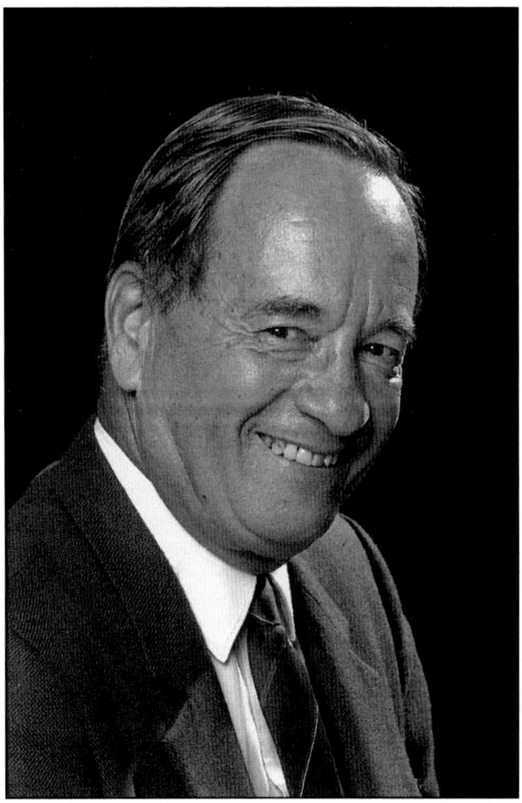

Under Alfred J. Fleischer, a member of the University City School Board for 15 years and its president from 1958 to 1968, the district gained national recognition for innovation and experimentation in education. The district experimented with team teaching, the initial teaching alphabet, independent study programs, and new methods of reporting progress to parents. The library in the high school was donated to the school district by Fleischer and named in his honor. (Photo Courtesy of Alfred J. Fleischer.)

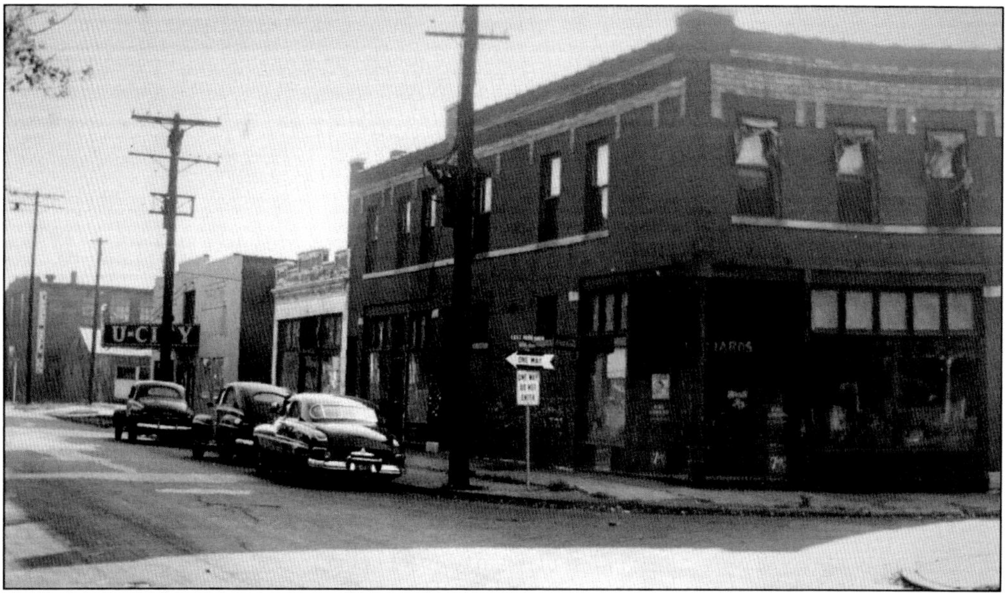

By the 1950s, the northeast section of the city, known as Cunningham Park, was beginning to show deterioration, so in 1962, citizens passed an urban renewal bond to revitalize the area. Cunningham Industrial Park is now located in this section of the community. (Photo Courtesy of the Archives of the University City Public Library.)

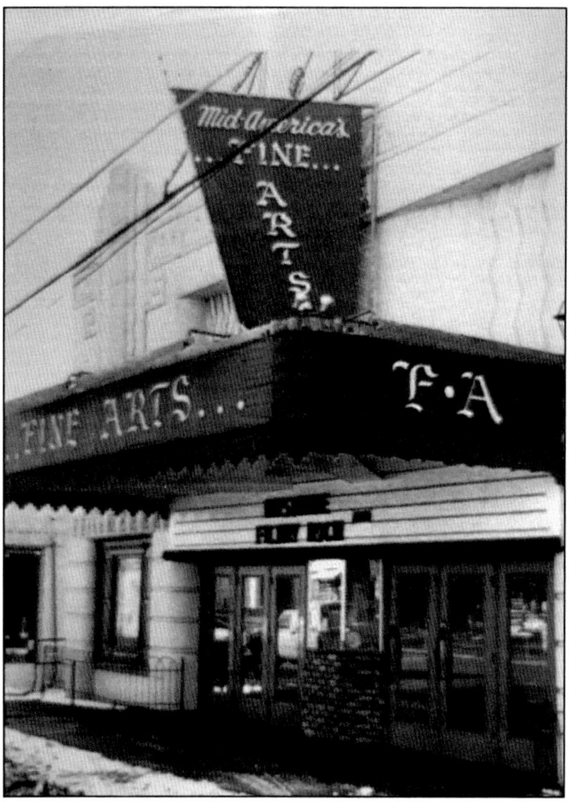

The old Beverly Movie Theater, like many movie theaters across the county, began to loose its appeal during the 1950s. It was later renamed Mid-America's Fine Arts Theater and specialized in sexually explicit films. The theater closed in the mid-1980s, after considerable protests from the community. (Photo Courtesy of the Mercantile Library.)

Four

CHALLENGES AND CELEBRATIONS

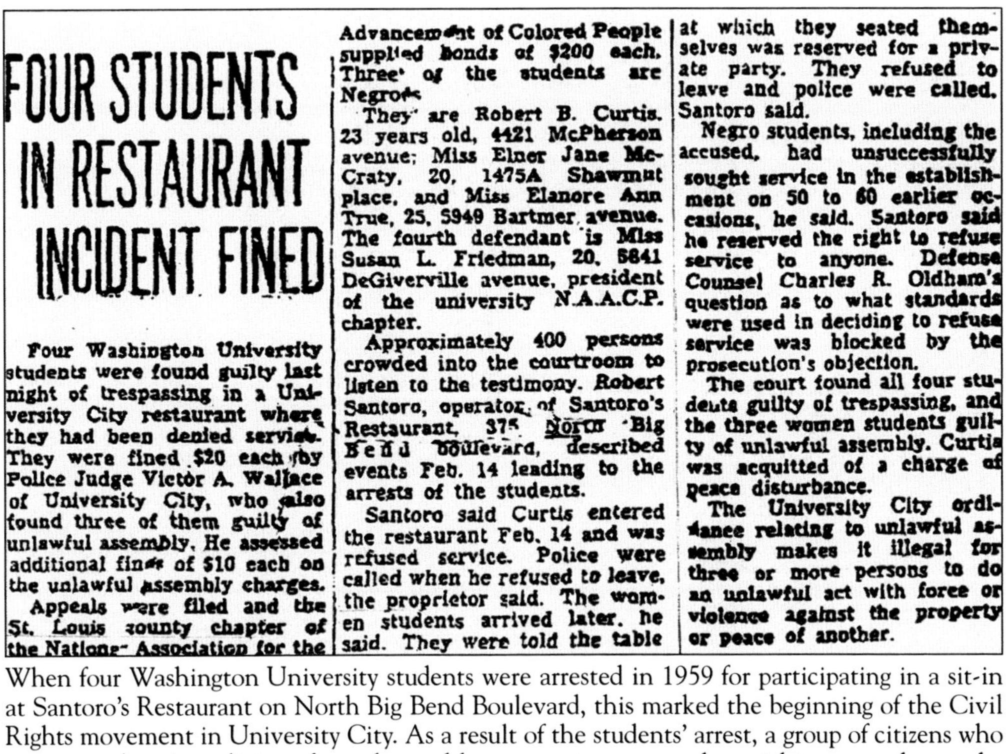

FOUR STUDENTS IN RESTAURANT INCIDENT FINED

Four Washington University students were found guilty last night of trespassing in a University City restaurant where they had been denied service. They were fined $20 each by Police Judge Victor A. Wallace of University City, who also found three of them guilty of unlawful assembly. He assessed additional fines of $10 each on the unlawful assembly charges.

Appeals were filed and the St. Louis county chapter of the National Association for the Advancement of Colored People supplied bonds of $200 each. Three of the students are Negroes.

They are Robert B. Curtis, 23 years old, 4421 McPherson avenue; Miss Elner Jane McCraty, 20, 1475A Shawmut place, and Miss Elanore Ann True, 25, 5949 Bartmer avenue. The fourth defendant is Miss Susan L. Friedman, 20, 5841 DeGiverville avenue, president of the university N.A.A.C.P. chapter.

Approximately 400 persons crowded into the courtroom to listen to the testimony. Robert Santoro, operator of Santoro's Restaurant, 375 North Big Bend boulevard, described events Feb. 14 leading to the arrests of the students.

Santoro said Curtis entered the restaurant Feb. 14 and was refused service. Police were called when he refused to leave, the proprietor said. The women students arrived later, he said. They were told the table at which they seated themselves was reserved for a private party. They refused to leave and police were called, Santoro said.

Negro students, including the accused, had unsuccessfully sought service in the establishment on 50 to 60 earlier occasions, he said. Santoro said he reserved the right to refuse service to anyone. Defense Counsel Charles R. Oldham's question as to what standards were used in deciding to refuse service was blocked by the prosecution's objection.

The court found all four students guilty of trespassing, and the three women students guilty of unlawful assembly. Curtis was acquitted of a charge of peace disturbance.

The University City ordinance relating to unlawful assembly makes it illegal for three or more persons to do an unlawful act with force or violence against the property or peace of another.

When four Washington University students were arrested in 1959 for participating in a sit-in at Santoro's Restaurant on North Big Bend Boulevard, this marked the beginning of the Civil Rights movement in University City. As a result of the students' arrest, a group of citizens who represented major religions formed an ad hoc committee to study racial issues, and to make recommendations. One of the committee's recommendations to the City Council was to pass a public accommodations law, but no immediate action was taken. A law was passed in 1963, however, making University City the first county municipality to pass such a bill. During that uncertain time, few would have thought that University City would have become a pioneer in Civil Rights. At that time, the city still had an ordinance requiring each African-American male who worked as a janitor or a porter to wear an identification badge with a photograph, name, and finger prints. (Article Courtesy of the Mercantile Library.)

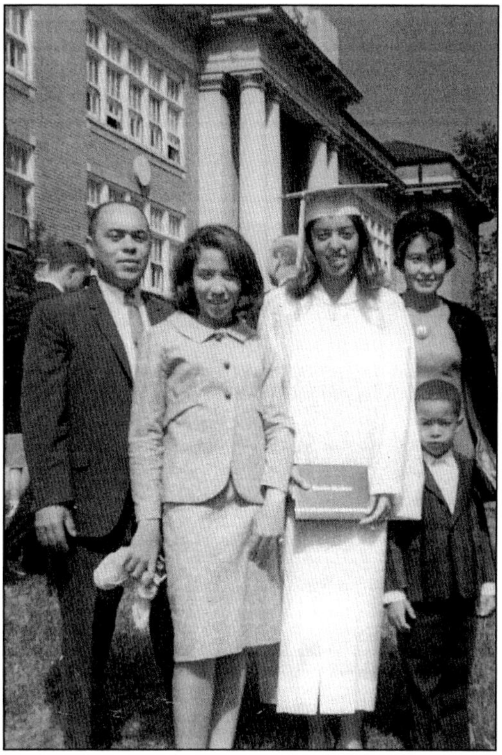

On April 12, 1963, John A. Whitfield and his family became the first African Americans to move onto the 7100 block of Pershing. Pictured here, from left to right, are John Sr., with daughters Pamela Y., Carma J., son John Jr., and wife Edna. According to the Whitfields, "For Sale" signs were soon on display up and down the block. Some realtors took advantage of the situation by using a tactic known today as "block busting" to cause panic selling. (Photo Courtesy of John and Edna Whitfield.)

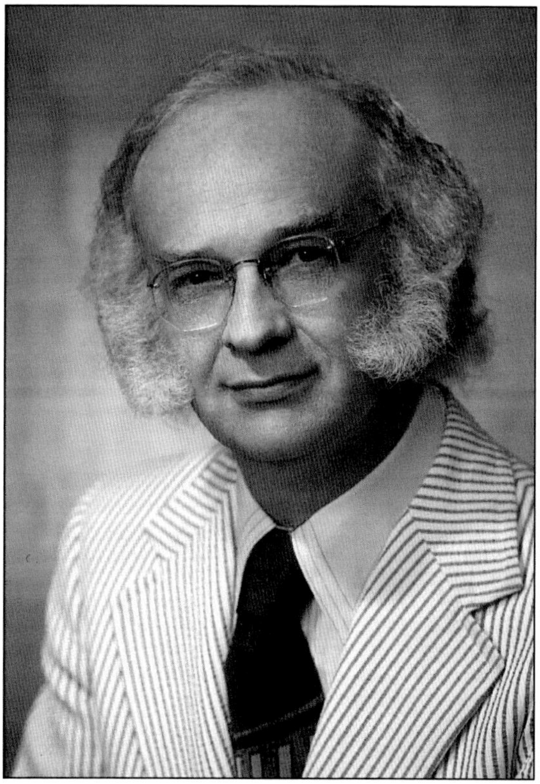

To help bring some sanity to the neighborhood, Dr. George Murphy, a Washington University psychiatrist and resident of the community, went door-to-door and convinced his neighbors to take their "For Sale" signs down.

At the time, restrictive covenants and agreements between members of the real estate business and the St. Louis Real Estate Board had not allowed integration to take place in many neighborhoods, and therefore many agents saw University City as a place to capitalize on panic-stricken whites. (Photo Courtesy of Dr. George Murphy.)

On February 3, 1963, when the last streetcar left University City, in a small, symbolic way, it signaled an end to an era. Little did many know that the years and events to follow would change University City forever. (Photo Courtesy of Washington University.)

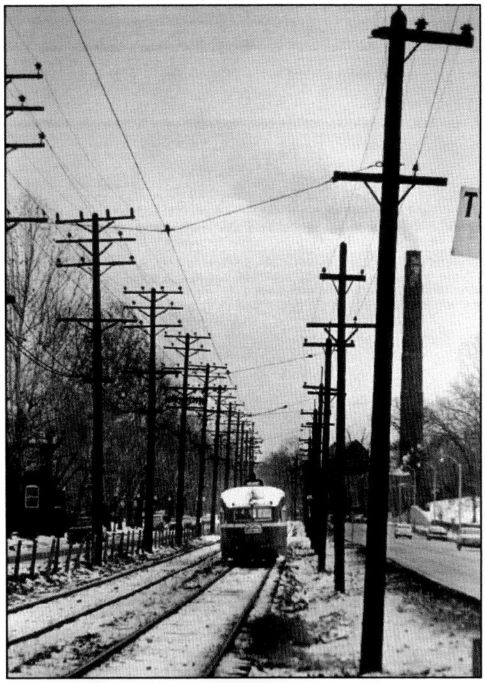

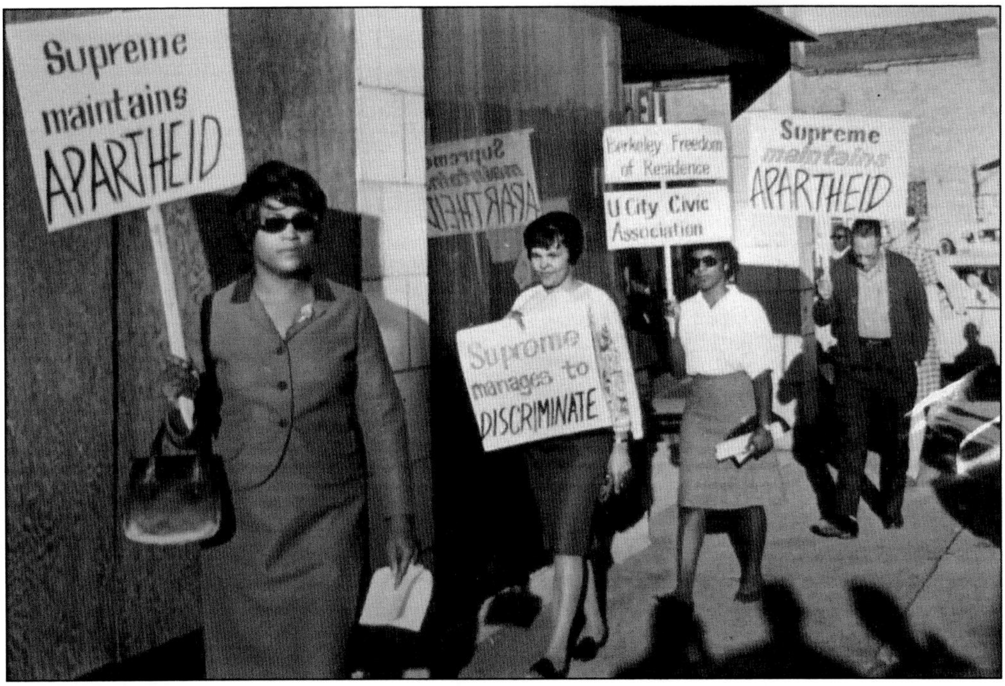

Not only was discrimination in housing challenged in University City, but so, too, were those individuals in University City who engaged in unfair housing practices. In 1966, members of the University City and Berkeley Freedom of Residence Committee, University City Civic Association, CORE, and ACTION began picketing in front of Supreme Management Corporation at 6621 Delmar Boulevard because of the housing practices in the City of Berkeley. (Photo Courtesy of Mercantile Library.)

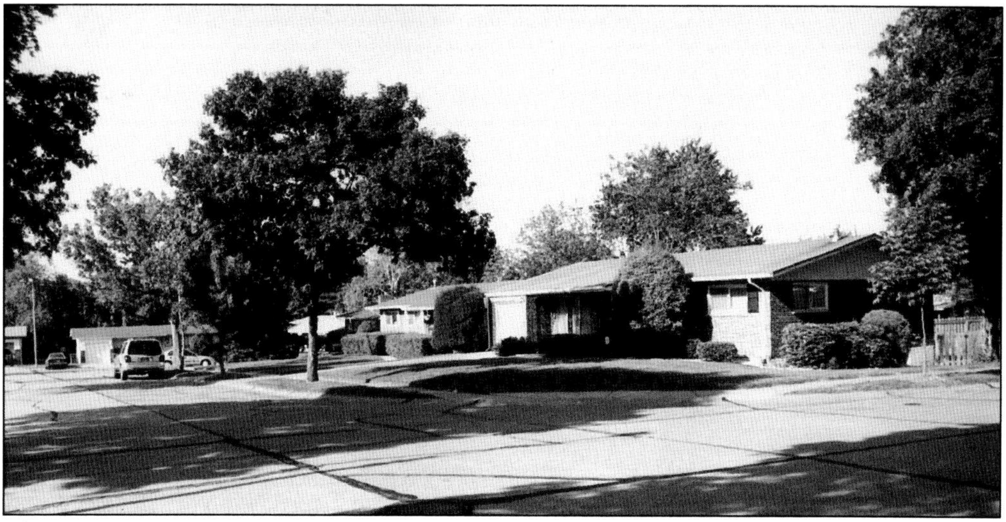

The Forest Green Court off Partridge Avenue played an important role in the integration of University City. When these homes were constructed between 1964 and 1965, they were purchased by African Americans. Since the ranch-style homes in this development were of the same size and quality of those in similar developments nearby, the area became instantly an integrated middle-class neighborhood. (Photo by John A. Wright.)

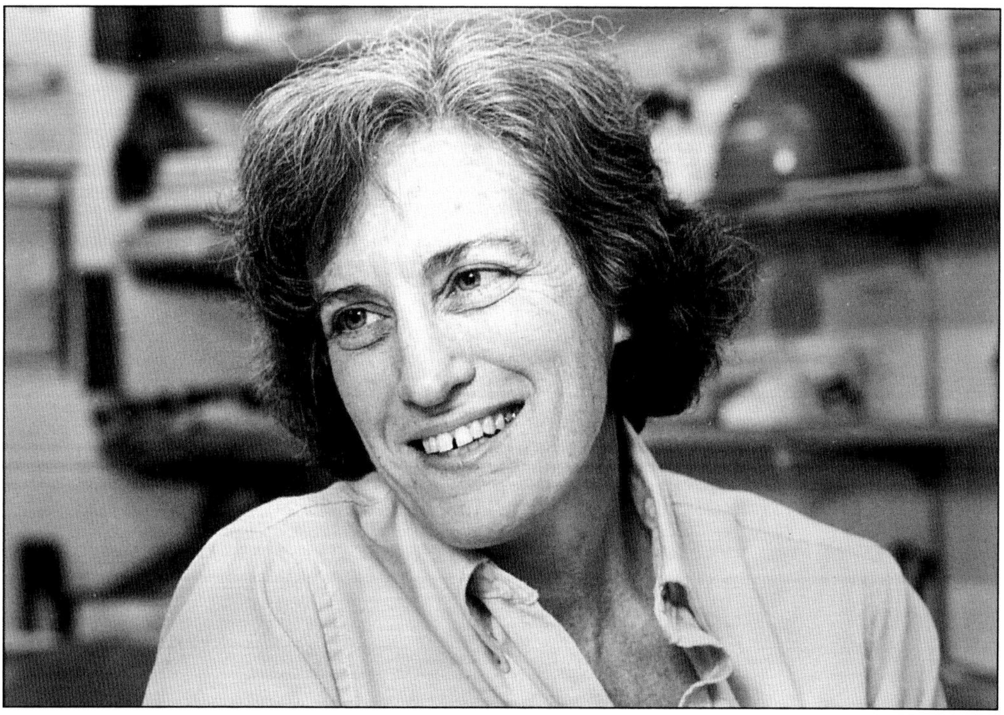

In 1968, under the leadership of Kay Drey, the University City Residential Service was incorporated. The goal of this non-profit organization was to preserve integrated communities in the city. The real estate agencies had red-lined University City, making mortgages difficult to obtain and insurance rates unfairly inflated. To head off panic, the city introduced the use of occupancy permits and a ban on "For Sale" signs. (Photo Courtesy of Kay Drey and Mike DeFilippo.)

In 1973, these university firemen and others succeeded in their efforts to avoid being required to man the city's Emergency Operation Center. However, success did not come easy in 1977 when the firemen went on strike over benefits for two fellow, partially-disabled firemen. A few days after the strike started, a fire broke out in the old United States Fiber Stopper Company built by E.G. Lewis. Because of the strike no firemen would cross the picket line and the building burned down. (Photo Courtesy of the Mercantile Library.)

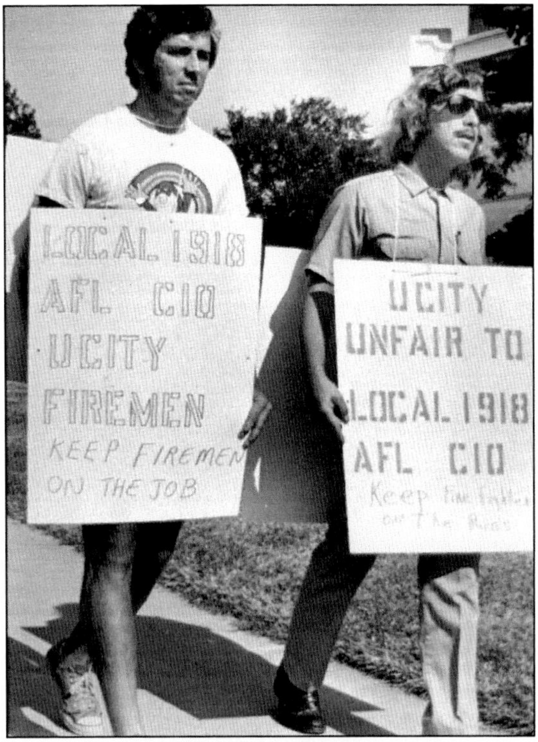

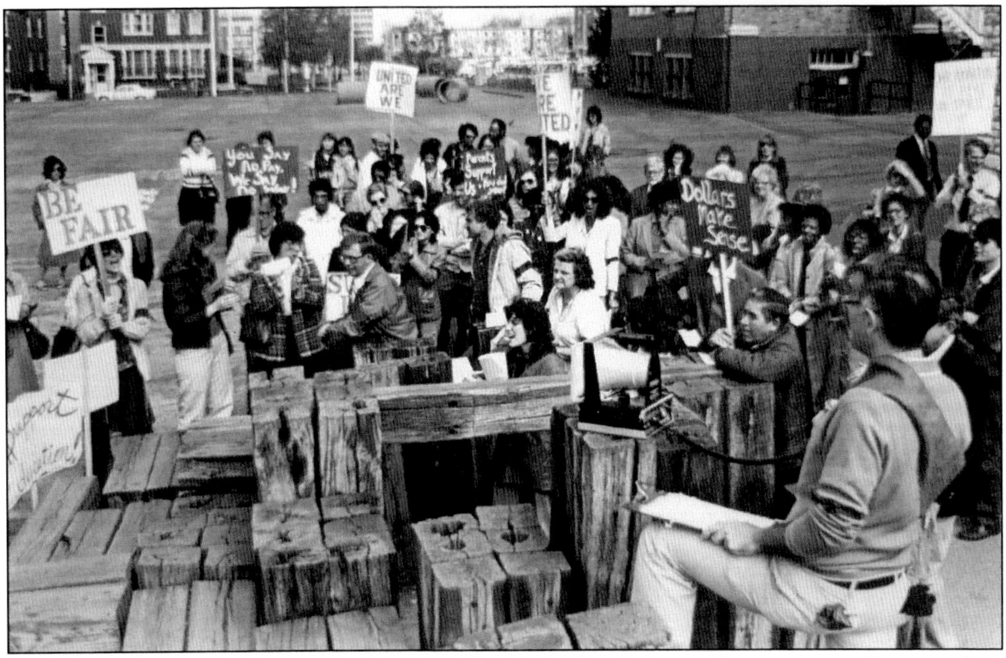

While the school system was attempting to adjust to a changing population, it was also struggling to provide funding for operations. These teachers are gathered in the Delmar-Harvard School yard to protest and to demand higher salaries. Because of the community's mainly residential status, voter approved higher taxes were constantly needed to maintain district operations. (Photo Courtesy of the Mercantile Library.)

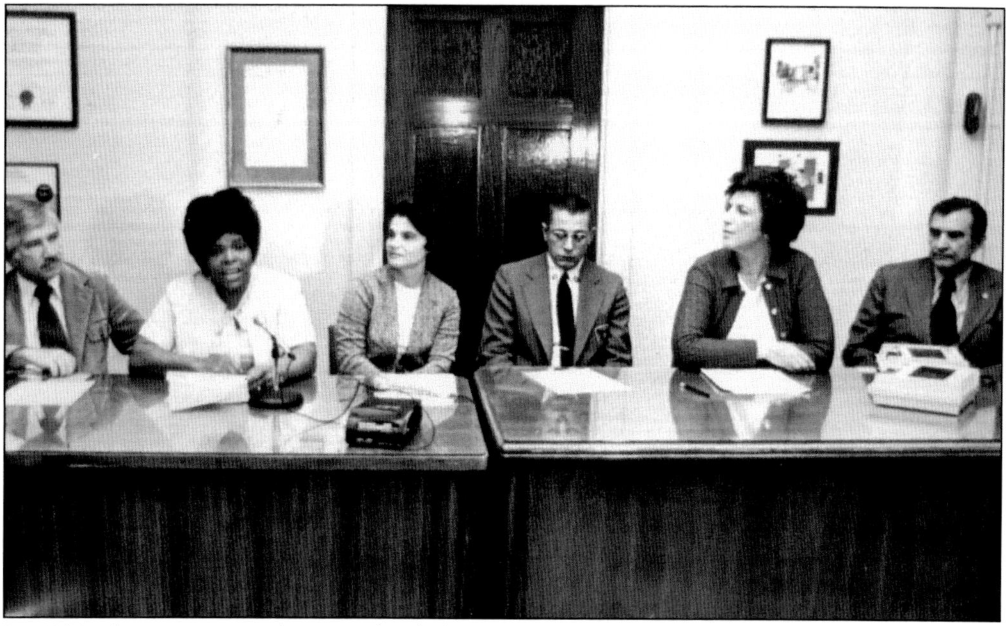

In 1970, the community became divided on the issue of school integration—neighborhood schools versus a more centralized concept. The neighborhood proponents won by obtaining three seats on the school board. After the election, African-American residents began to monitor the schools through such organizations as Black Watch, to ensure equal educational opportunities were being provided for all students. Resident Betty Thompson is pictured here, second from the left, in the late 1970s, with University City municipal and school officials, expressing her concerns about school issues. (Photo Courtesy of the Mercantile Library.)

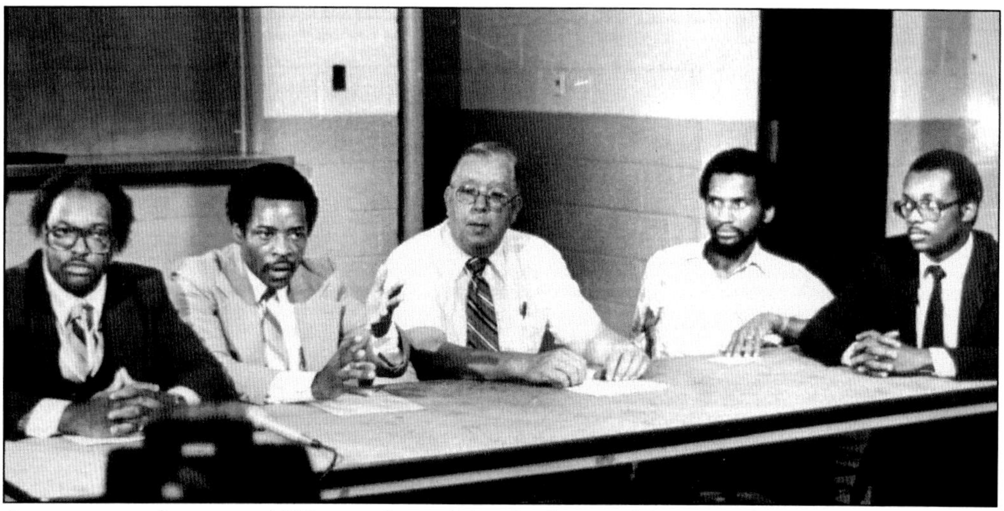

At a news conference in 1983, members of the Coalition of Concerned Citizens of University City announced plans for a possible economic boycott of several city businesses. The conference was held at the Baptist Church of the Holy Communion. Present, from left to right were Rev. Ron Vail; Rev. Sterling Lance, chairman of the Coalition; Bud Hage, manager of Thomas Market; and coalition members James Redd and Byron Price. (Photo Courtesy of Mercantile Library.)

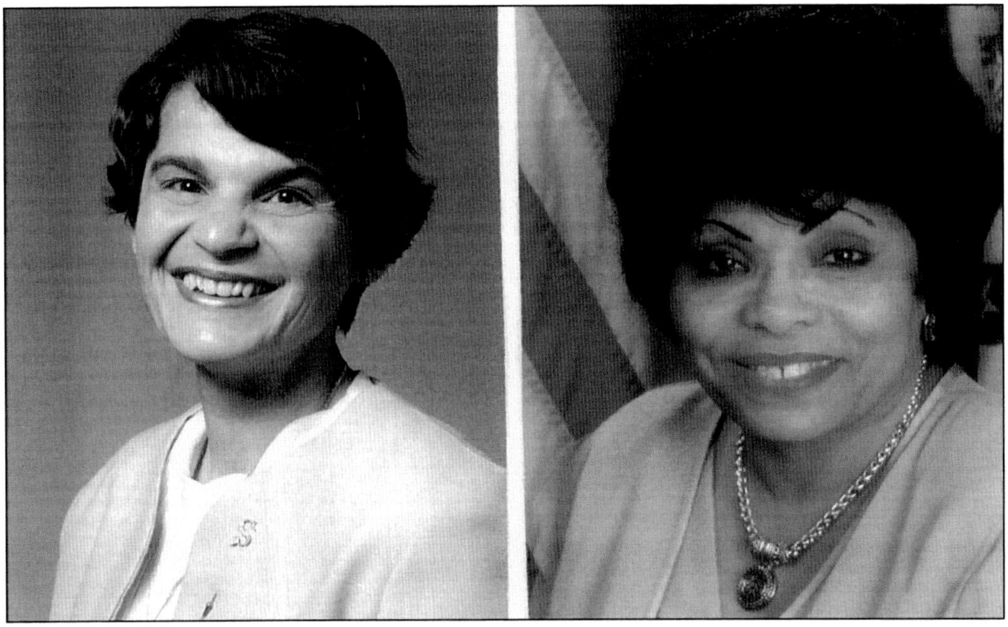

Sheila Lumpe (left) and Betty Thompson (right) went on to serve the community as state representatives. Sheila Lumpe, after serving on the school board from 1973 to 1981, was elected to the state House of Representatives and served from 1981 to 1997. Betty Thompson was elected to the state House of Representatives in 1997, after she served 18 years on the University City Council. Thompson presently serves as the Minority Whip. (Left Photo Courtesy of Sheila Lumpe. Right Photo Courtesy of Betty Thompson.)

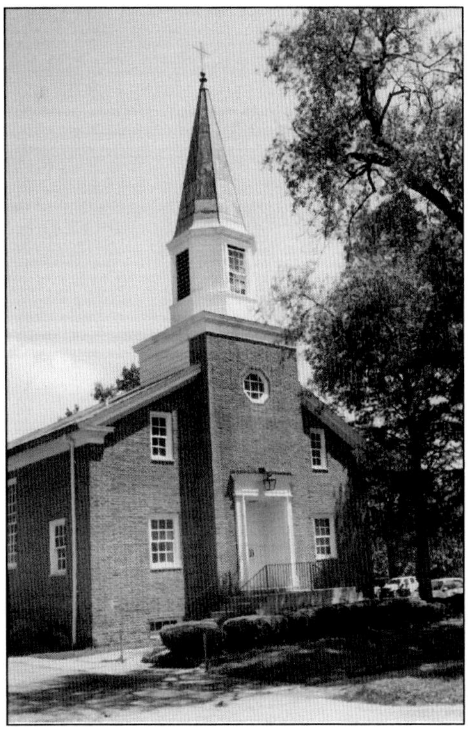

During the early years of the Civil Rights movement in University City, the Baptist Church of the Holy Communion at 7515 Melrose Avenue was the site of many organizational and planning meetings of African Americans. (Photo by John A. Wright.)

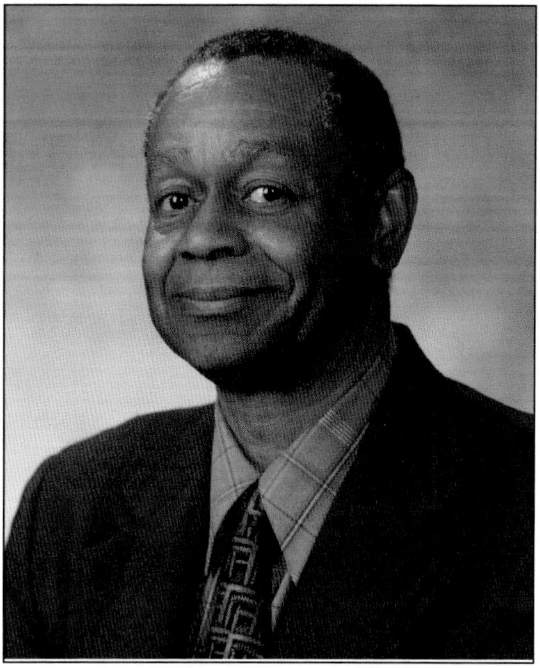

In 1967, Washington University Professor Jack Kirkland became the first African American elected to the University City School Board. The Board of Education at the time was concerned with racial balance in the schools. The African-American population followed the housing patterns of the city and was not evenly distributed. When Kirkland came up for re-election in 1970, he left the board, along with two others, and the neighborhood candidates became the majority on the board. The election left a divided community. (Photo Courtesy of Jack Kirkland.)

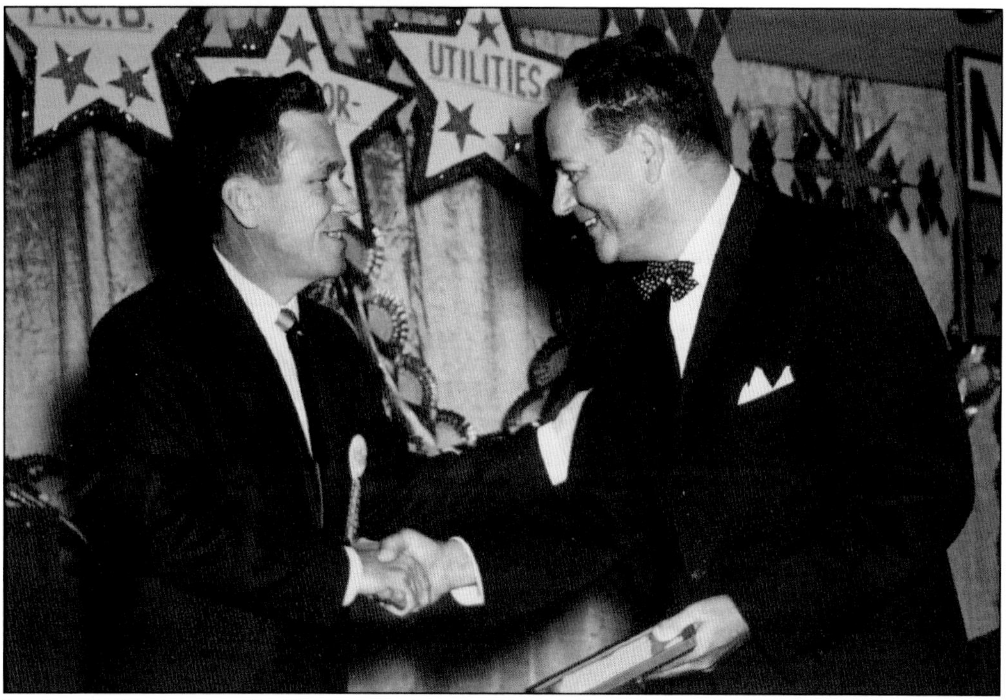

In this 1965 photograph, University City Mayor Nathan B. Kaufman is seen receiving the Certificate of Merit from Governor Warren Hearnes on behalf of the city. When Kaufman was elected councilman-at-large in 1958, he became the city's first Jewish mayor. He went on to serve as head of the municipal government longer than any of his predecessors and guided the community through some of its most difficult periods into a stable environment. (Photo Courtesy of the Archives of the University City Public Library.)

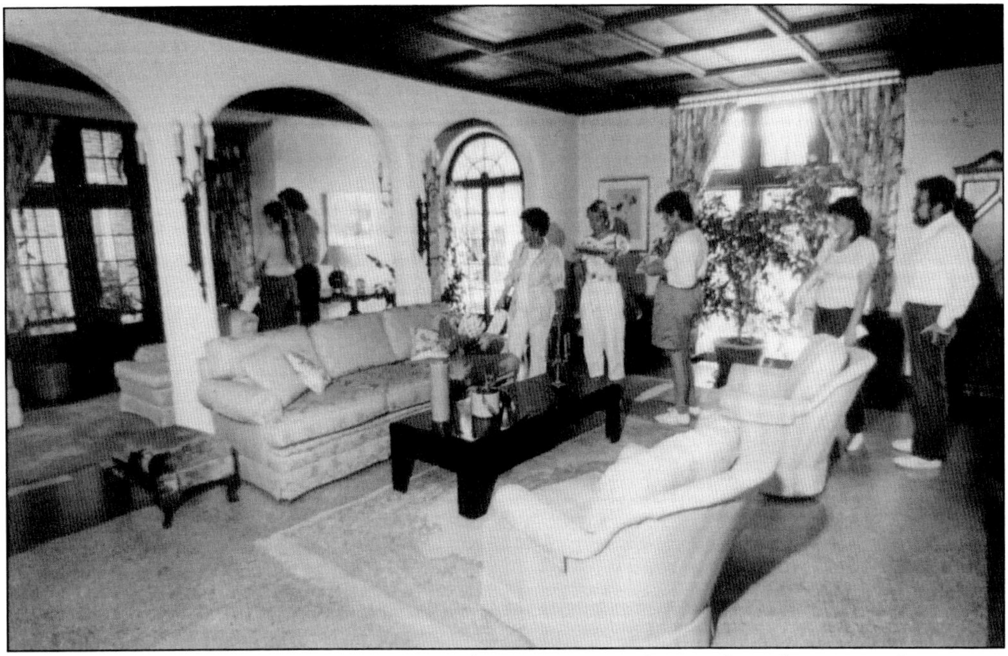

To promote and showcase University City, the city promoted a number of events and activities such as the Annual House Tour under the leadership of City Manager Charles Henry. City officials knew University City had some of the best housing stock in the area and potential buyers were not being shown the community by real estate agents who wanted to cash in on white flight. (Photo Courtesy of the Mercantile Library.)

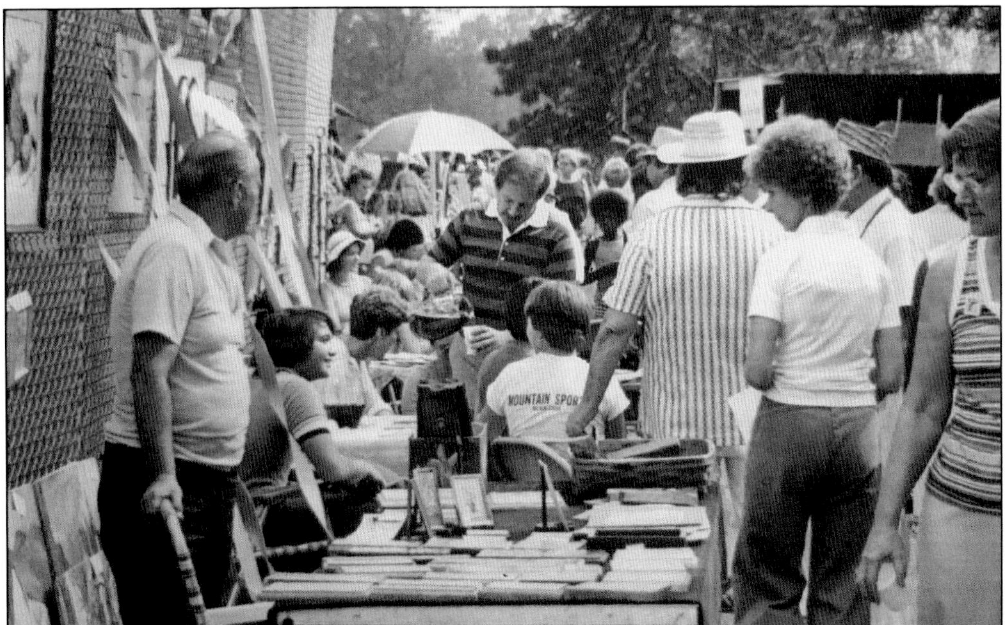

Among the events used by University City to promote the city was the Moonlight Ramble (a bicycling event), Annual Photo Contest, Starlight Concerts, the Memorial Day Run, and Sunday in the Park, pictured here. (Photo Courtesy of the Mercantile Library.)

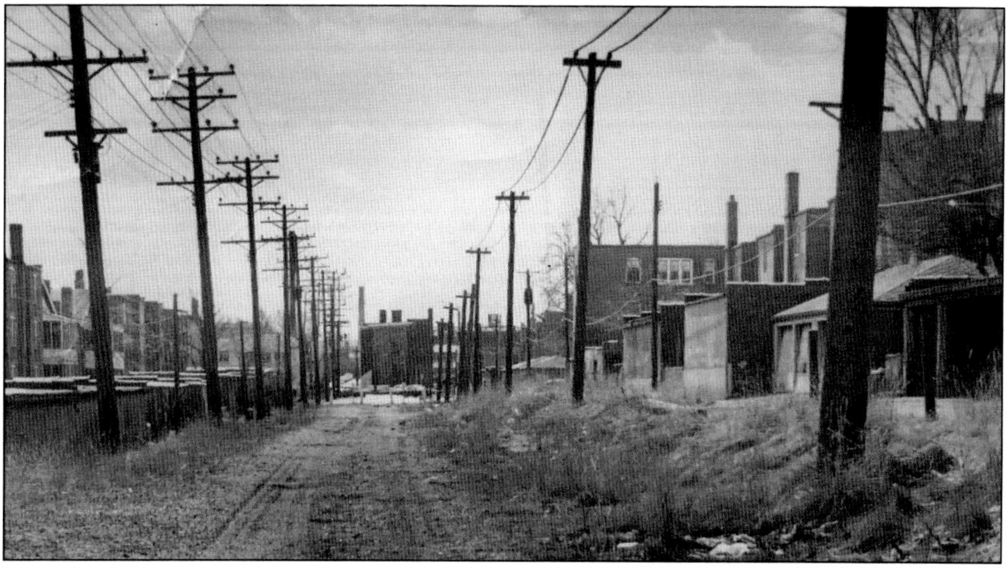

In 1962, the citizens of University City passed an urban renewal bond issue by 85 percent, for the renewal of a 190-acre area bounded by the City of St. Louis on the east, Kingsland on the west, Washington Avenue on the south, and Olive Street Road on the north. It also included an adjacent tract north of Olive, now known as Cunningham Industrial Park. The plan included the use of the old route of the Kirkwood-Ferguson streetcar line between Delmar Boulevard and Olive Street Road. (Photo Courtesy of the Archives of the University City Public Library.)

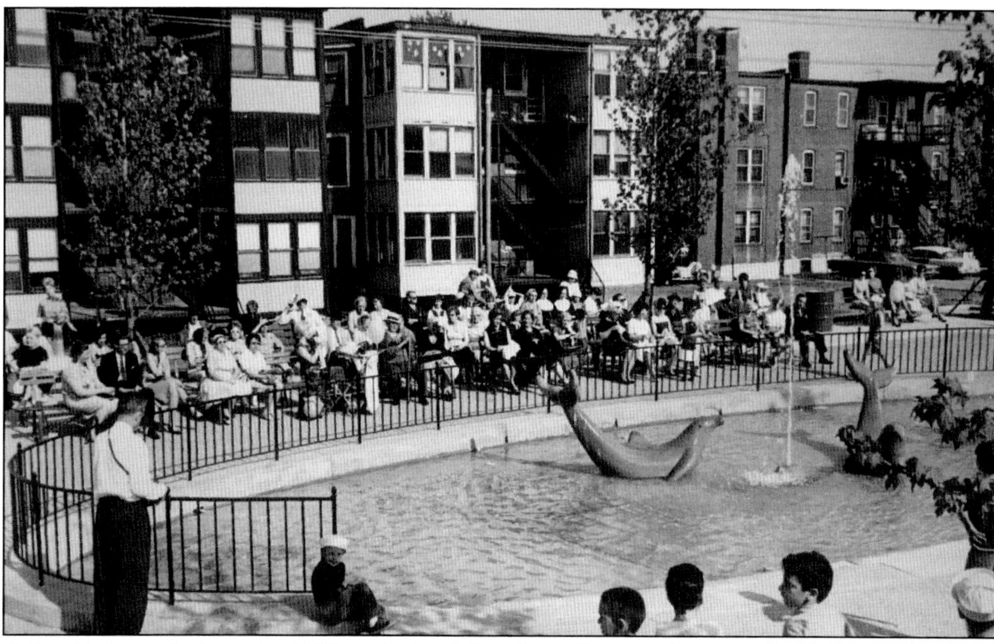

Ackert Park was dedicated in 1967 on the land abandoned by the old route of the Kirkwood-Ferguson Streetcar. The city's goal was to renew this area of the city while at the same time making sure that it would not result in a high-rent district. The city officials were fully aware that many of the residents of the Eastgate-Westgate area did not enjoy the same income level as many other University City citizens. (Photo Courtesy of the Archives of the University City Public Library.)

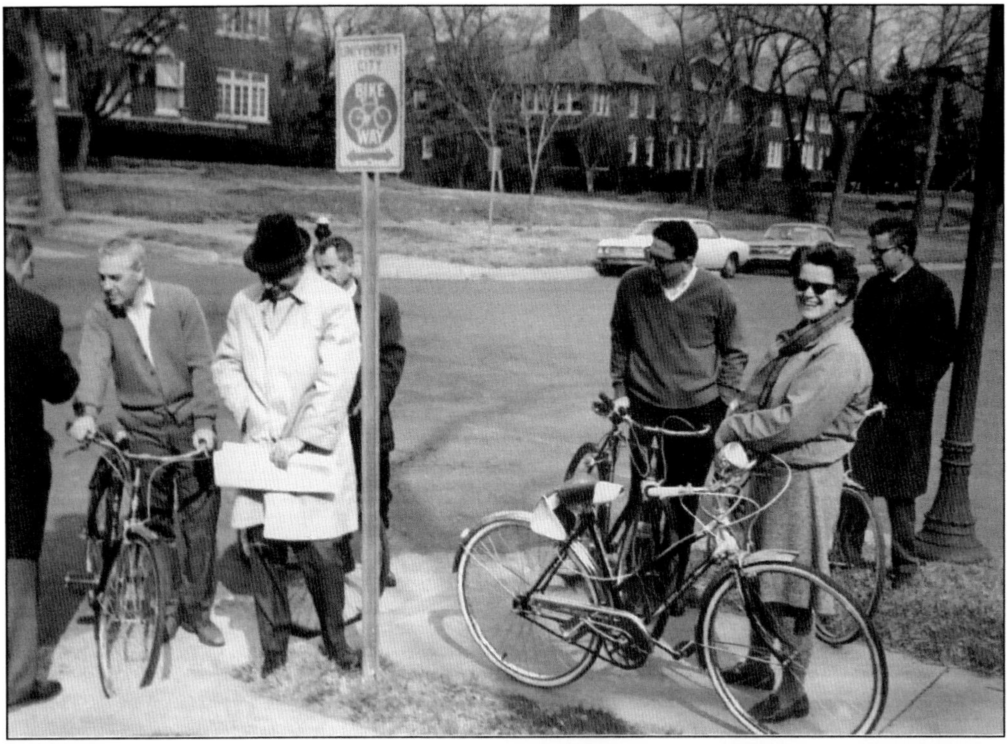

Among many of the programs initiated by University City was a Bike Path that opened in 1967. These residents are among the first to take a test ride. (Photo Courtesy of the Archives of the University City Public Library.)

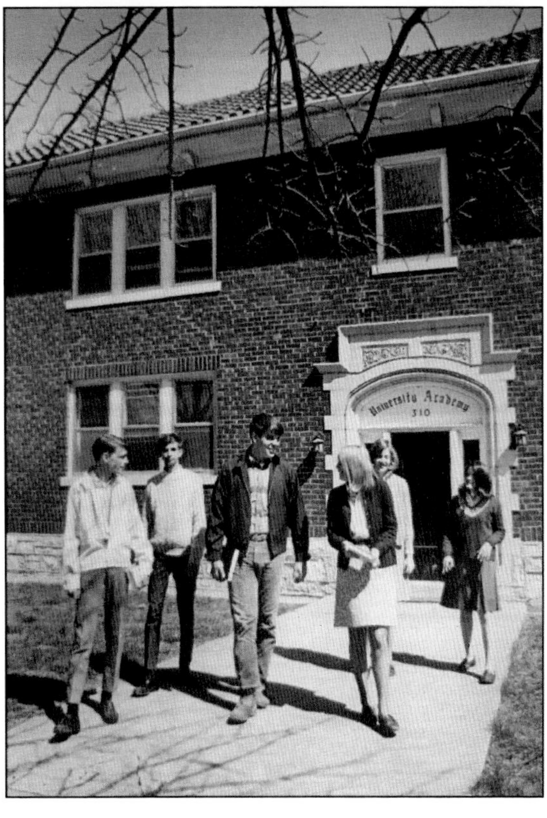

The University Academy was founded in the early 1960s by Mrs. J. Davin Burger, who wanted a school for bright youngsters dissatisfied with public education. A great deal of the work to prepare the school, located in an apartment building at 310 Melville Avenue, was performed by students. The school was never solvent and closed in 1968, after its fifth graduating class. (Photo Courtesy of the Mercantile Library.)

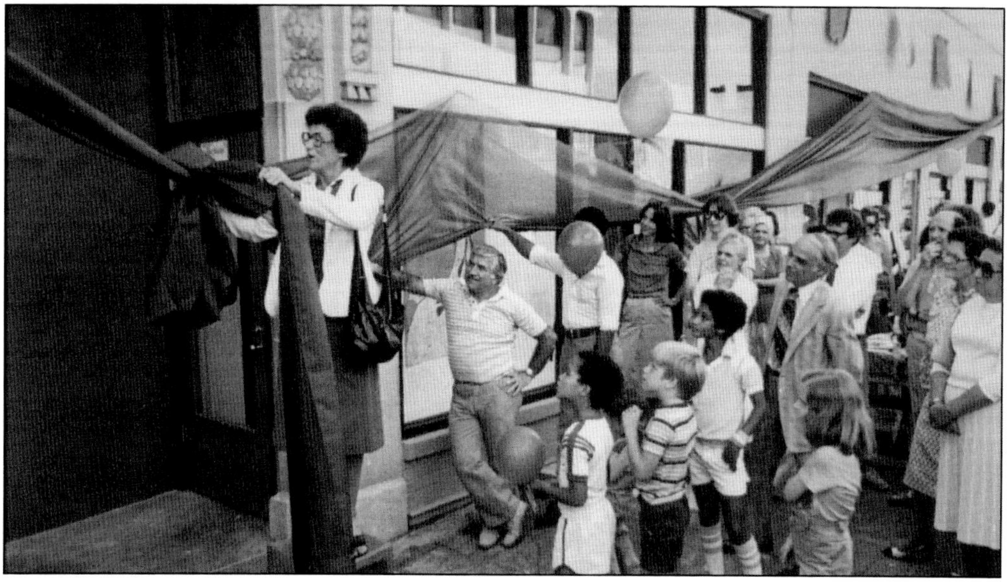

Councilwoman Harriet Woods was photographed in 1970 cutting the ribbon for the opening of Craft Alliance. The Craft Alliance, a not-for-profit group, moved to the University City Loop from its Central West End quarters and established quality gallery space with a wide array of educational programs. (Photo Courtesy of the Archives of the University City Public Library.)

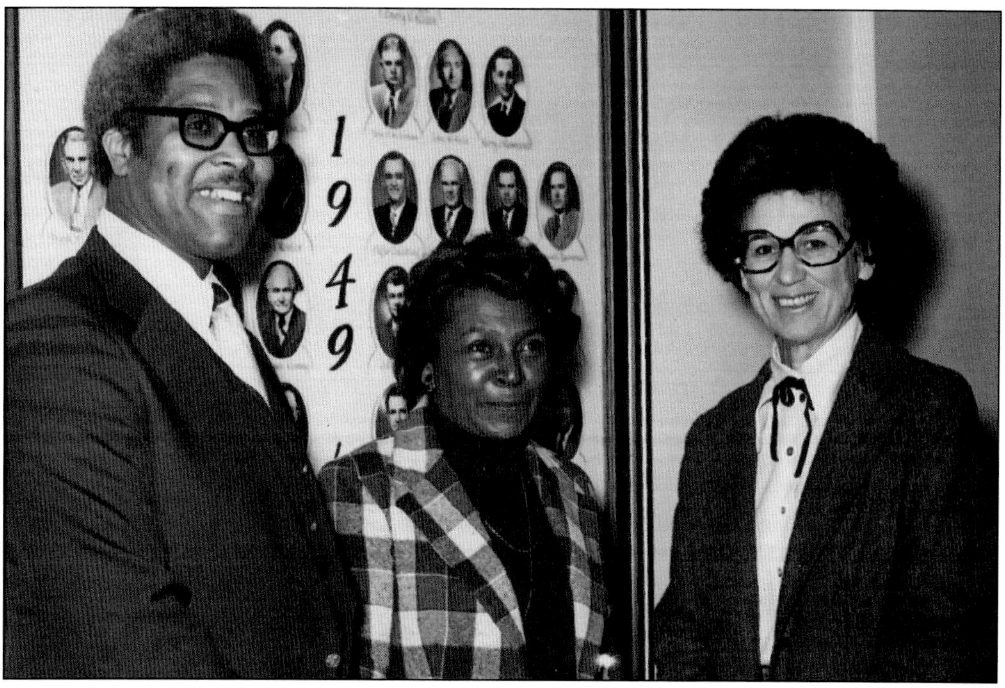

Councilwoman Harriet Woods, after leaving the City Council, was elected state senator, representing the community. In 1985, she was elected lieutenant governor of Missouri, becoming the first woman elected to a statewide office in Missouri. Woods is pictured here with University City residents John A. Wright and Carrie Bash, representing the Governor's Advisory Council on Vocational Education. (Photo Courtesy of Harriet Woods.)

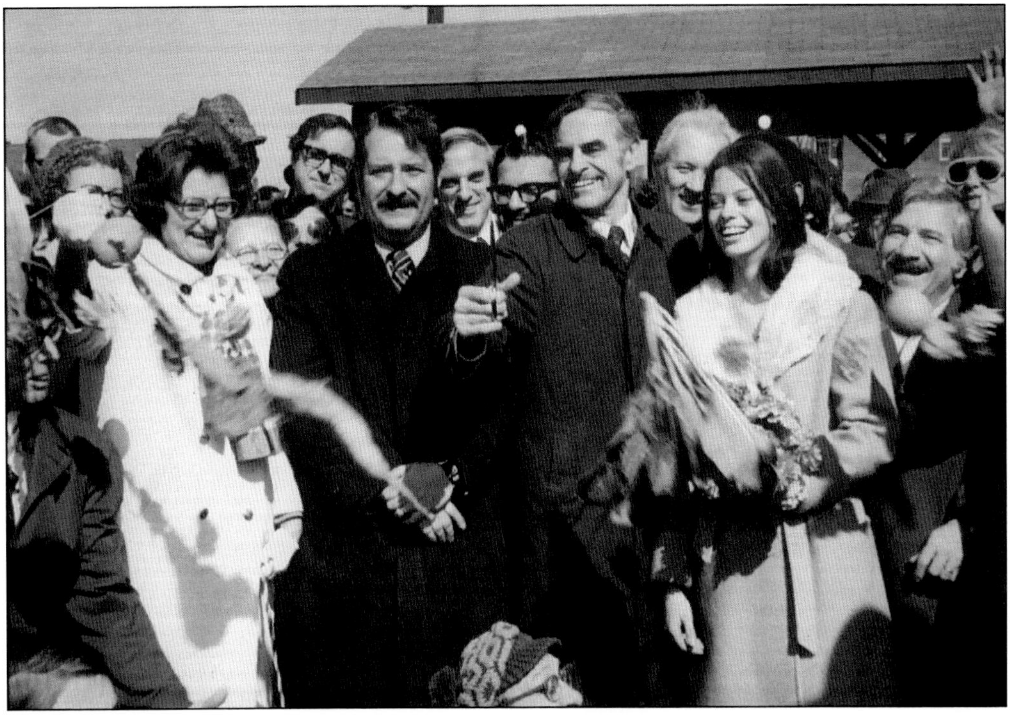

University City's Farmers Market was constructed in 1974, in the Loop. The National Guard supplied the labor with the Land Clearance and Redevelopment Authority paying for the materials. The market was constructed on land cleared after a fire had destroyed Schenber's Market, one of the Loop's last remaining grocery stores. Pictured from left to right at the ribbon cutting in 1975 are Charles Henry, George Cohn, Elsie Glickert, Larry Lumpe, Kenneth Rothman, Charles Warner, Fred Mishow, Hadley Grimm, Deana Jarboe, and Larry Lieberman. Sitting in front is Martin Manta. (Photo Courtesy of the Archives of the University City Public Library.)

One of the major anchors in the Loop has been Blueberry Hill, under the ownership of Joe Edwards. Since its opening in 1973, it has expanded several times and is now a well-known community landmark. Edwards has provided vital leadership for many of the activities that have made major contributions to the revitalization of the Loop, such as the "Sidewalk of Fame," the renovation and opening of the Tivoli Theatre, and the new Pageant Theatre. (Photo Courtesy of Joseph and Hope Edwards.)

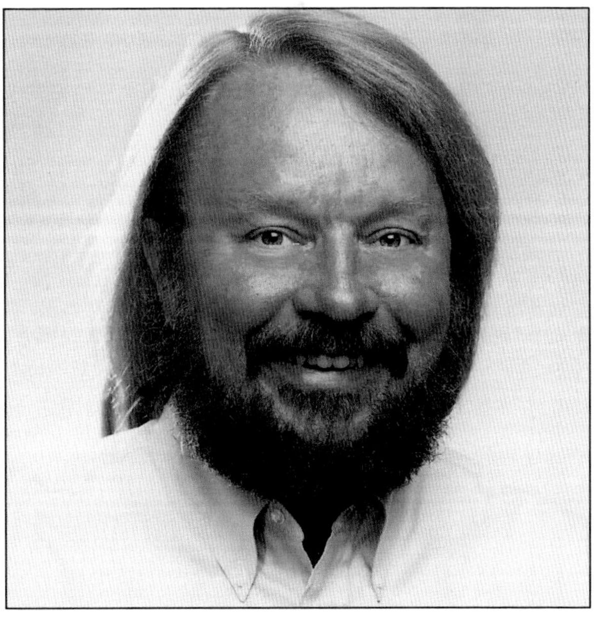

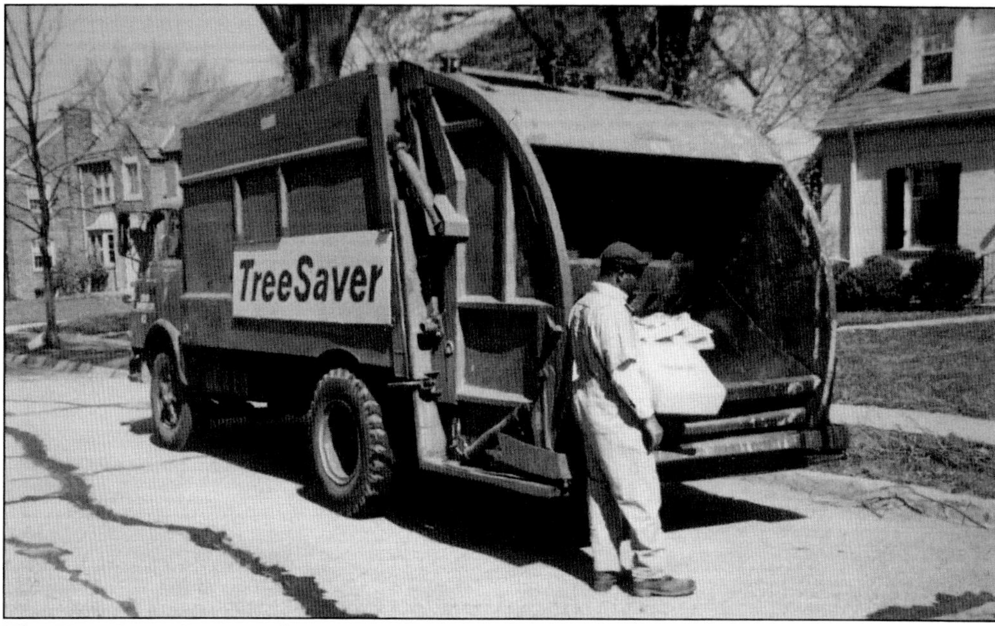

The Tree Saver Program began in University City in 1973 out of citizen concerns for the environment. In the first 10 years of the program, over 10 million pounds of newspapers were collected. (Photo Courtesy of the Archives of the University City Public Library.)

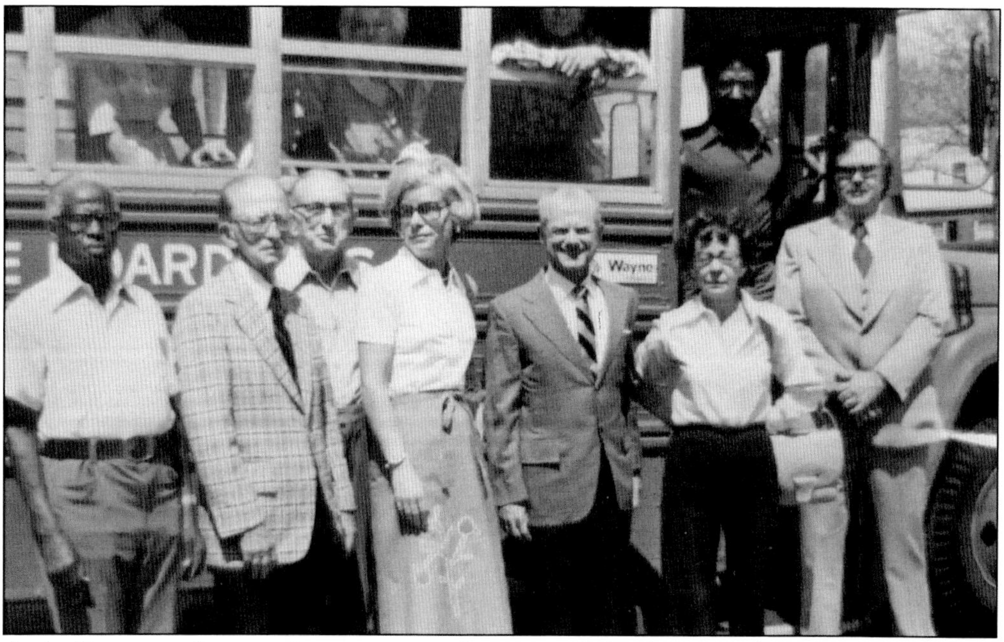

As the University City population continued to grow and develop, consideration was given to its senior population. The old public library on Trinity Avenue was converted into a Senior Center and an Older Adult Bus Service Program was initiated. City Manager, Victor A. Ellman (fifth from the left) is seen in this 1977 photograph, with University City agency representatives, at the delivery of the senior service bus, which served the St. Andrews and Delcrest dining centers. (Photo Courtesy of the Mercantile Library.)

One of the most prestigious honors in the law enforcement profession was bestowed upon both the University City Police Department and Chief James Damos in October of 1981. When he was elected President of the International Association of Chief of Police, Damos became the third person in Missouri so honored since the formation of the organization in 1893. (Photo Courtesy of the Archives of the University City Public Library.)

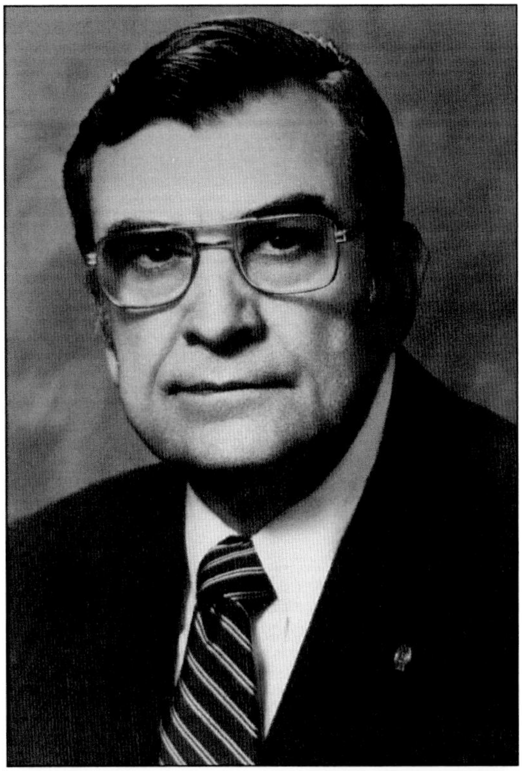

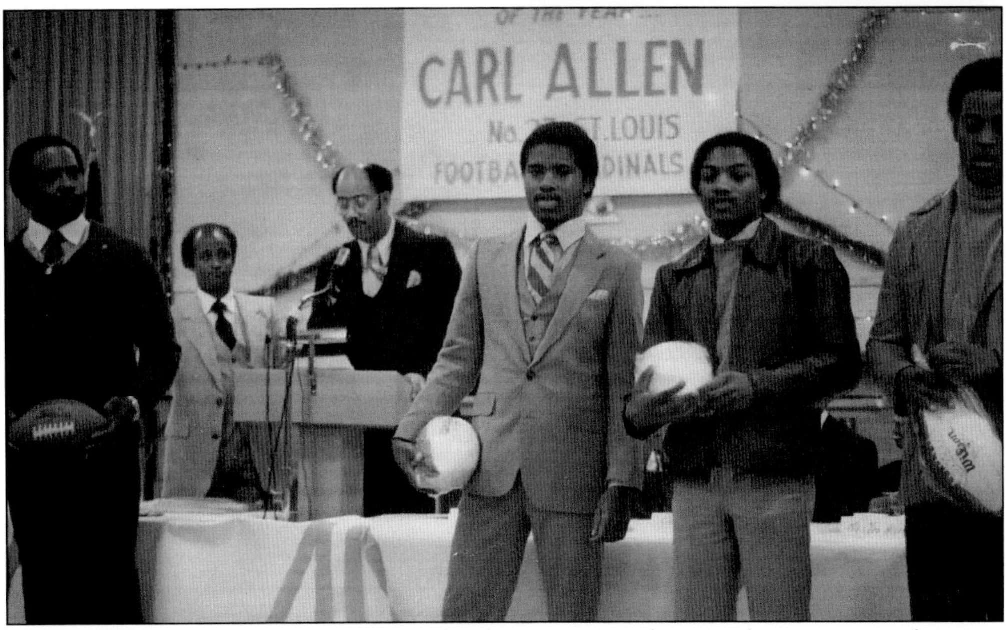

The University City Sports Association has been a major player in the community for many years, serving young people of all ages. Under the leadership of Charles Alphin (behind the microphone), the association brought in a number of sports personalities to the community to recognize young athletes. These young men are being recognized by Carl Allen of the St. Louis Football Cardinals as Sportsmen of the Year. (Photo Courtesy of John A. Wright.)

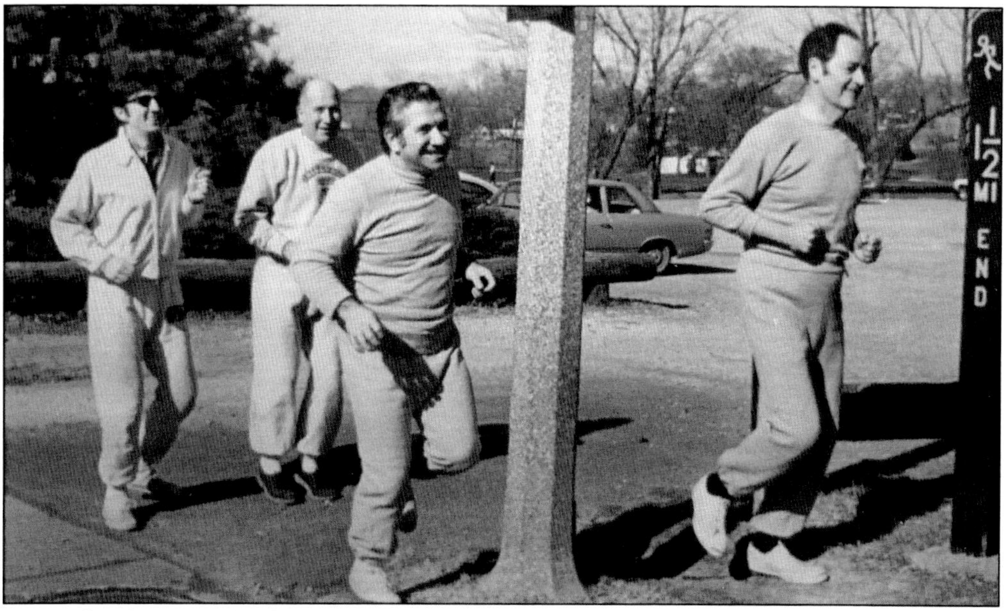

City Officials are pictured here taking the first lap on the city's new jogging course in Heman Park in 1971. The one and one-half mile course starts at the Shaftsbury entrance to the park. From left to right are Walter Barry, assistant director of Human Resources; Chauney Linhart, director of Parks, Recreation, and Forestry; Councilman Lawrence Leiberman; and Mayor Nathan B. Kaufman. (Photo Courtesy of the Mercantile Library.)

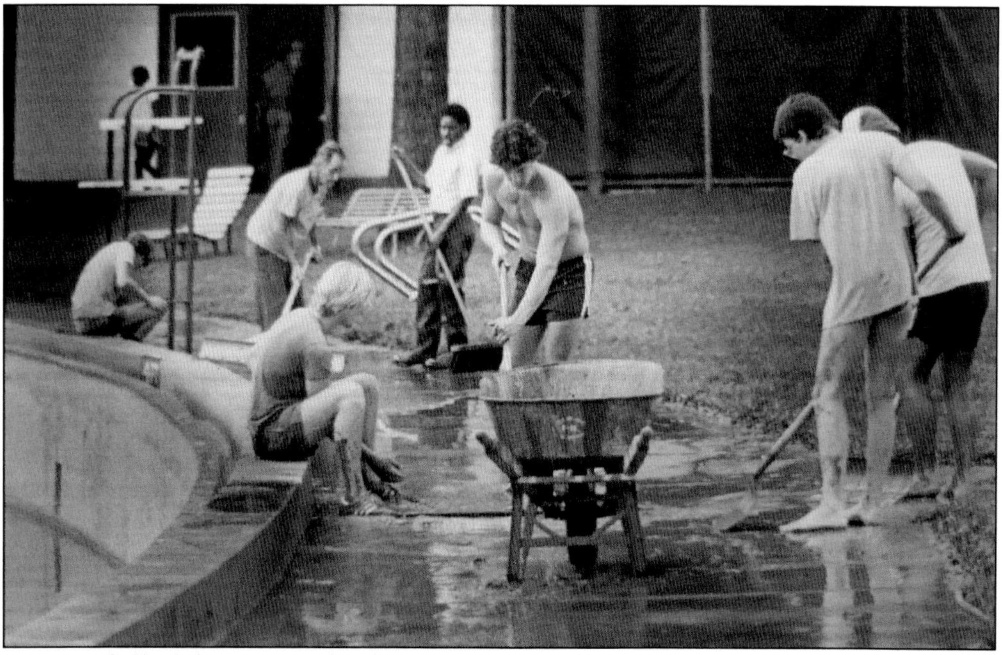

In spite of all of the positive development in the community, until the late 1990s residents still had to contend with the rituals of clean-up after a long, heavy rain and overflow from the River Des Peres. These young workers are cleaning the city pool after a heavy 1981 rain. (Photo Courtesy of the Mercantile Library.)

Five

University City Today

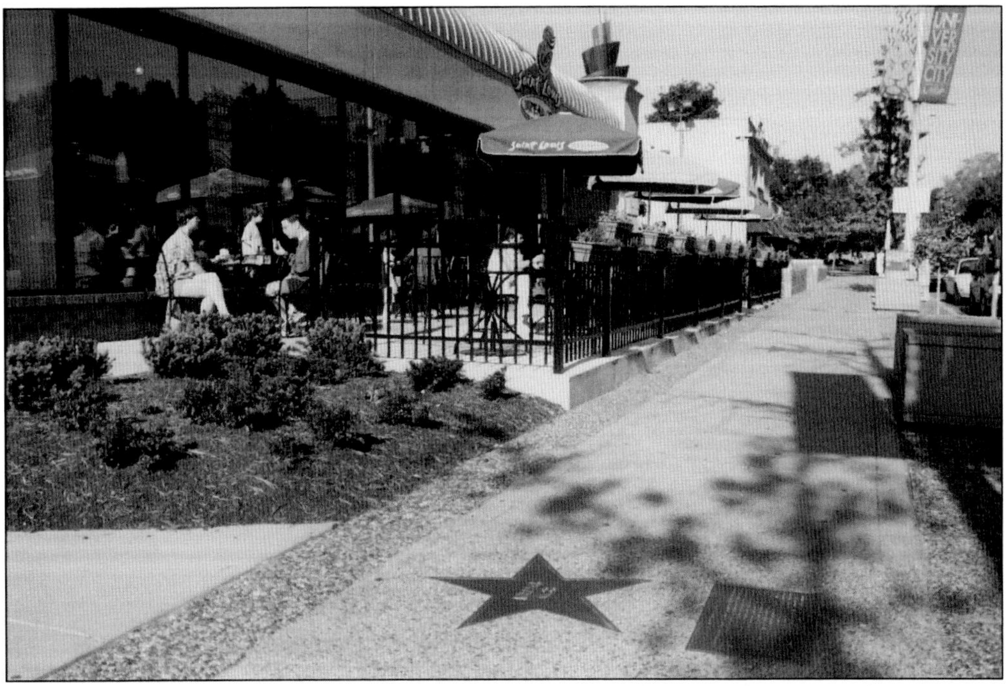

Today, the University City "Loop" offers a welcome to all who enter the city. In the Loop, one can dine among the stars on the city's Walk of Fame. The sidewalk plaques recognize almost 100 influential and famous St. Louisans such as Tina Turner, Chuck Berry, Charles Lindbergh, and Stan Musial.

A great deal of the area around the Loop is designated as an historic district on the National Register of Historic Places. University City is proud of the fact that it has saved a large number of its buildings and areas from decay. The city now stands as a national example of what can be done by citizens working together for a common goal. Because of their efforts, the beauty of the city is preserved to be enjoyed by present and future generations. (Photo by John A. Wright.)

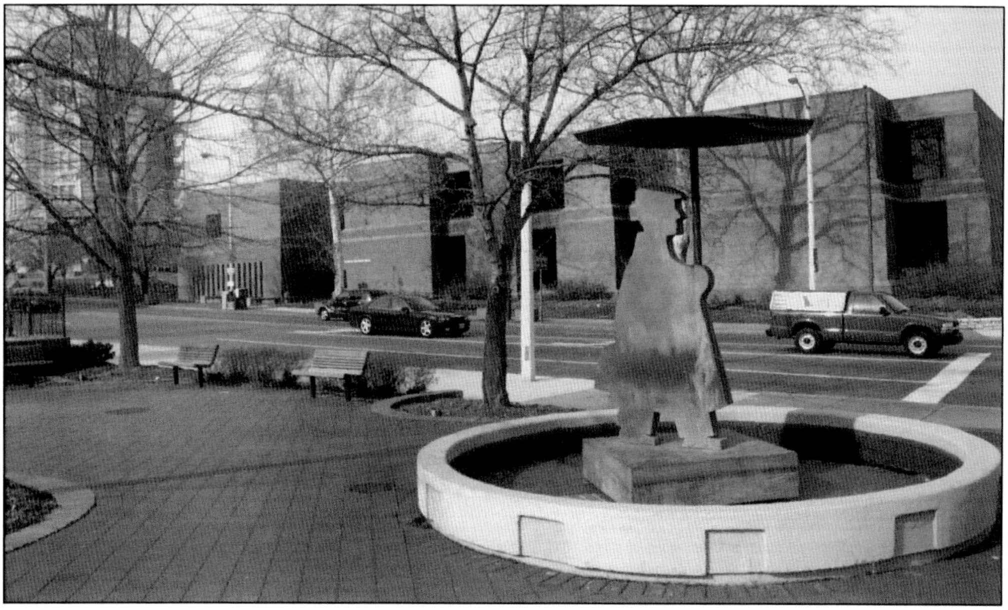

Epstein Plaza with Rainman provides a welcomed stop in the plaza for the Loop walkers. It is named for Milton and Zelda Epstein, who both served on the City Council for eight years. Milton also served on the City's Charter Commission and helped establish the first Civil Service and Human Rights Commissions. Zelda was very active in the community, working with older adults. She was also involved in the development of the senior citizens' building at McKnight Road and Delmar Boulevard. (Photo by John A. Wright.)

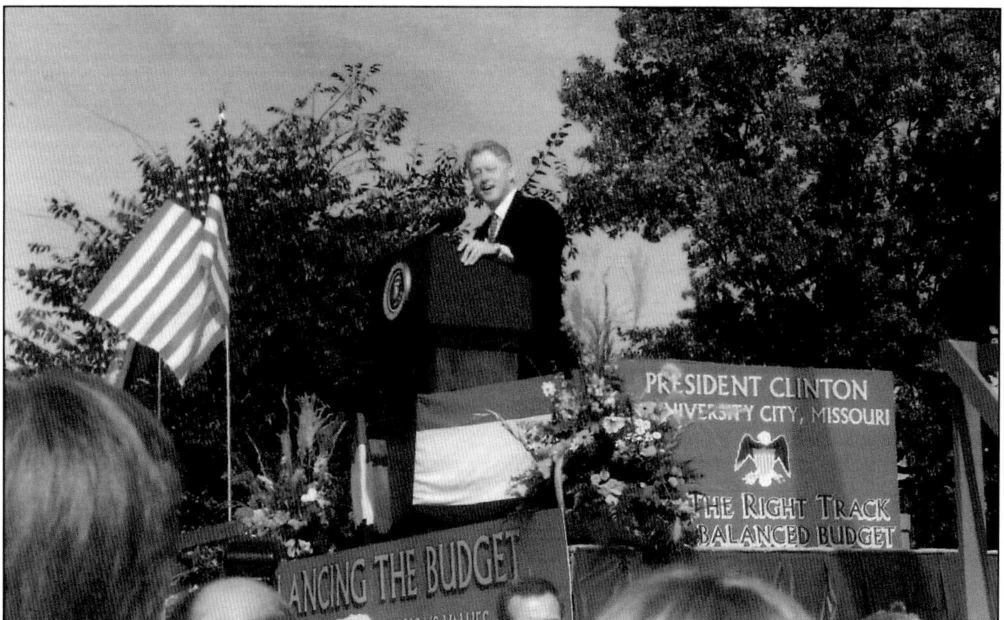

President Bill Clinton made the University City Plaza a stop on his campaign trip to St. Louis before a presidential debate at Washington University in 1996. (Photo Courtesy of the City of University City.)

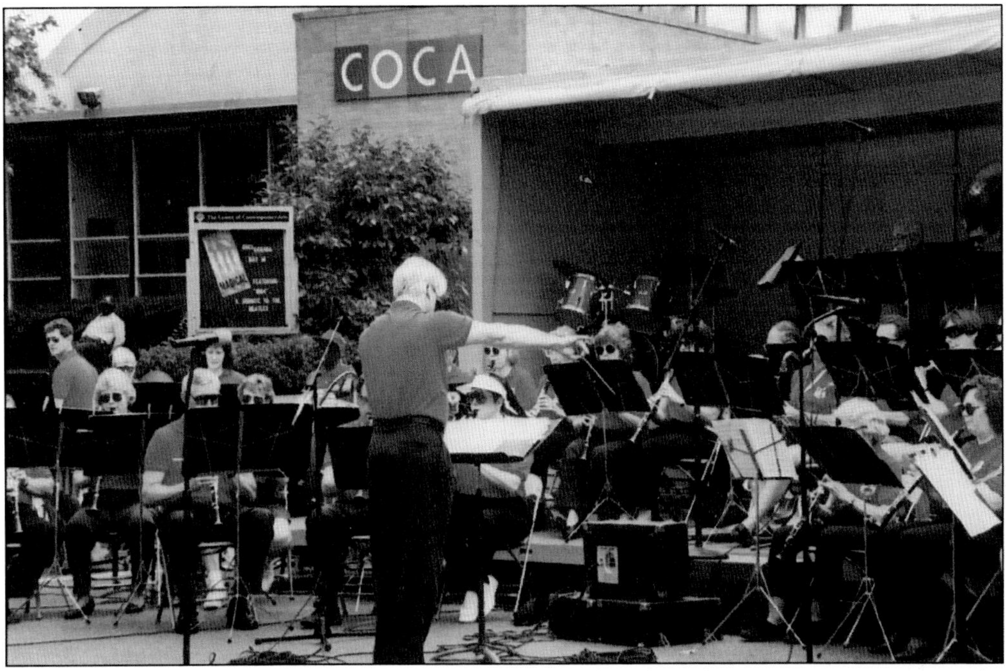

The Center for Contemporary Arts (COCA), a visual and performing arts center, provides affordable arts programs to the St. Louis Community. It is located in this landmark B'nai Amoona Synagogue, designed by the German architect Eric Mendelsohn and constructed between 1946 and 1950. The building, at the time of its construction, represented a radical departure from conventional thinking about religious architecture. In 1984, it was listed on the National Register of Historic Places. The St. Louis Symphony Community Music School Adult Concert Band is seen here in 1994 performing outside the building. (Photo Courtesy of University City Hall.)

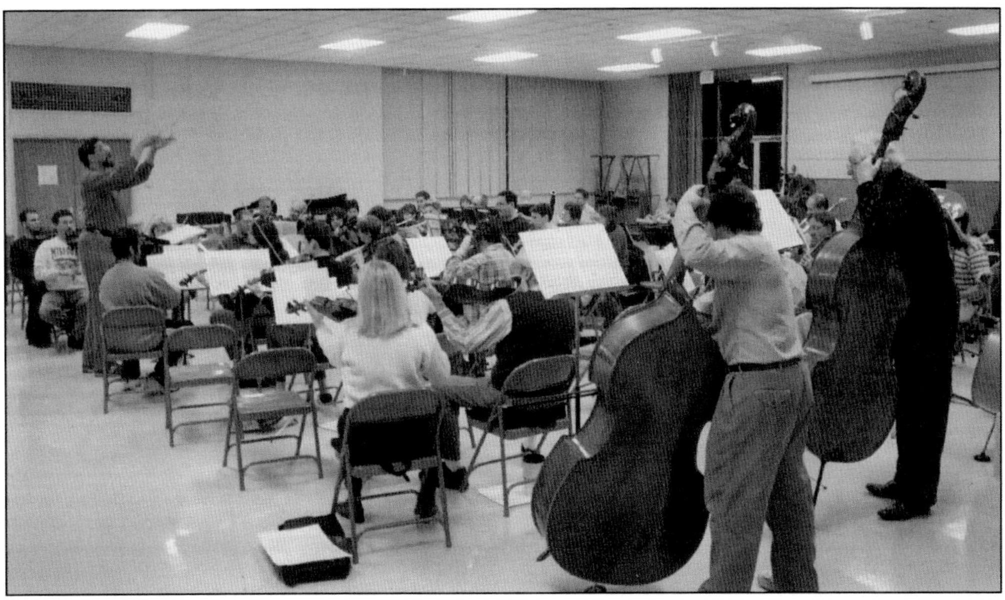

The University Symphony Orchestra still thrives and performs after many years under the direction of Leon Burke Jr. (Photo by John A. Wright.)

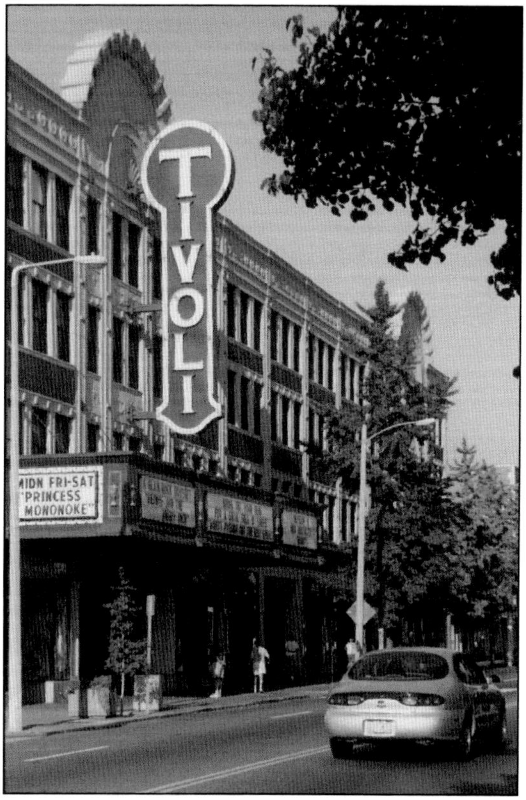

The Loop area of University City, once the site of a race track and amusement park, is now the home of more than 100 specialty shops, eclectic restaurants, galleries, and more. By being on the western edge of the City of St. Louis, less than ten minutes from Clayton and within walking distance from Washington University, it attracts people of all ages and ethnic groups. The Tivoli Theater at 6350 Delmar Boulevard, built in 1924, has been remodeled and now carries the best new independent films (plus classics). (Photos by John A. Wright.)

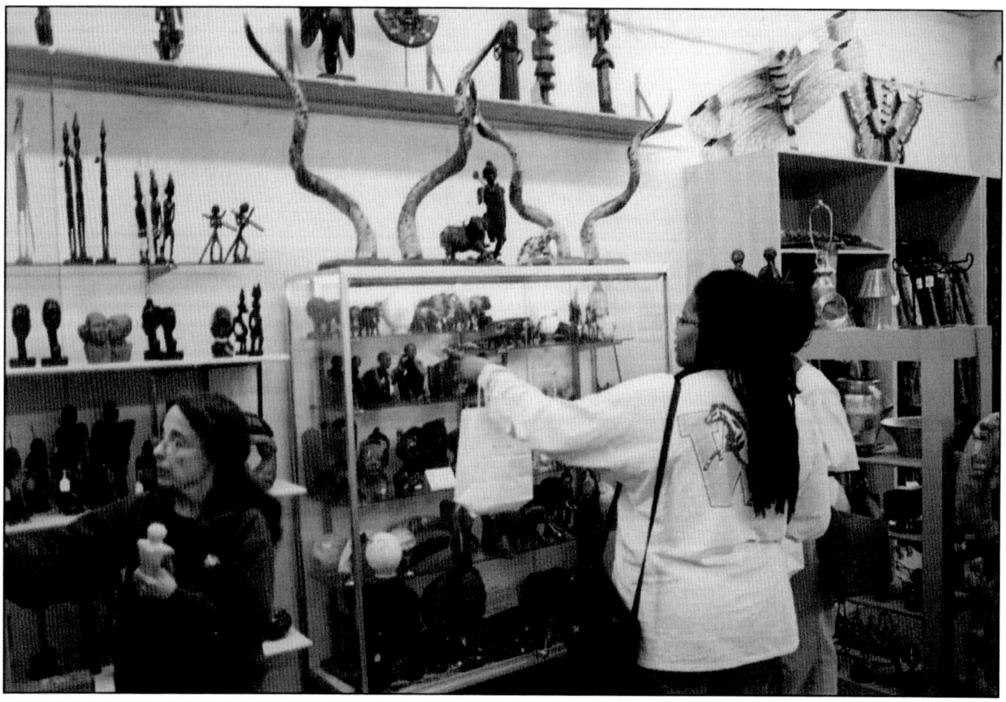

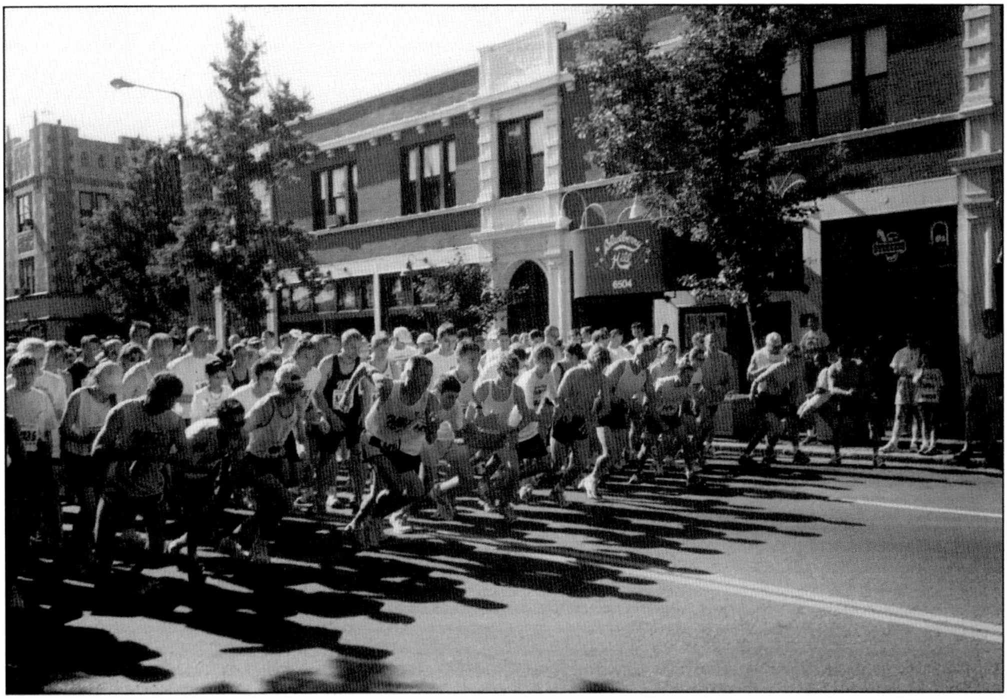

University City sponsors numerous events each year that attract thousands such as the Memorial Day Run (above), which raises funds for the library's book fund. the Loop in Motion Art Festival (below) is held each fall. It plays host to bands, artists, and ethnic cuisine. Other city events include the Starlight Concert Series, Sculpture Series, Photo Show, House Tour, Loop Holiday Walk, and the Martin Luther King Community Celebration. (Top Photo Courtesy of Lindard Ballard. Bottom Photo by John A. Wright.)

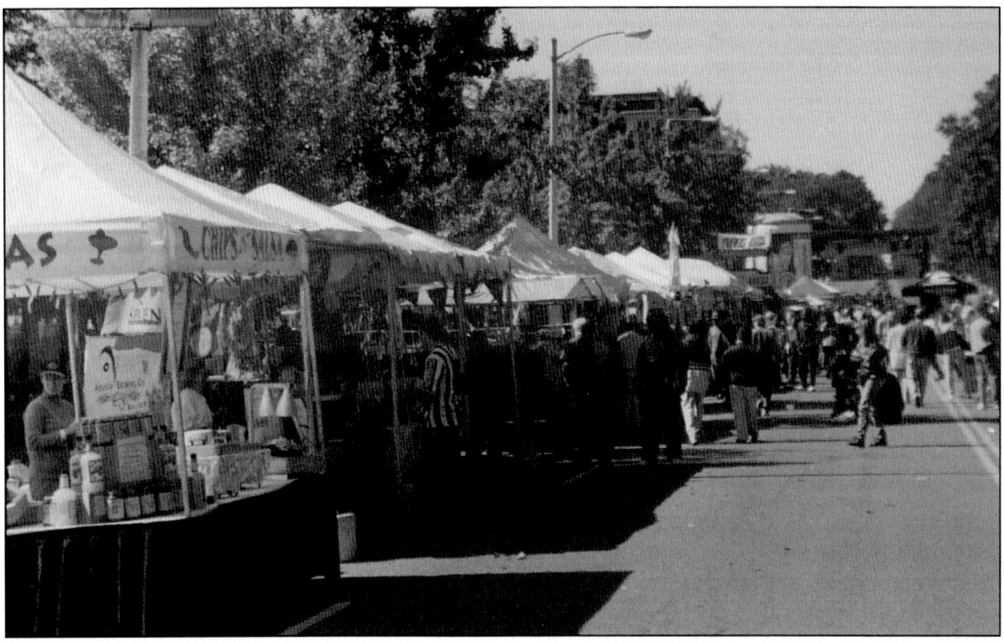

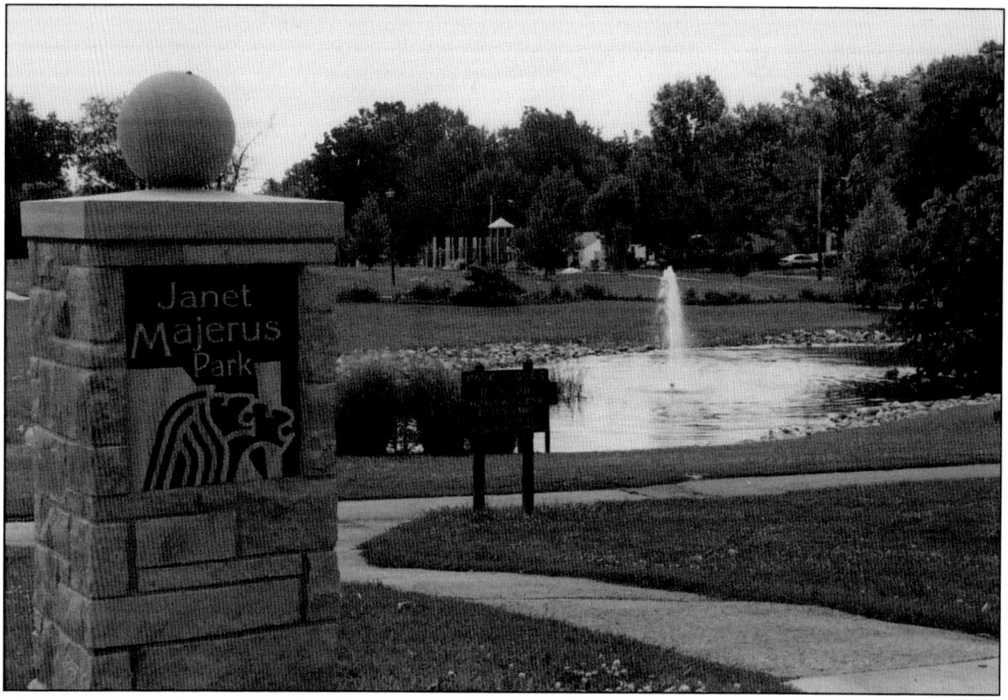

University City has 17 parks which provide its residents with a municipal swimming pool, tennis courts, children's playground, jogging track, fitness stations, recreation facility with a fitness center, community center, nine-hole golf course, picnic areas and shelters, football fields, Little League baseball diamonds, regular baseball diamonds, and paved basketball courts. Ackert, Flynn, Fogerty, Heman, Kaufman, Janet Majerus, Lewis, Metcalfe, Millar, Rabe, and Ruth Park are named for former University City mayors. (Photo by John A. Wright.)

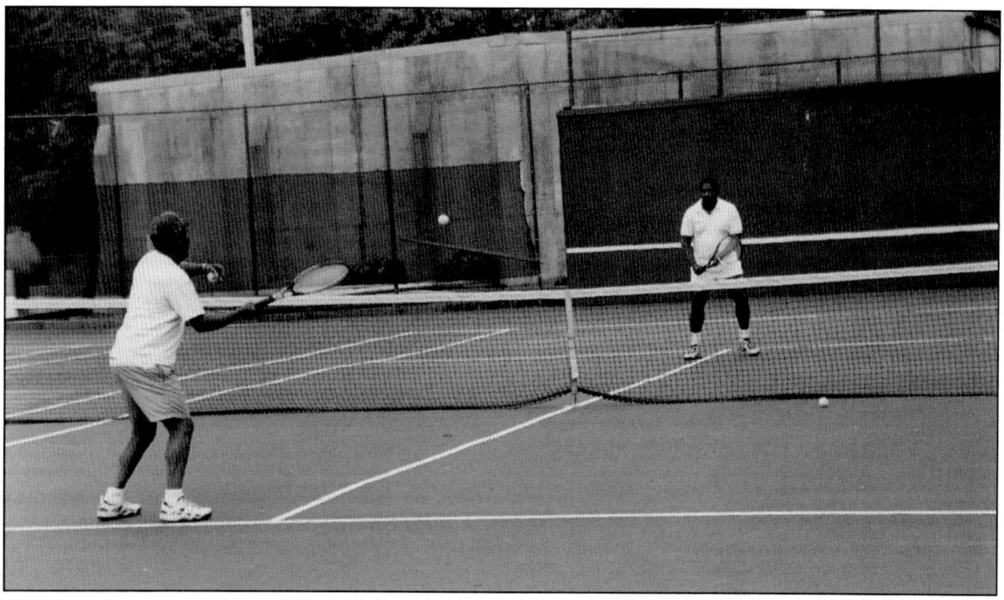

The City has over 19 tennis courts, which can be found at Heman, Flynn, and Kaufman Parks. (Photo by John A. Wright.)

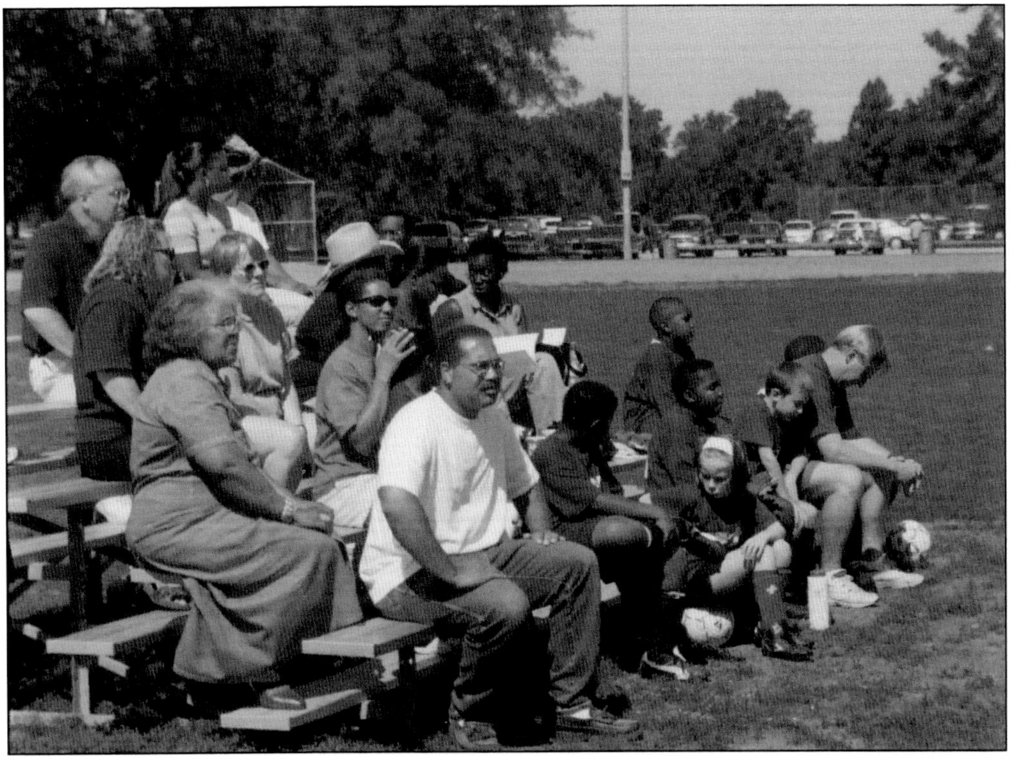

University City's parks provide an opportunity for neighbors and parents to come together and watch their children and friends participate in a variety of sporting activities year round. (Photo by John A. Wright.)

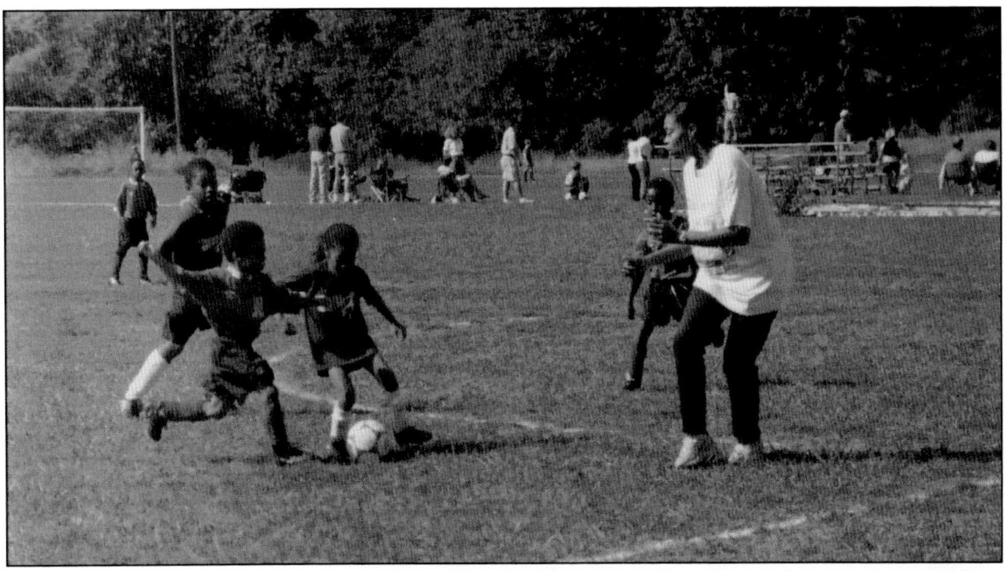

Through many sporting activities organized by the University City Sports Association, children in the community are able to come together and get to know each other, and develop the skills of good sportsmanship that can carry over in their lives beyond the field and into adulthood. (Photo by John A. Wright.)

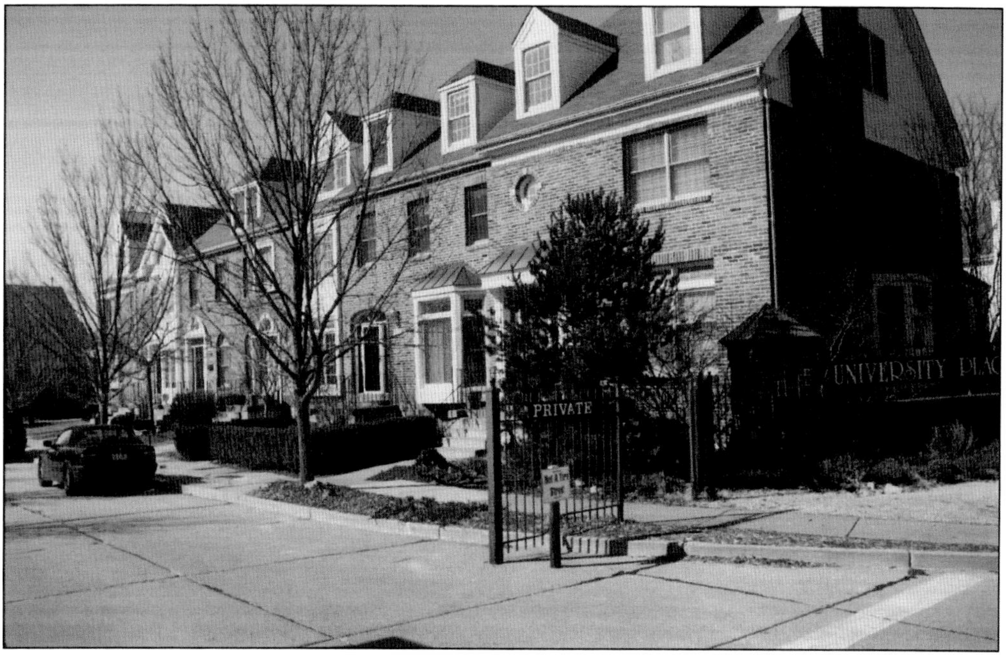

While many community landmarks have remained, some have disappeared to make way for new developments such as University Place (above), which now occupies the site of Hanley Junior High School, and Schnucks University City Square (below), which now occupies the site of Mercy High School. (Photo by John A. Wright.)

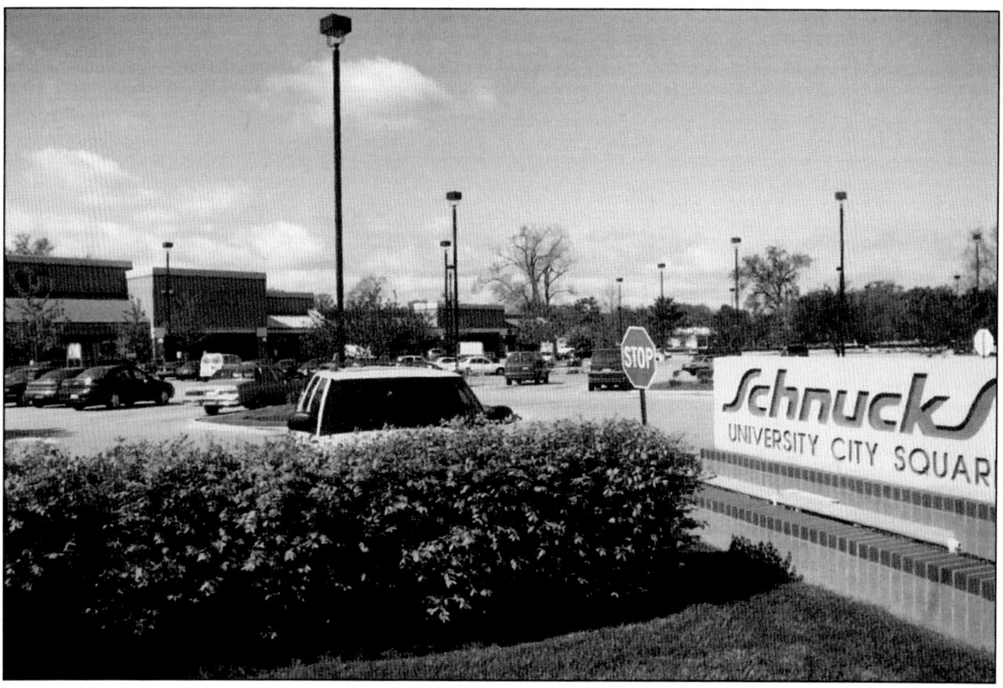

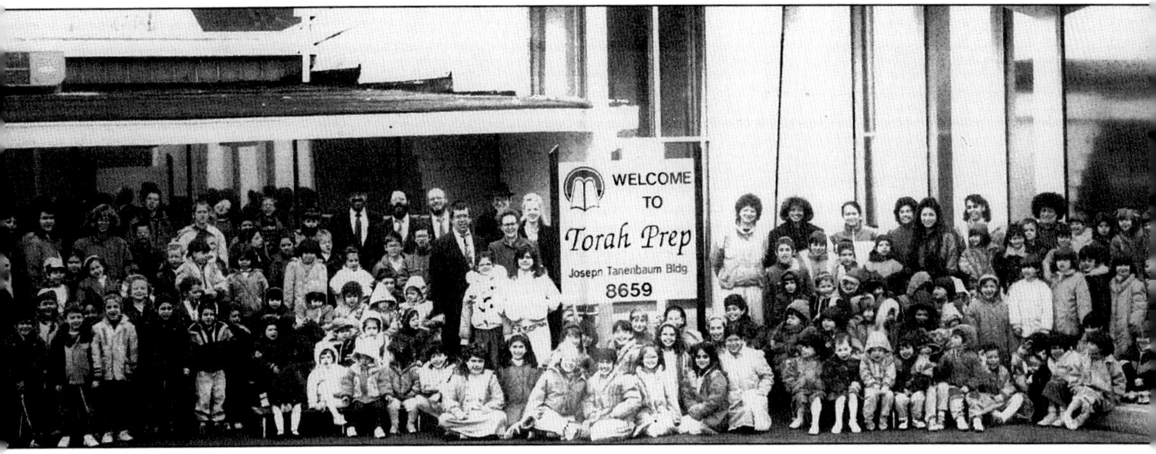

While some landmarks disappear, others take on different purposes such as the former St. Patrick's Catholic Elementary School on Olive Street Road. It is now the home of Torah Prep (above), which is accredited by the North Central Association of Schools and Colleges. The mission of the school is to have students embrace the Torah and the importance of Middos Tovos as life's major directives.

The former Jewish Community Center Association (JCCA) on Olive Street Road is now occupied by Agape Academy and Child Development Center (bottom photo). The center has received National and State Accreditation. Agape students ranked in the top 10 percent on the national level for CAT testing. Starting in 1990 with 13 children, the population now exceeds 350 students. The student body is diverse in ethnicity, religious affiliation, and economic status. (Top Photo Courtesy of Torah Prep. Bottom Photo by John A. Wright.)

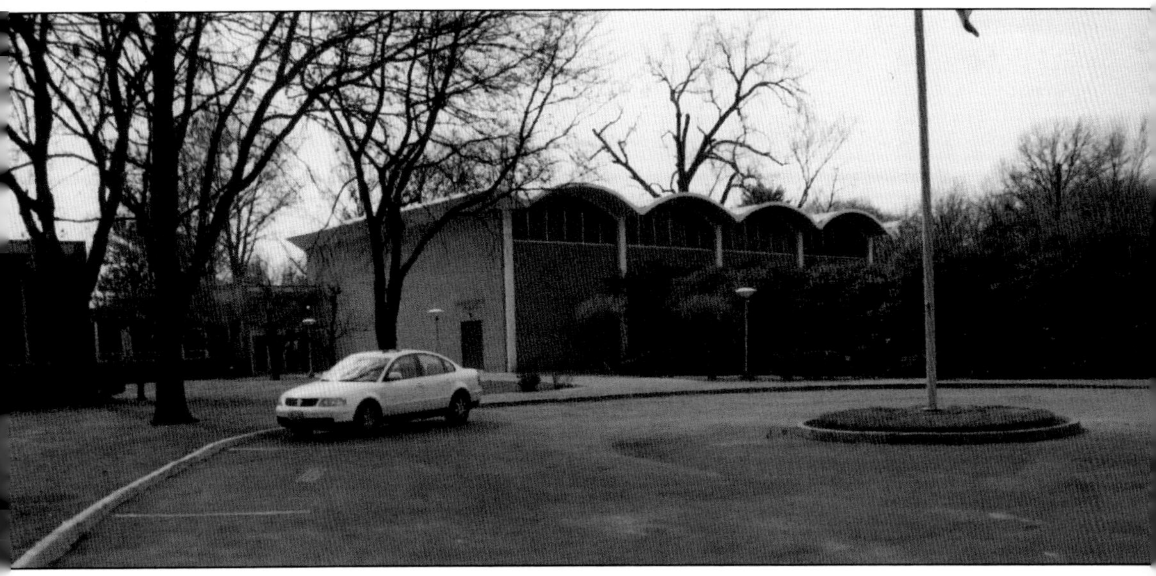

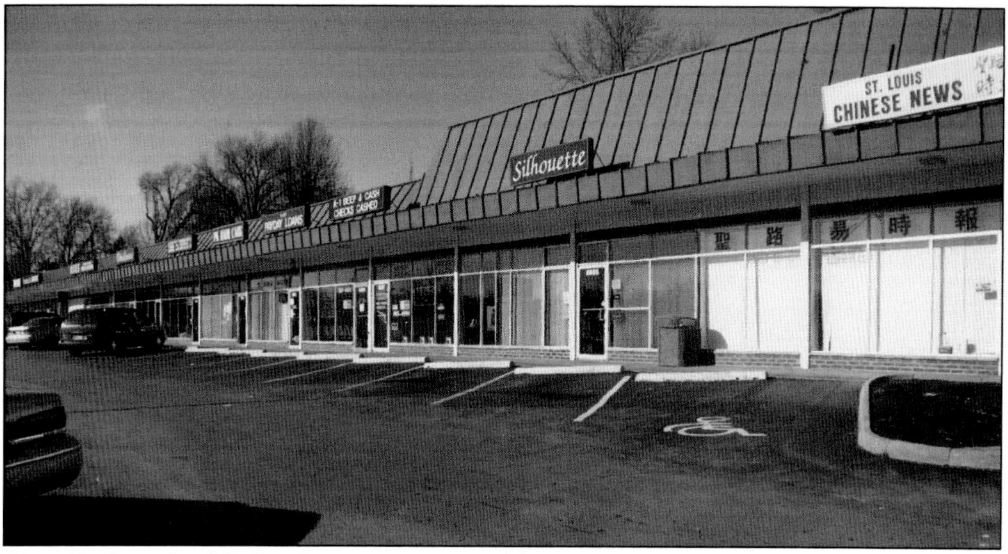

Olive Boulevard is filled with numerous strip malls, small businesses, ethnic restaurants, retail shops, and other businesses that reflect the diverse population of University City. Cunningham Industrial Park, near Olive and Skinker Boulevards, is home to wholesale suppliers, professional offices, automotive services, industrial production, and warehousing. (Photo by John A. Wright.)

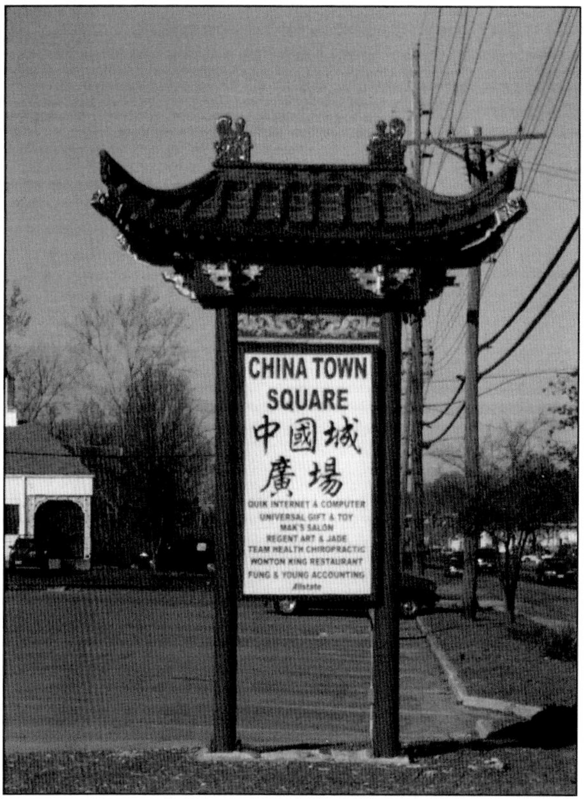

One can find one of the largest concentrations of Asian restaurants, markets, and businesses in the region on Olive Boulevard. (Photo by John A. Wright.)

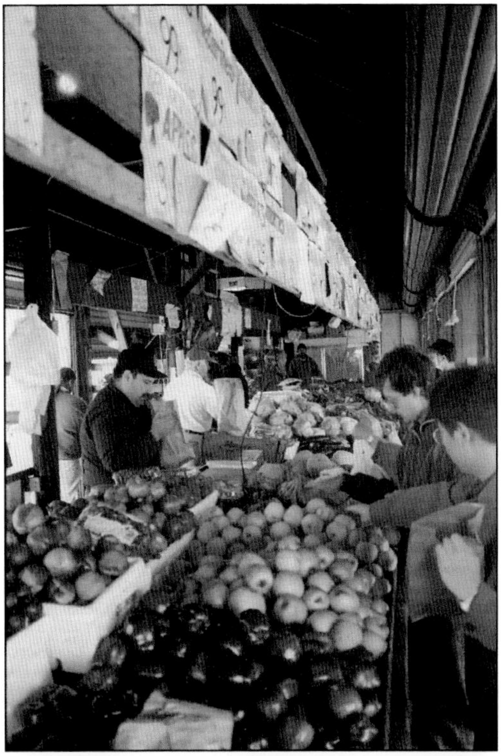

The market in the Loop holds a special attraction for locals as well as visitors on weekends with its large selection of fresh produce, food court, and outdoor events. (Photo by John A. Wright.)

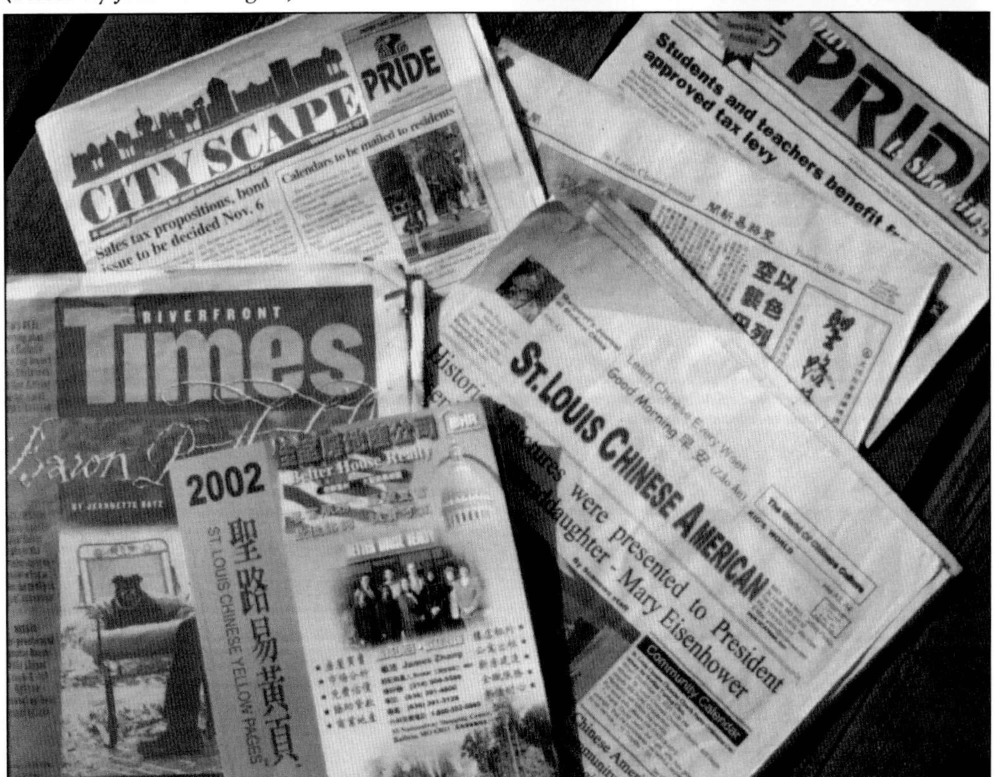

University City today, as yesterday, is a city of learners and readers. Located in the city are the home offices of the *St. Louis Chinese American*, *St. Louis Chinese Journal*, *Riverfront Times*, *St. Louis Chinese Yellow Pages*, and *St. Louis Journalism Review*. The city and the public school system, along with numerous neighborhood associations and organizations, publish periodic publications to keep citizens informed. (Photo by John A. Wright.)

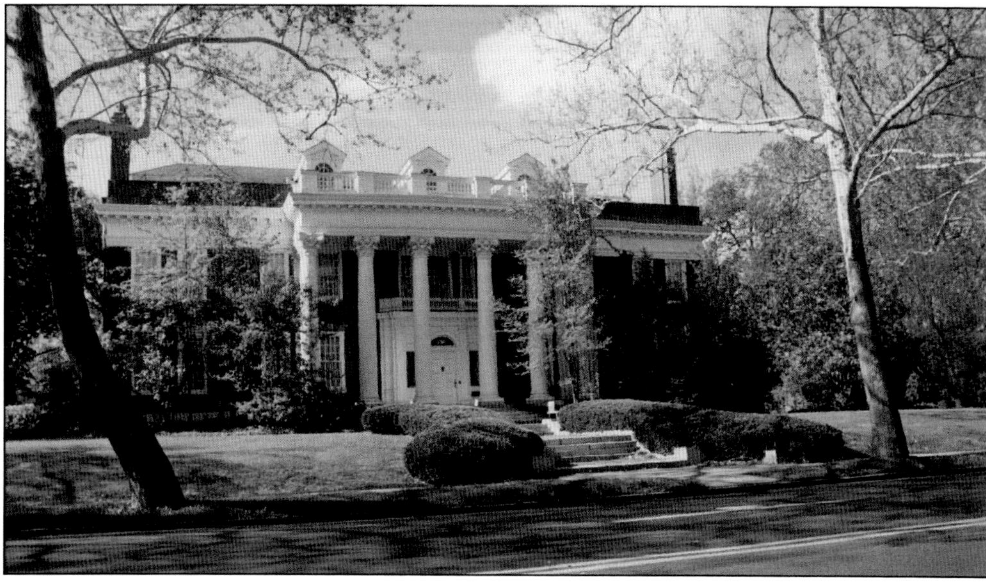

University City has one of the widest ranges of quality housing, with craftsmanship unequaled by most communities in the metropolitan area. One can find large mansions dating back to 1911, like the one above, or an apartment, a single family two-story home, ranch-style structure, or a two-family unit, like the one below, for young families. Property values in the city increased 44 percent between 1997 and 2001, and city officials expect values to continue to rise. (Photos by John A. Wright.)

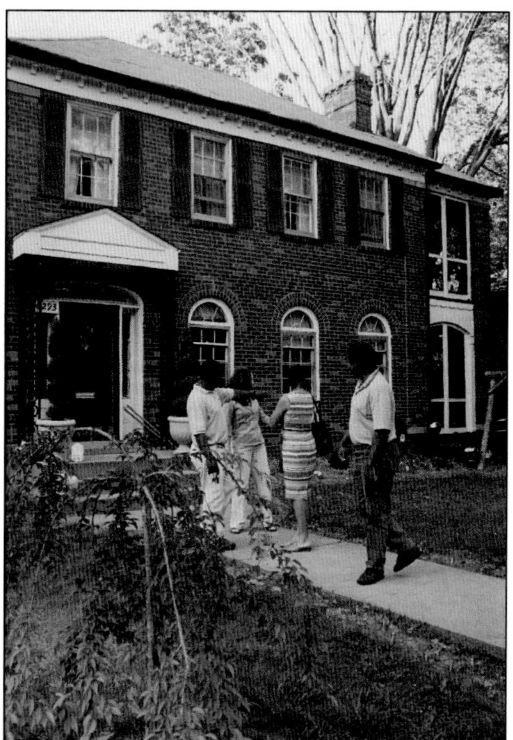

University City's dedication to learning and culture is demonstrated in its public library's 150,000 volumes, with additional collections of records and compact discs, audio and video cassettes, business materials, historical data, and large print books for vision-impaired residents. The library's gallery showcases the work of local and national artists. Year-round quality programs for children preschool age and older are offered through the children's library. The library is part of the Municipal Library Consortium, which enables residents to borrow books from St. Louis City, St. Louis County, and St. Charles. (Photo Courtesy of the Archives of the University City Public Library.)

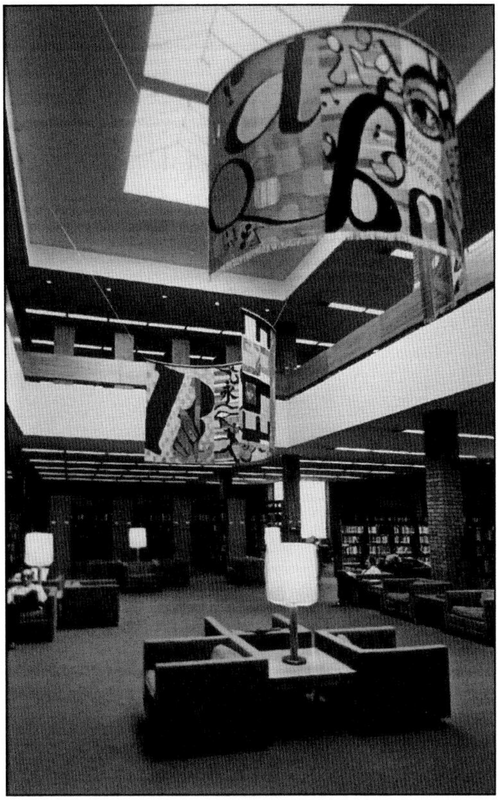

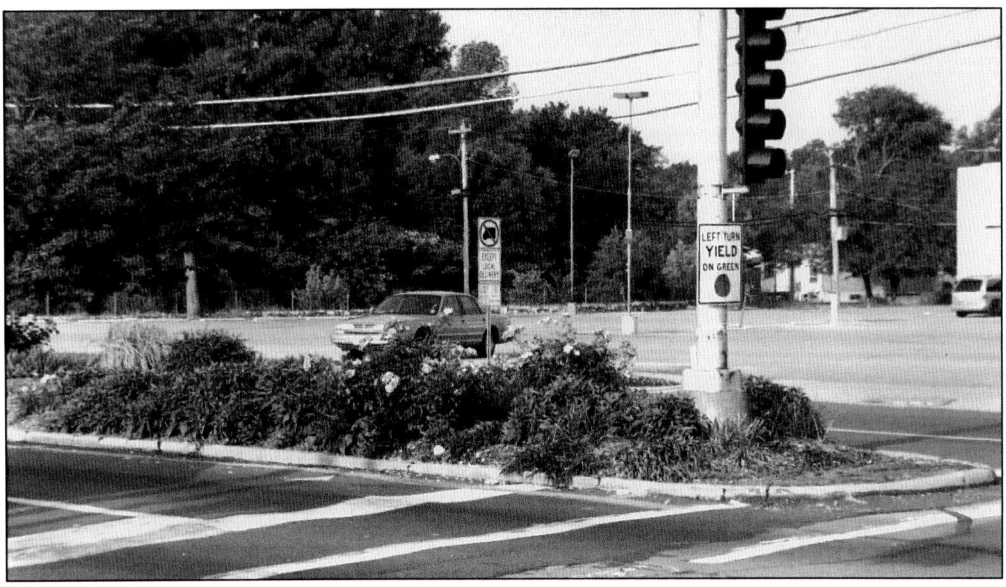

Named a "Tree City USA" by the National Arbor Day Foundation, the city has approximately 30,000 trees growing on public land. In addition, U. City in Bloom, a volunteer gardening group started by University City Park Commissioners Jane Schaeffer and Susan Hopper in 1985, maintains more than 300 public gardens such as the one pictured here at Midland Boulevard and Olive Street Road. (Photo by John A. Wright.)

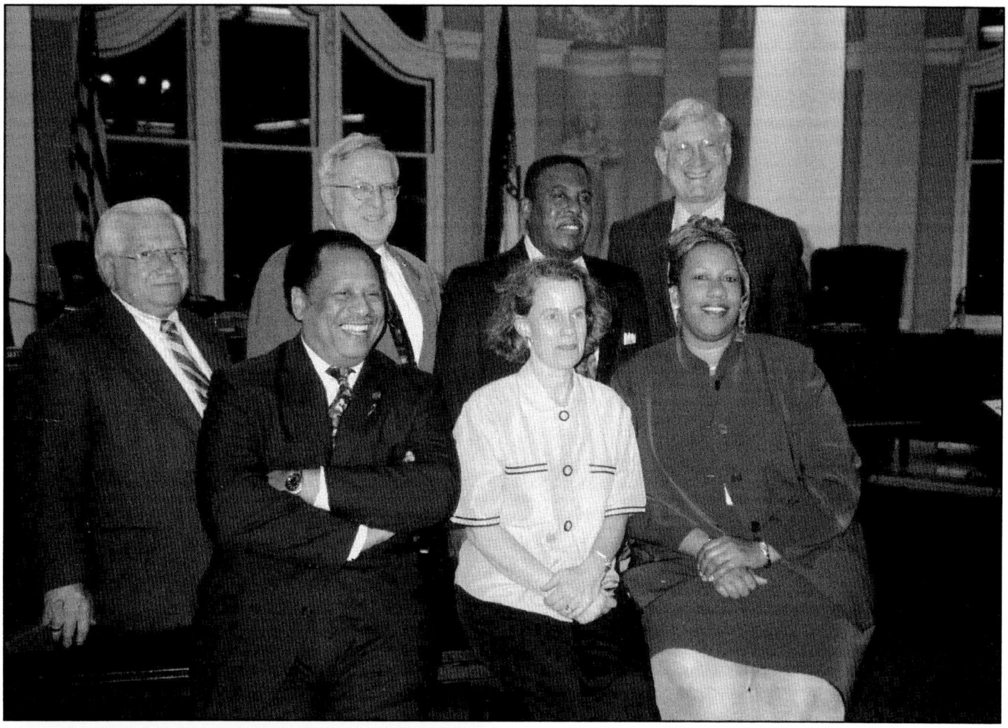

The City operates under a council-manager form of government. The City Council, which has seven members, meets twice a month. The Council sets policy, passes legislation, and adopts an annual budget. One of the council members serves as mayor. The city manager is the chief executive responsible for administering city services. Council members, from left to right, are (front row) Mayor Joseph Adams, Shelley Welsch, Cassandra Colquitt; (back row) Larry Lieberman, Wayne Munkel, Arthur Sharpe Jr., and Robert Wagner. (Photo Courtesy of University City, City Hall.)

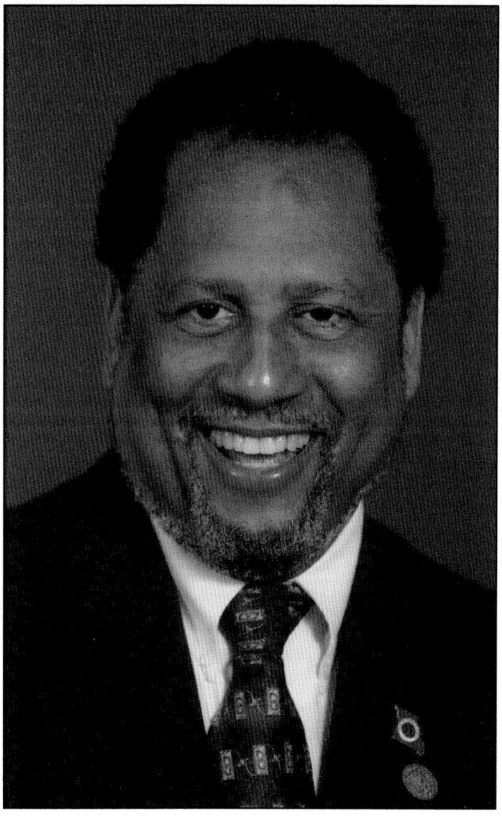

Joseph Adams, a 31-year history professor at St. Louis Community College at Meramec, was appointed Mayor of University City in 1995 and elected the following year, becoming the city's first African-American mayor. Prior to his election as mayor, Adams served as a councilman for 21 years. Adams ran unopposed in his last election in 2002. (Photo Courtesy of University City, City Hall and Ann Appelbaum Widner.)

Lee Payne has been with the University City Police Department since 1970. He moved up through the ranks and became Chief in 1993. He received his Bachelor of Arts Degree in Criminal Justice from Maryville College, and graduated from the 137th Session of the FBI National Academy in Quantico, Virginia. Chief Payne has 84 uniformed police officers under him, the largest department in St. Louis County. The department takes a proactive stand against crime by educating residents through services that includes Neighborhood Watch and a Victim Service Unit. (Photo Courtesy of Lee Payne.)

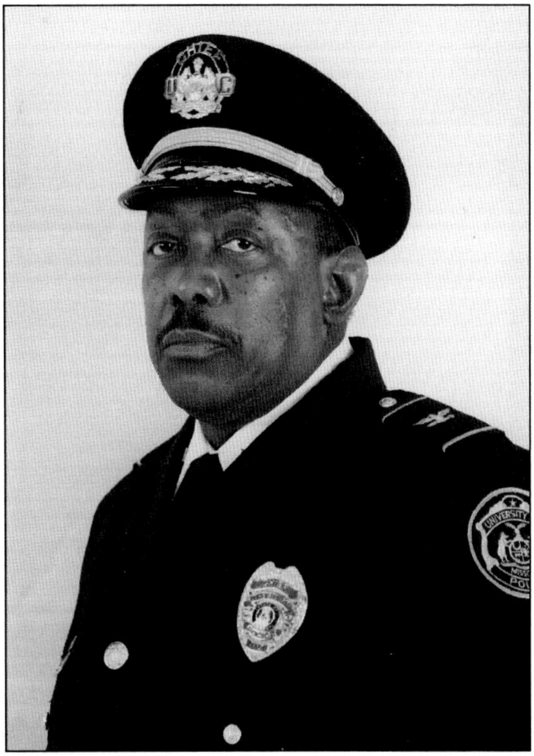

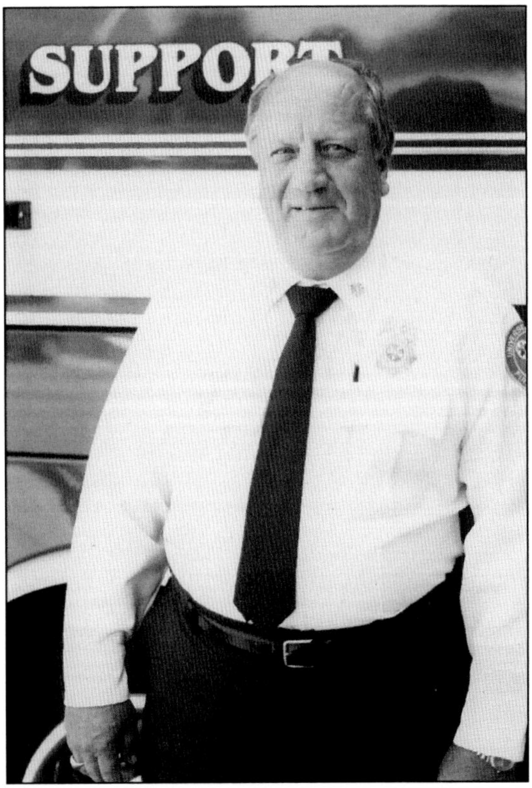

The University City Fire Department is under the leadership of Robert Metcalf, who has a Bachelor of Fire Science from Central Missouri State University. Metcalf moved through the ranks in the fire department from firefighter to fire chief in 1989. He oversees a 50-member department, which includes 25 paramedic firefighters staffing two engine houses. University City was the first municipality in St. Louis County to require firefighters to also be paramedics. (Photo by John A. Wright.)

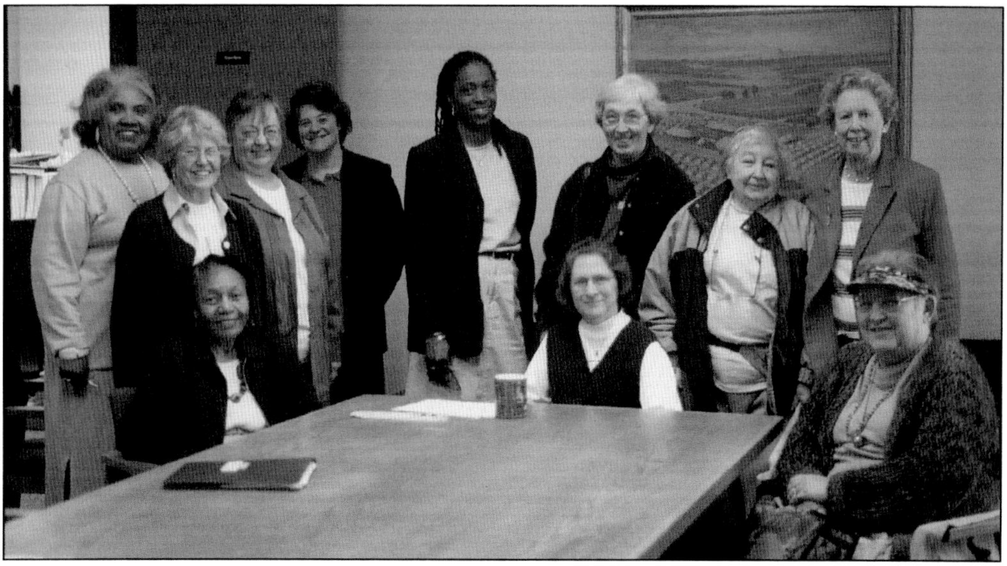

University City has 200 or more residents who volunteer on city boards and commissions that have advisory powers to the City Council. The Historical Society and The Friends of University City Library are two such boards. The Friends of the University City Public Library provide programs and activities to support the library. Members, as of March, 2000, pictured from left to right are (seated) Sarah Lewis; Linda Ballard, Director of Library; and Pat Nelson; (standing) Sylvia Wright, Norma Vavra, Carol Raziq, Nan Rochberg, Njoki Redding, Joyce Best, Sarah Nadler, and Ruth Harding. (Not shown: M. Strominger, J. Seltzer, R. Klasskin, R. Abelson, D. Davison, R. Madden, C. St. Clair, and M. Pinckney.)

The University City Historical Society works to preserve the community's rich history and provide educational programs. Members, pictured from right to left, are Ralph Bowser, Vi Ruesing, Barbara Santoro, Katherine Bailey, President Patricia Perryman, Judy Little, Paul Marsh, Evelyn Stacy, Peter Wollenberg, and Myra Vandersall (Not shown: Carol Diaz-Granados, Brian Gordon, Dea Hoover-Burniski, Bob Kaufman, Kevin Moloney, Sue Rehkopf, and Sigrid Renner.) (Top Photo by John A. Wright. Bottom Photo by Peter Wollenberg.)

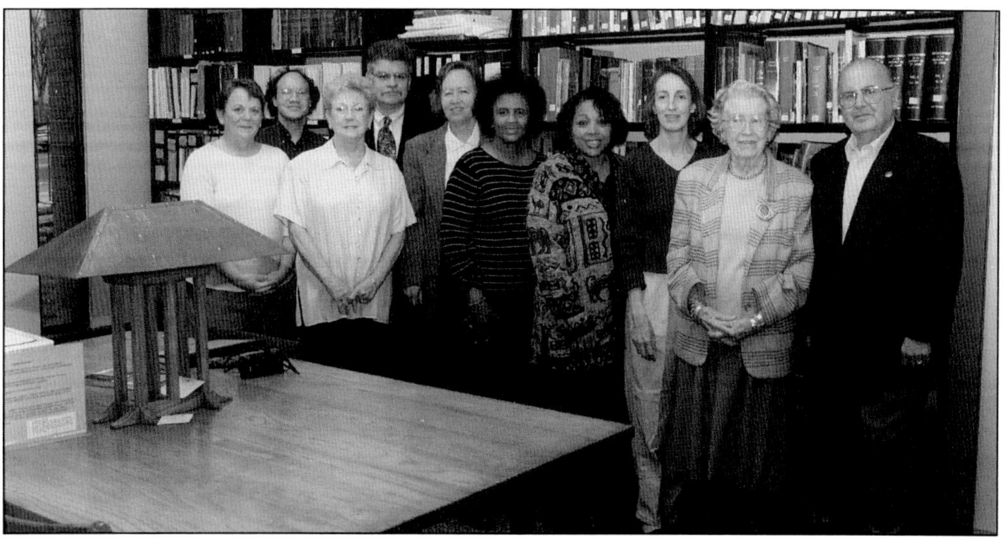

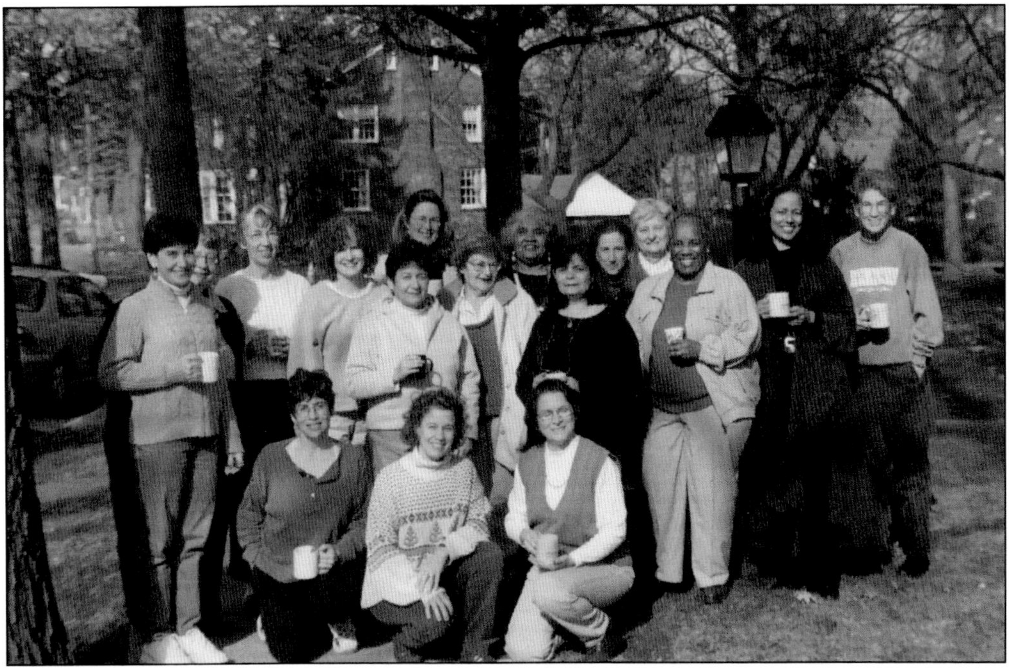

Many community residents come together on their own to discuss and work for ways to improve the community, with programs and action such as Women in the Neighborhood (WIN) and the Roth Neighborhood Association. WIN is a group of women who meet monthly in each others' homes to discuss community and neighborhood issues and to search for solutions. Members, from left to right, are (front row) Sarah Heyman, Shelley Welsch, and Linda Ballard; (back row) Betty Marver, Judy Baernstein, Jen Jenson, Mary Quigley, Susan Block, Mary Wertsch, Jean Hazelton, Sylvia Wright, Phyllis Shapiro, Kristin Sobotka, Elsie Glickert, Christine Long, Marsha Lacour-Little, and Harriet Woods.

University City has more than 75 subdivision trustees and neighborhood associations that interact with city officials. The Roth Neighborhood Association, under the leadership of Richard Dockett, is pictured here at its monthly meeting, at the community center. (Photos by John A. Wright.)

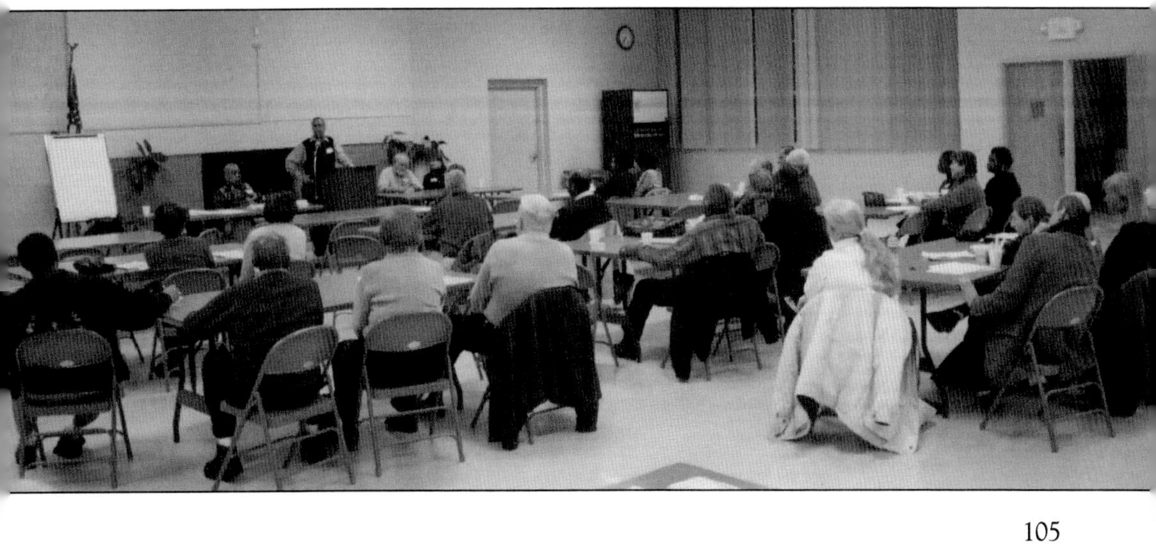

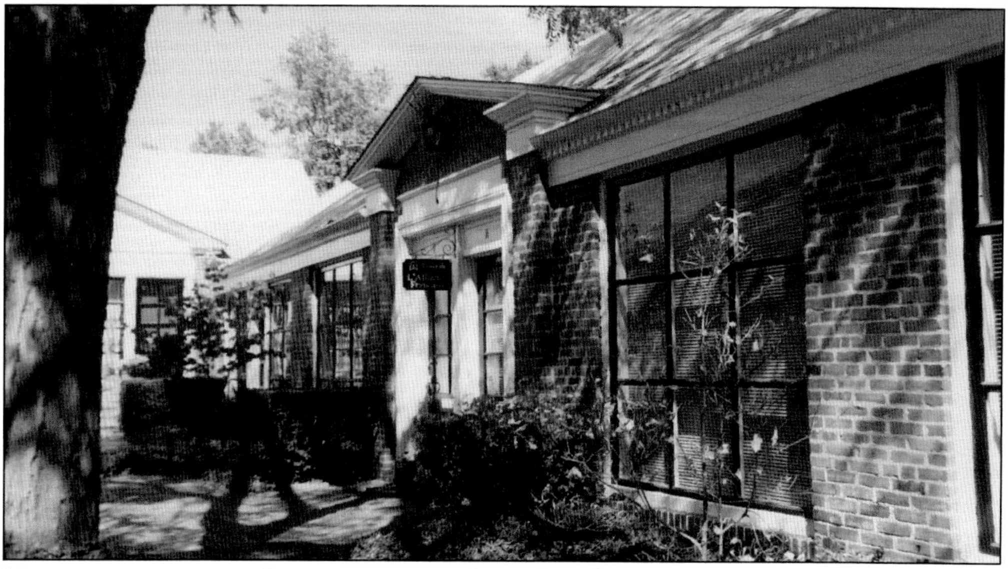

Many organizations in the community, such as the Chinese Cultural Center, The English Language School, and The Alliance Francaise de St. Louis at 8505 Delmar Boulevard, attest to the international flavor and diversity of University City. The Alliance provides classes on French language and culture. (Photo Courtesy of the Alliance Francaise de St. Louis.)

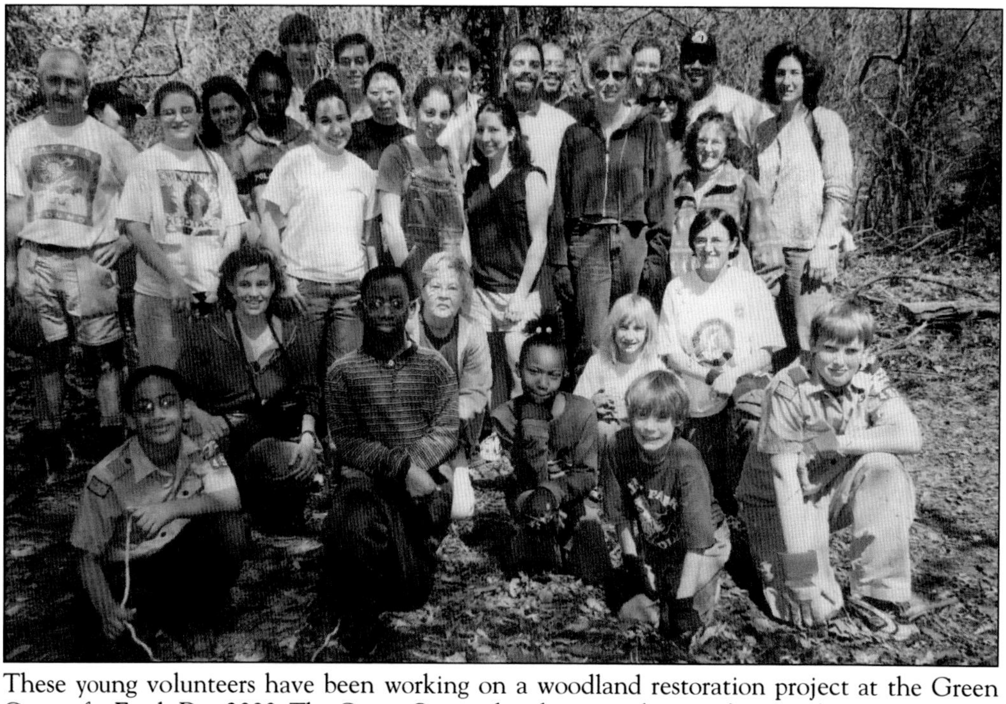

These young volunteers have been working on a woodland restoration project at the Green Center for Earth Day 2000. The Green Center, headquartered in Kaufman Park, was founded in 1997 by a committed group of University City volunteers. The work of the center takes place in its outdoor spaces, which include learning/demonstration gardens on the headquarter's grounds, a half-acre prairie, a restored wetland, the 26-acre Ruth Park Woods, and arboretum in Heman Park. (Photo Courtesy of Green Center.)

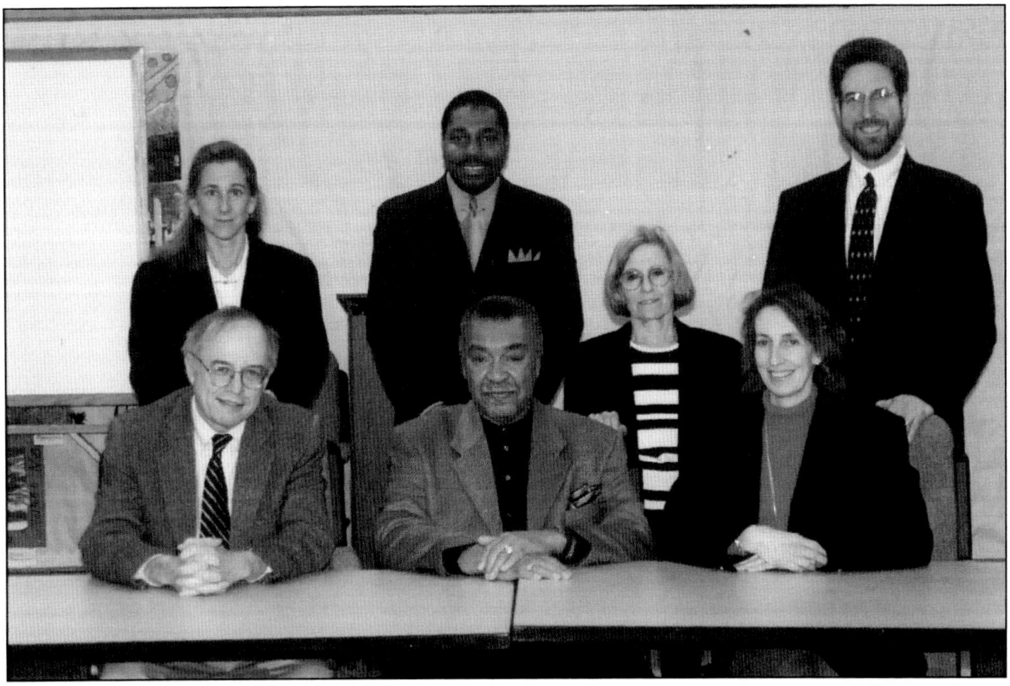

The University City School Board plays a vital role in the operation of the school district. They develop and approve policies to guide a school system of approximately 4,250 students and more than 550 employees. The members of the school board, as of January of 2002, from left to right, are (seated) Rory Ellinger, President Edgar Burnett, and Barbara Santoro; (standing) Kristin Sobotka, Rev. E. G. Shields, Joy Lieberman, and David Harris. (Photo Courtesy of Joy Lieberman.)

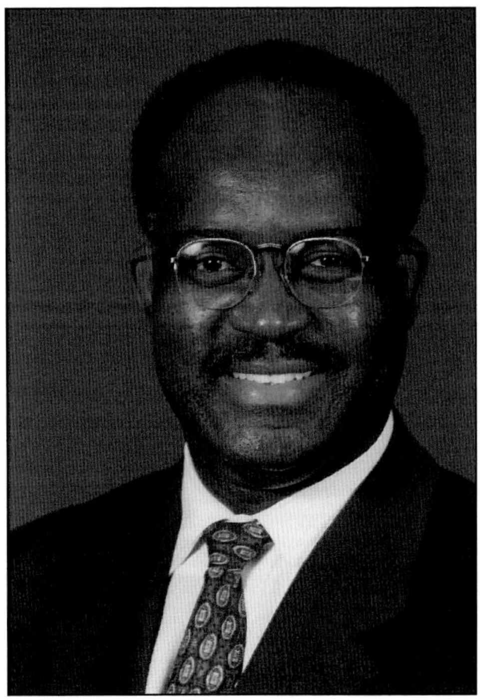

Dr. Vern Moore is the school district's 15th superintendent in its 91-year history. Dr. Moore succeeded Dr. Lynn Beckwith Jr., who retired at the end of the 1999–2000 school year. He served as Deputy Superintendent of the Oklahoma City Public Schools before coming to University City. Oklahoma City Public Schools, which was 39 percent African American, 34 percent Caucasian, 19 percent Hispanic, nearly 3 percent Asian, and slightly more than 5 percent Native American, prepared Dr. Moore well for the diversity of University City. (Photo Courtesy of the University City School District and Ann Appelbaum Widner.)

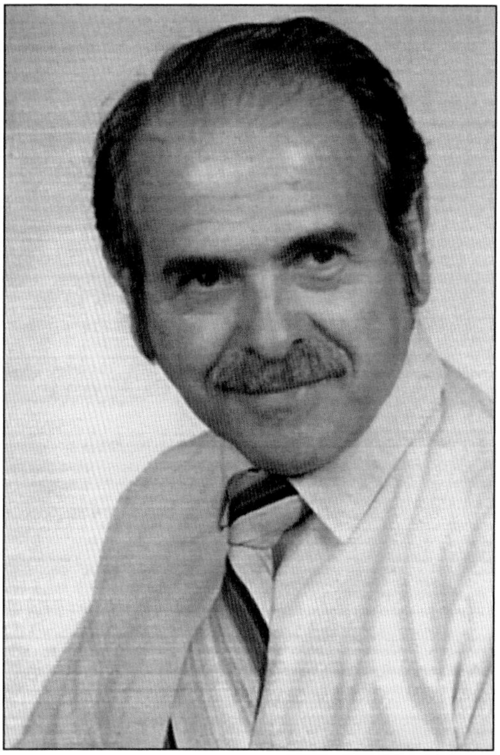

University City High School has many outstanding alumni who have made contributions, but Wallace Klein of the class of 1940 stands out from the crowd. Mr. Klein has never really left the high school or the school district. Following his graduation from Washington University with a master's degree in political science and history, he spent 29 years teaching German at UCHS. He is the recipient of the first Distinguished Service Award of the Foreign Language Association of Greater St. Louis. Since retirement in 1983, he has given thousands of volunteer hours to the school district, including coordination of alumni activities. (Photo Courtesy of Wallace Klein.)

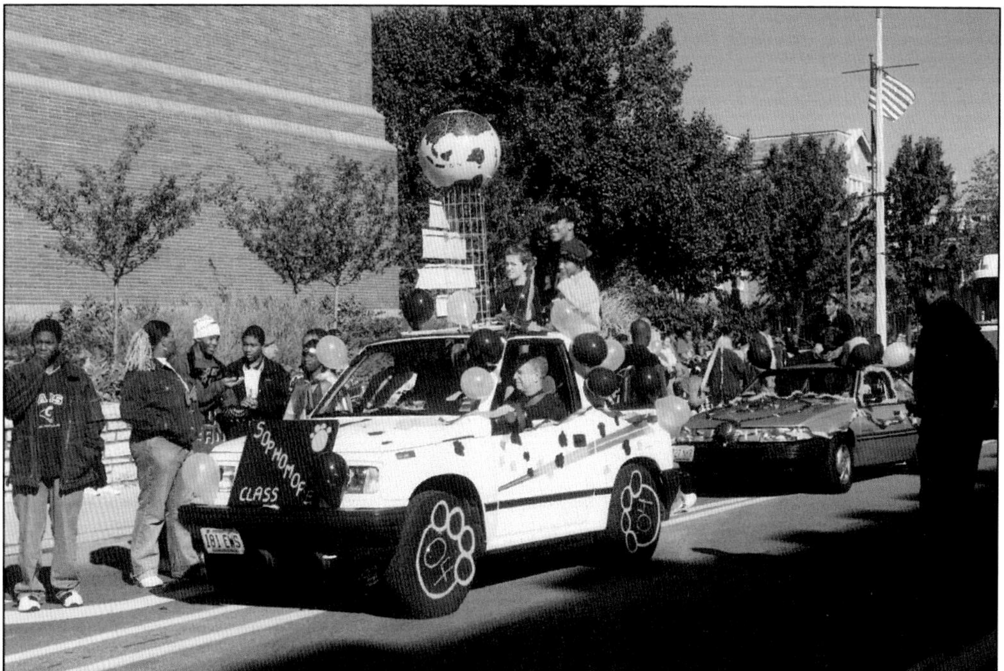

The University City High School Home Coming Parade is a major annual community event. Many residents young and old take part in the viewing of the parade as it winds its way through the city. (Photo Courtesy of University City Public Schools.)

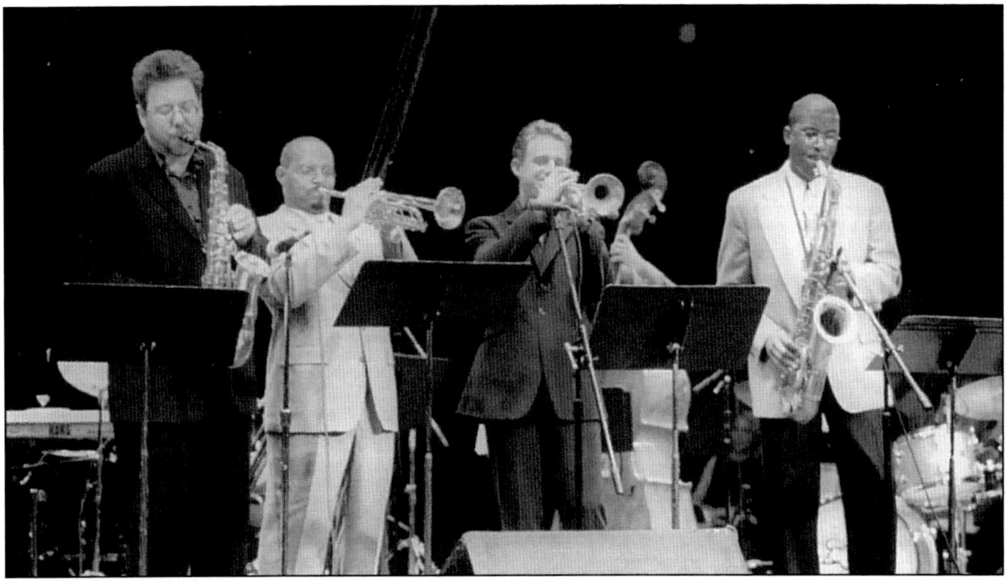

On June 12, 1999, University City High School alumni, David Berger, Ronnie Burrage, Neal Caine, Henry Claude, Jeremy Davenport, Wayne du Maine, Mary Ehrlich, Melissa Fathman, Peter Martin, Chris Thomas, Todd Williams, and Mike Wilner returned to University City to perform in the "Lions of Jazz" Concert for the benefit of the University City Education Foundation. University City alumnus Donald Wolff, "Mr. Jazz," served as master of ceremony. (Photo Courtesy of Wiley Price and the University City Education Foundation.)

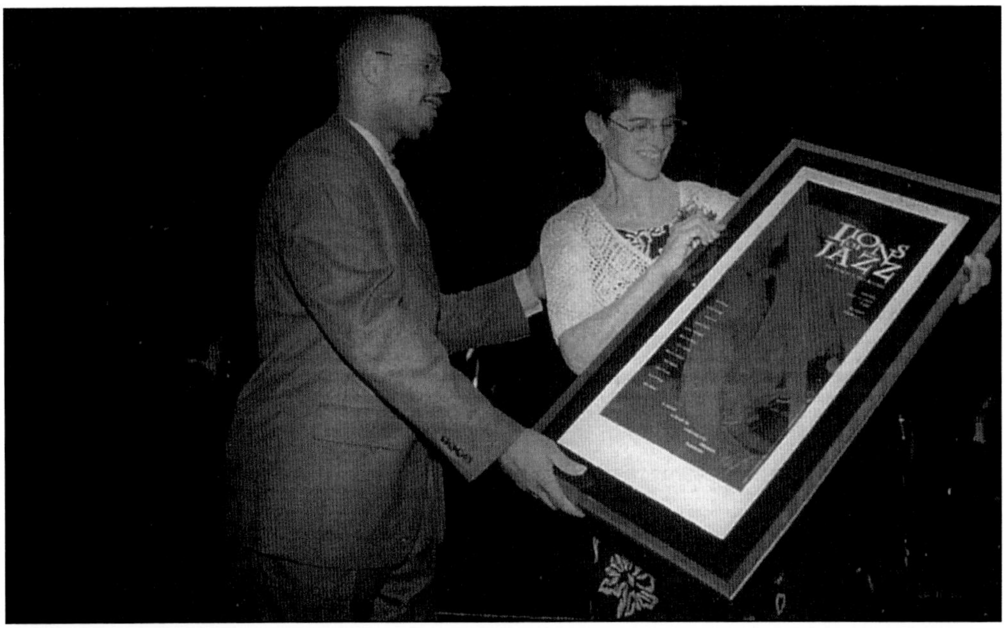

University City alumnus and Hall of Famer Wayne du Maine is presenting Mary Schuman a framed copy of the "Lions of Jazz" Concert. Schuman was the organizer behind the successful concert. The illustration and poster design is by University City High School alumnae Saaba Buddenhagen, Traci Moore, and Eleanor Safe. (Photo Courtesy of Wiley Price and the University City Education Foundation.)

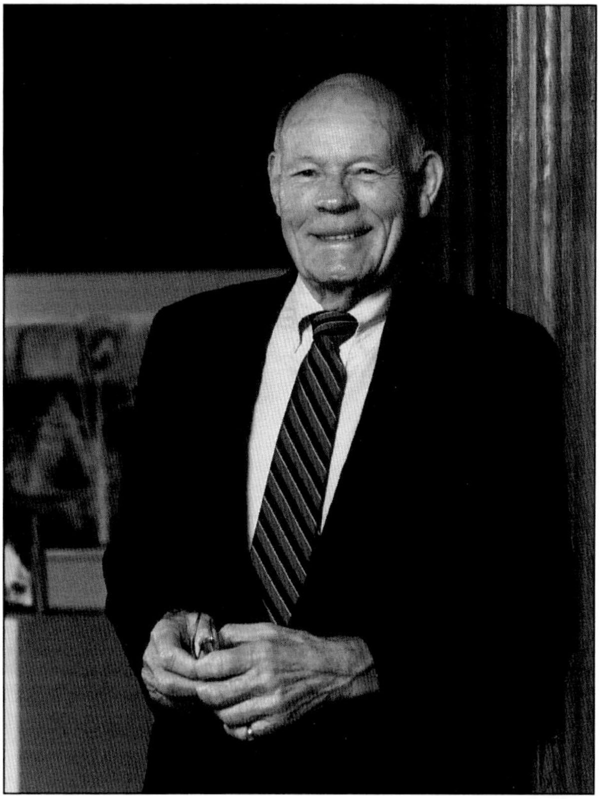

E. Desmond Lee, known as one of St. Louis' most prominent philanthropists and one of the top 100 givers in America, according to *Worth* magazine, is a 1936 University City High School graduate. Lee is a major contributor to the arts. A concert hall at Webster University's Community School in University City is named in his honor. He is a proud sponsor of Washington University's Total Quality Schools program, an improvement process in which several University schools now take part. (Photo Courtesy of the University City Public Schools.)

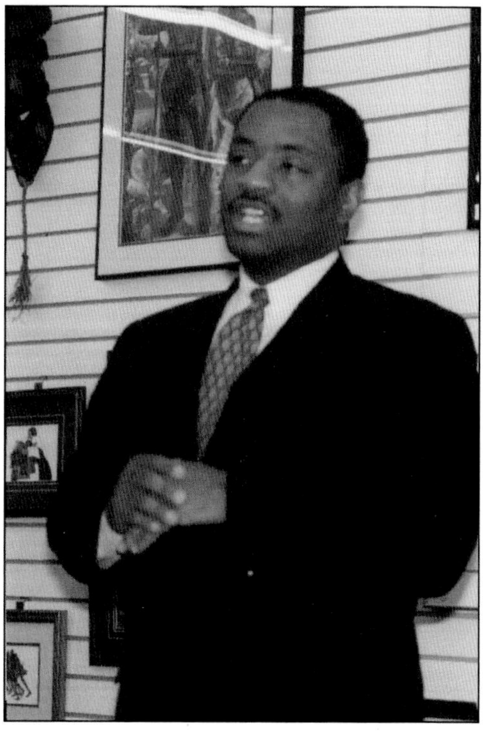

The 1978 University City High School alumnus and CEO of Kwame Building Group, Anthony Thompson, founded his company in 1991. It is a certified minority-owned business that has grown from four employees to 80 in its first ten years of existence. Two-thirds of the employees at Kwame are minorities and one-third are women. More than half of the management positions are held by women. For this diversity, Kwame last year received the Diversity Development Award in the Associated General Contractors of St. Louis Construction Keystone Award Program. (Photo Courtesy of Betty Thompson.)

Cornell Haynes also known as "Nelly" has risen from a local personality to an international star, since his days at University City High School. He entered University City High School in 1990 as a freshman and was very athletic, participating in football, baseball, and basketball. Early in 2002, Haynes produced a video to promote the City of St. Louis. (Photo Courtesy of Michael Thacker.)

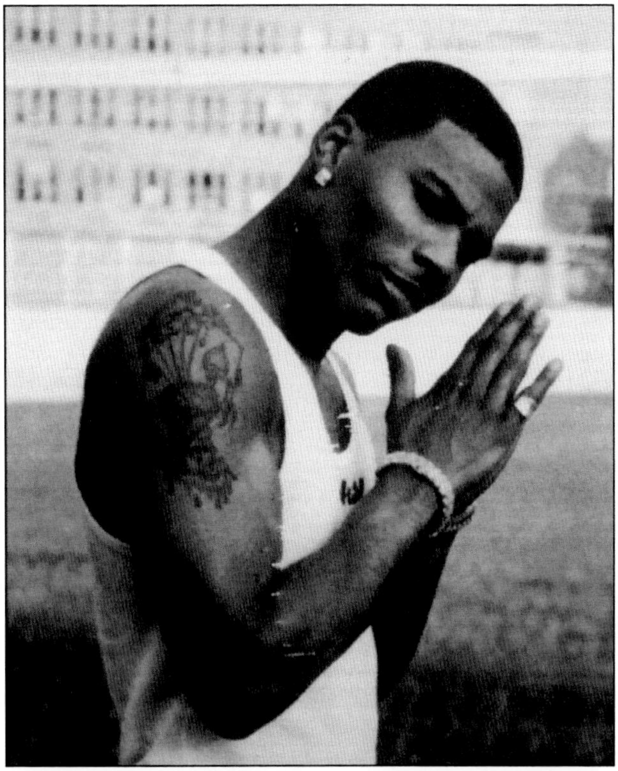

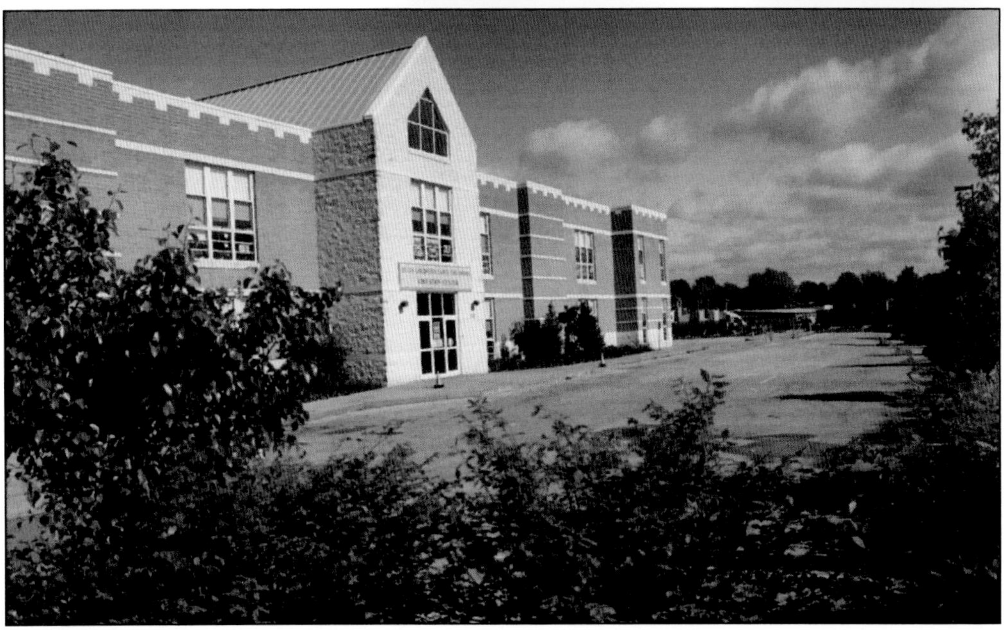

In 1996, the University School District opened the Julia Goldstein Early Education Center. The center was named in memory of the late Ms. Goldstein, an early childhood educator for more than 60 years. In 1986, Goldstein founded the PEEP (Partners for Educational Excellence Program) now called ACT (Adults and Children Together). She was named one of President George Bush's "Thousand Points of Light" in 1990. (Photo by John A. Wright.)

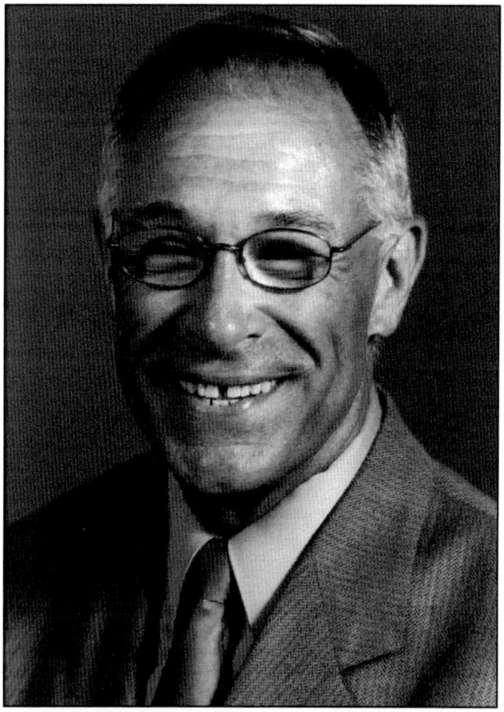

University City has made considerable progress under the leadership of City Manager, Frank Ollendorff. Since Ollendorff assumed his position in 1980 the city has had considerable growth and development. Property values and selling prices continue to rise. New $500,000 homes have recently been completed on North and South Road and Jackson Avenues and the first new homes in 40 years have been constructed recently in the northeast area of the city. (Photo Courtesy of University City Hall and Ann Appelbaum Widner.)

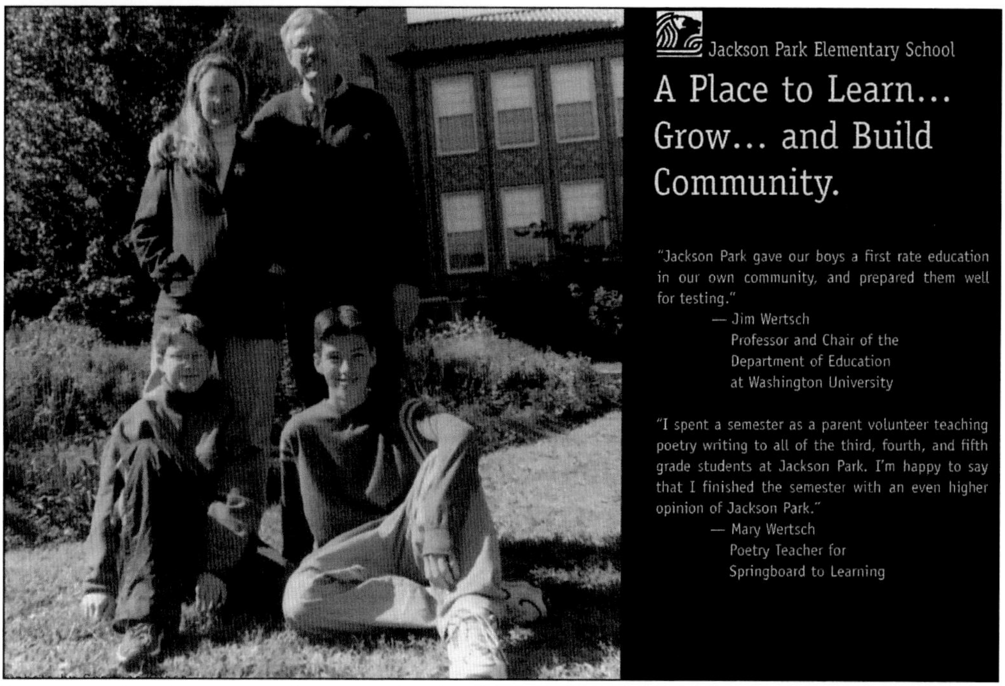

University City has an excellent accredited public school system that has won many awards. The city also has a wide range of educational options at the following private and parochial schools: Our Lady of Lourdes, Christ the King, Bethel Evangelical Lutheran, Agape Academy and Child Development Center, Inc., Torah Prep, Bais Yaakov and Block Yeshiva High Schools, and Frederick Douglass Institute. (Photo Courtesy of Candace Glass and Jackson Park PTO.)

Six

HILLTOP NEIGHBOR

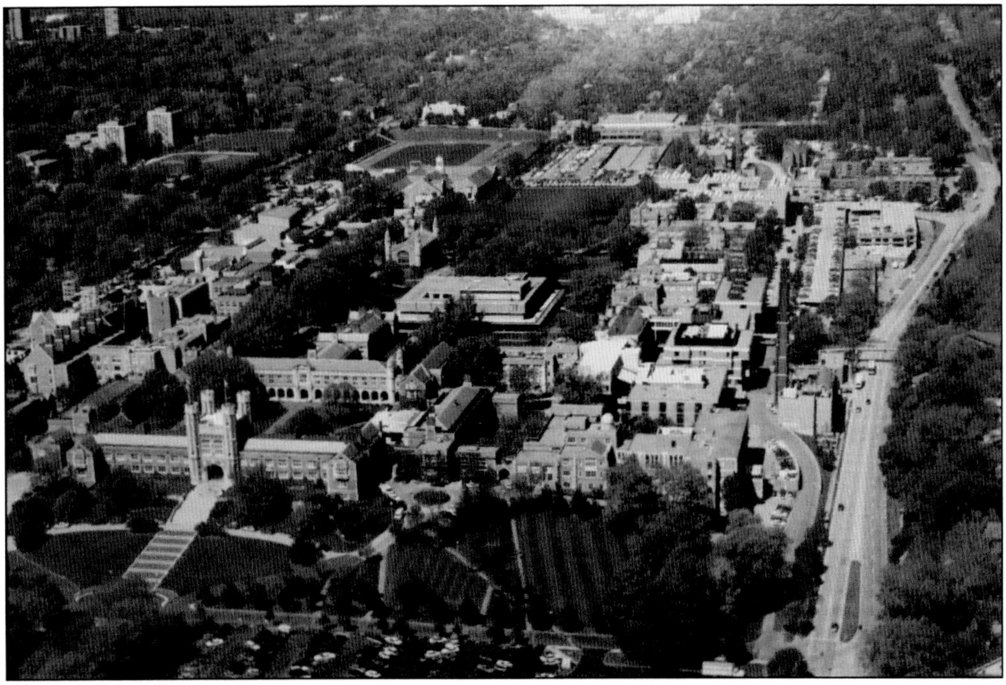

Since its founding, University City has had a close relationship with Washington University, its hilltop neighbor. The city and the University began their development in the area around the time of the 1904 World's Fair. It was Washington University that provided E.G. Lewis, University City's founder, inspiration for the city's name.

Washington University was founded in 1853 by William Greenleaf Eliot, a Unitarian minister, and Wayman Crow, a St. Louis merchant and state senator. The two were close friends as well as free spirits of the frontier who possessed strong social consciences. The University, from its beginning, held a great deal of promise and passed through many stages to get to its present image and international standing. The institution has over 2,600 on its instructional faculty and more than 10,000 employees with a $1.2 billion operating budget. (Photo Courtesy Washington University Archives.)

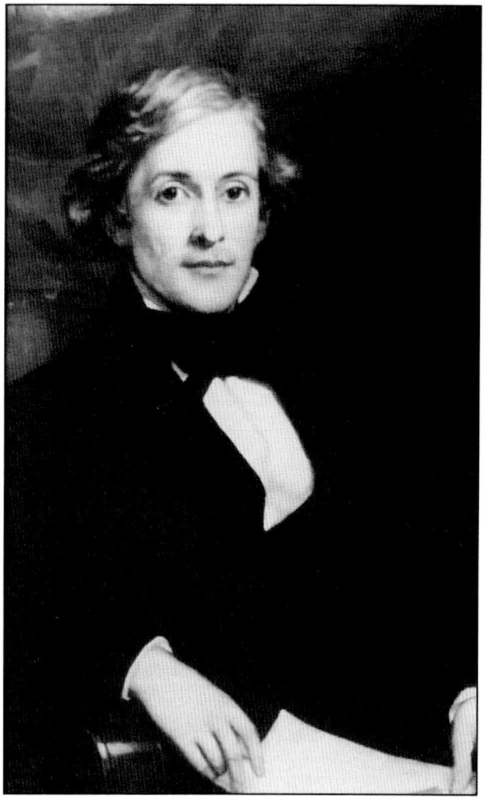

William Greenleaf Eliot, one of the University's founders, is credited with the founding of the St. Louis Public School system, Mary Institute, the now closed Smith Academy, and the Manual Training School. He is also credited with organizing the Mission Free School which, in turn, would become the Provident Association, the Community Chest, and the United Way. Eliot opposed slavery and preached in favor of prohibition and women's suffrage. (Photo Courtesy Washington University Archives.)

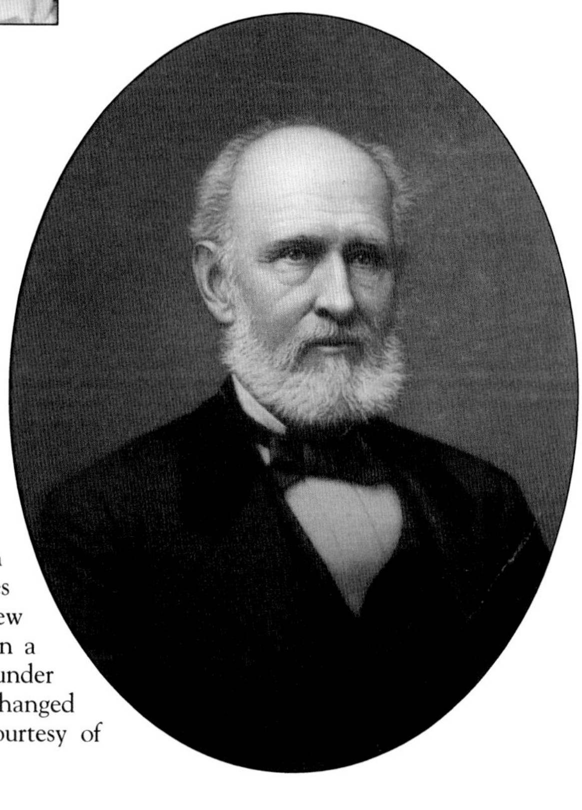

Wayman Crow, like Eliot, was a free spirit with a social conscience. According to Eliot, Crow was responsible for getting the University's Charter adopted without consultation with anyone. He selected the names of 17 personal friends and made a few modifications to a charter he found on a colleague's desk. The charter was issued under the name of Eliot Seminary and later changed to "Washington Institute." (Photo Courtesy of Washington University Archives.)

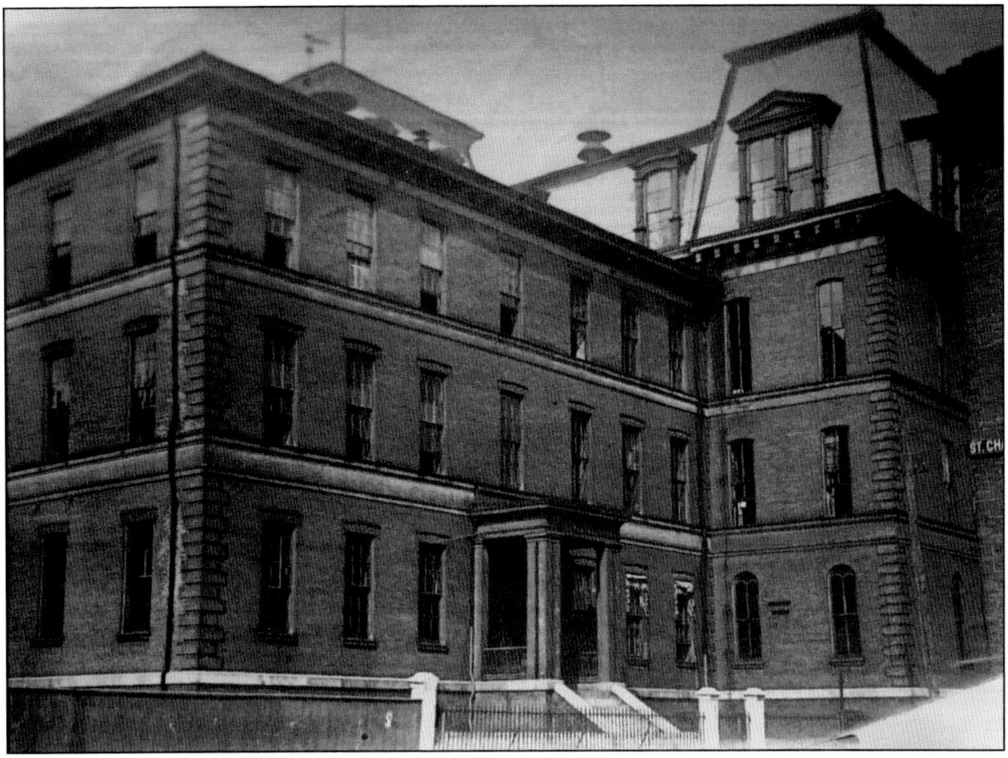

This is one of Washington University's first buildings on its downtown campus near 17th Street and Washington Avenue. The first of the University's educational ventures was an evening school for adults which opened on October 24, 1854, in the Benton School House on Sixth Street between Locust and St. Charles Streets. The following year the school moved into its own building on Seventh and Chestnut Streets under the name O'Fallon Polytechnic Institute which it had been renamed the previous year. (Photo Courtesy of Washington University Archives.)

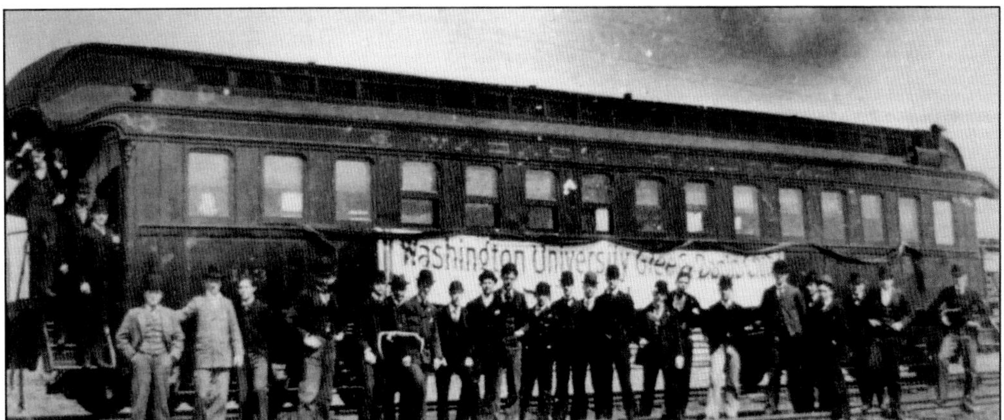

These young men are members of one of the early Washington University Glee Clubs. (Photo Courtesy of the Washington University Archives.)

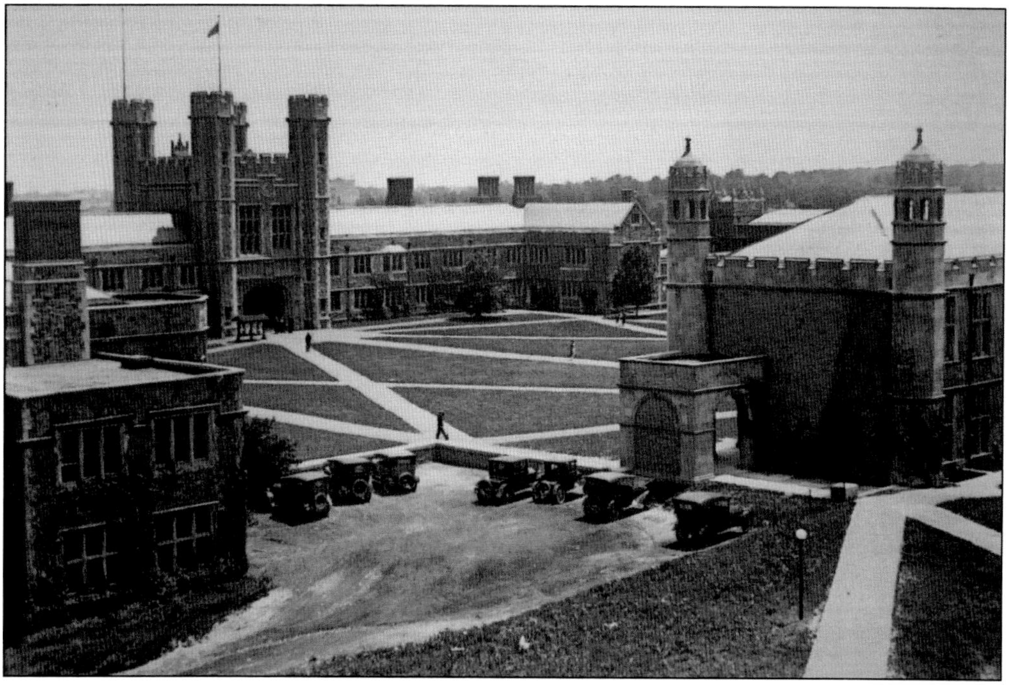

Brookings Hall, now the central administration building at Washington University, was the administration building of the 1904 World's Fair. Students were disappointed when they could not move on to the campus after it was completed. However, Robert Somers Brookings, president of the University's Board of Trustees, and a smart businessman, had leased the buildings to the Louisiana Purchase Exposition, so that he could use the money to construct additional buildings. (Photo Courtesy of the Washington University Archives.)

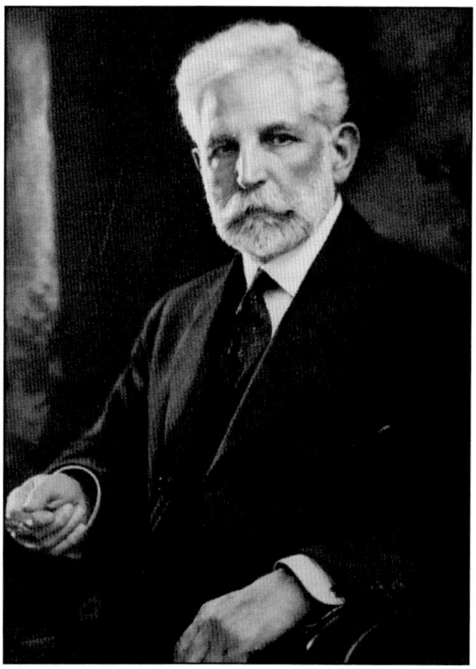

Robert Somers Brookings, a St, Louis woodenware merchant who retired at 46 as a millionaire, was president of the Board of Trustees for Washington University. He is credited with selecting the site for the University. It has been reported that shortly before the turn of the century he rode his horse up a slope west of Forest Park and decided on the present site for the University. The University at the time was in cramped, dingy, downtown quarters and struggling for survival due to a lack of funds. (Photo Courtesy of the Washington University Archives.)

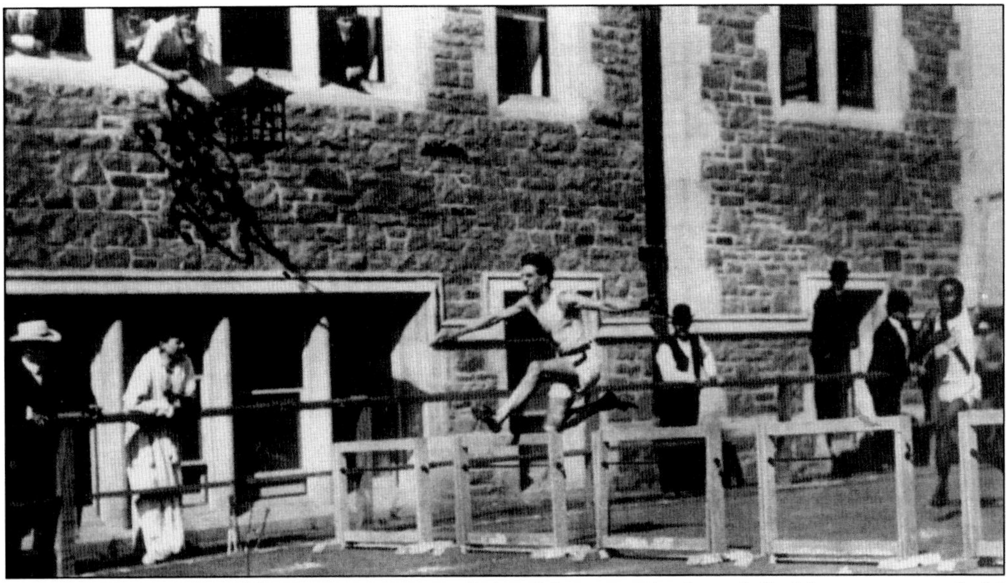

During the 1904 World's Fair, a portion of the Olympics Track and Field events were held at Washington University. George Poage, an African-American instructor at Sumner High School (on the right), finished third in both the 200 and 400 meter hurdles. Poage was the first African American to compete in the modern day Olympics. (Photo Courtesy of Julia Davis.)

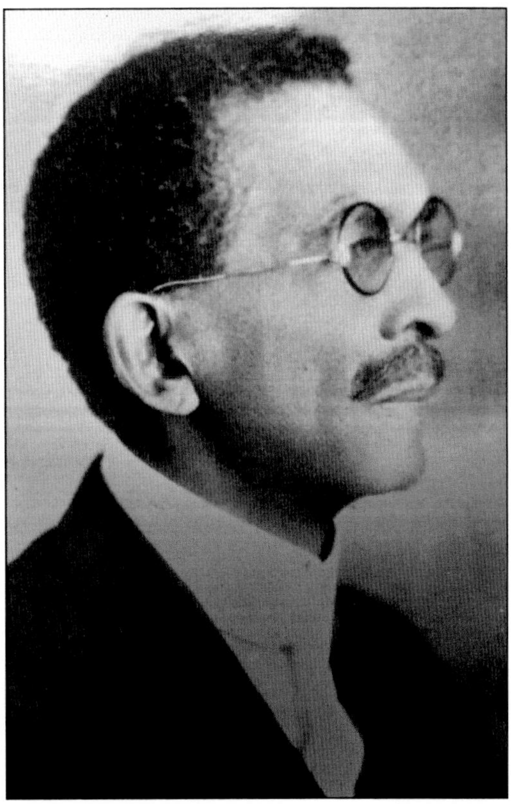

In the early history of Washington University, it accepted applications from African-Americans but stopped doing so shortly before moving to its present location. George Farmer, pictured here, graduated with honors from the University's Law School in 1887. Through the efforts of Attorney David Grant, president of the St. Louis Branch of the NAACP whose organization threatened to push for the University to be placed on the city's tax roll, African Americans were admitted again to the University's evening school in 1944. In 1945, students voted over 77 percent for the admission of African Americans into the undergraduate program. (Photo Courtesy of Washington University Archives.)

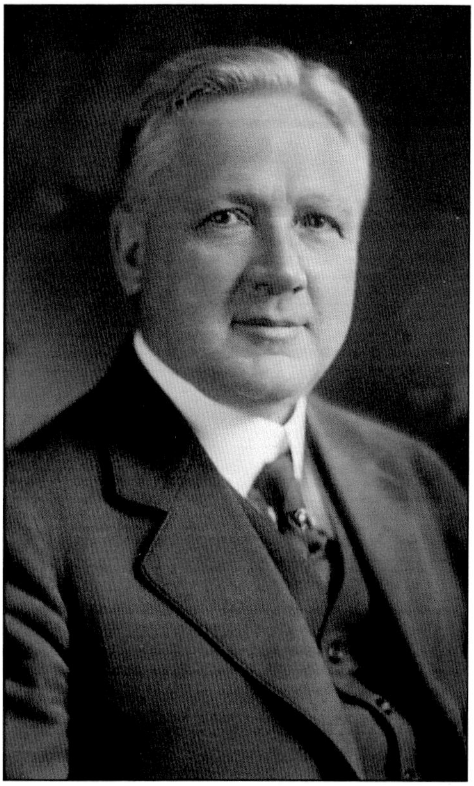

Professor F.W. Shipley, Dean of the College of Liberal Arts of Washington University, played a vital role in the early history of the University City School system. He was one of 13 residents and freeholders who signed the meeting notice for its organization. He went on to serve as vice-president and president of the University City Board of Education from 1917 to1924. (Photo Courtesy of Wallace Kline.)

In the spring of 1937, after years of negotiations, Mayor Matt C. Fogerty signed a contract with the Rock Island Railroad giving University City title to the then abandoned right-of-way. This east-west traffic relief artery running through the southern part of the city was completed in 1938 and named Millbrook Boulevard in honor of Mayor David Millar and President Robert S. Brookings of Washington University. These officials are viewing a plaque placed on Washington University's Campus on Millbrook Boulevard on March 22, 1941, commemorating its naming. (Photo Courtesy of the Archives of the University City Public Library.)

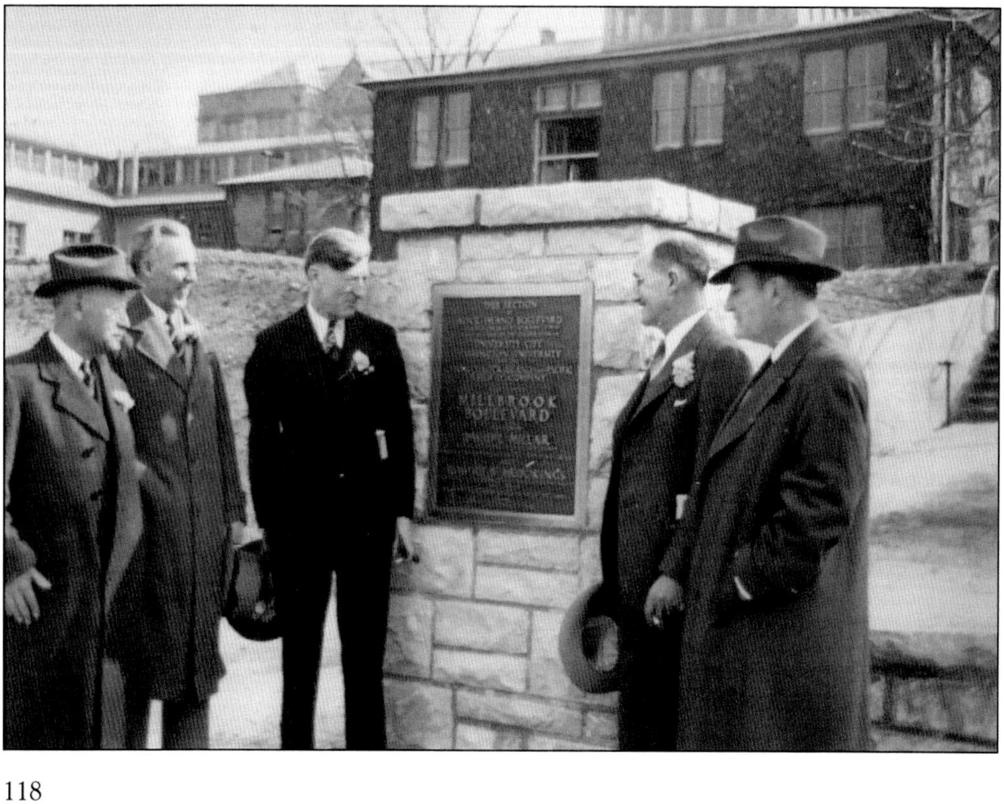

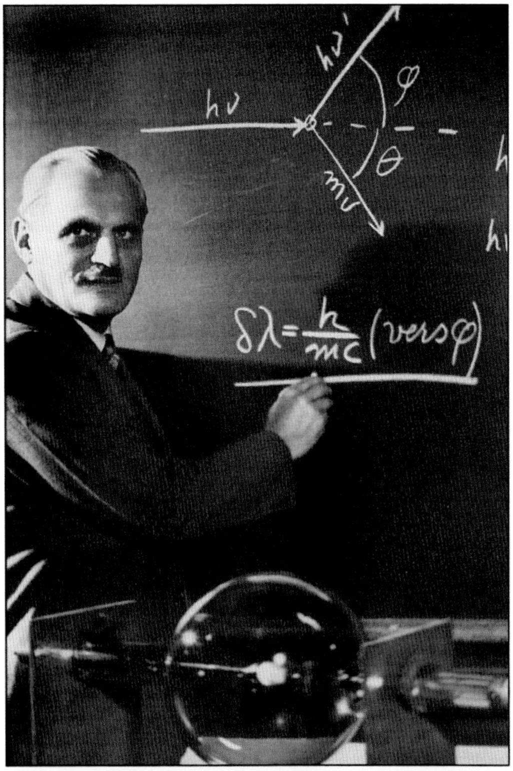

The election of Arthur Holly Compton, internationally known scientist and Nobel Prize physicist, as chancellor at the end of World War II marked the beginning of a new era at the University. Compton had served as a physics professor at the University 29 years earlier and had done the work at the University that earned him the Nobel Prize. As chancellor he is credited with leading a renaissance at the University. He administered the creation of new departments, the construction of new buildings, and the appointment of many noted and new faculty members. (Photo Courtesy of Washington University Archives.)

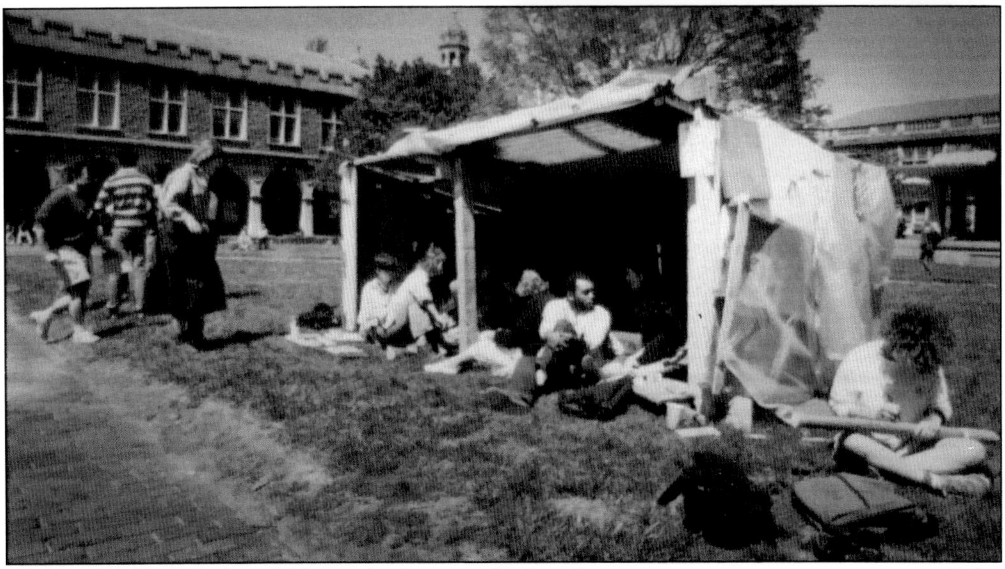

The 1950s through the 1980s marked a period of student protest on various issues around the country and at Washington University. Washington University students spoke out against a segregated restaurant in the late 1950s in University City. They spoke against the ROTC on campus in the 1960s and some were involved in the burning of the ROTC building at the corner of Millbrook Boulevard and Big Bend Avenue. These members of the Association of Black Students in 1986 are protesting the university's support of the apartheid system in South Africa. (Photo Courtesy of the Mercantile Library.)

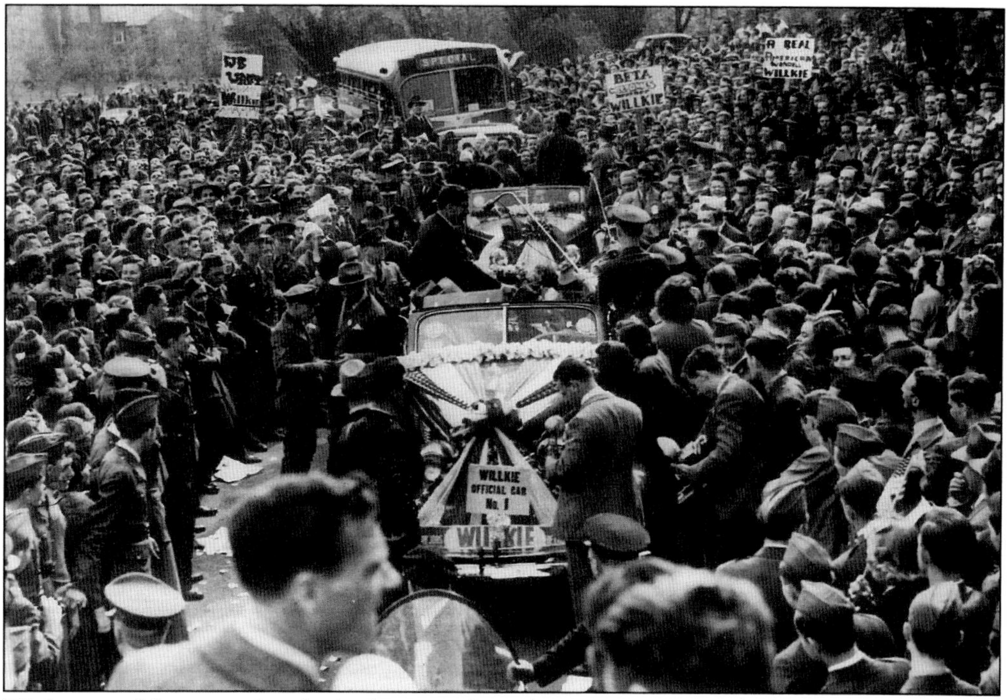

Washington University has had a history of involvement in national elections. In 1940, the Republican Presidential candidate, Wendell Wilkie, came to visit the campus during his tour. Mr. Wilkie lost to Franklin Delano Roosevelt, the Democratic candidate. (Photo Courtesy of the Mercantile Library.)

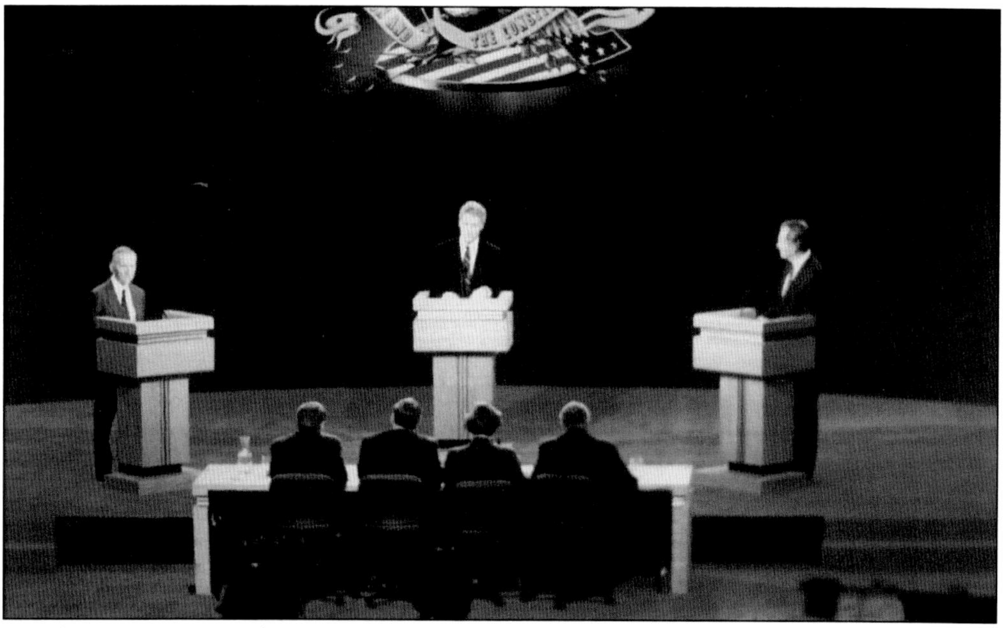

President George Bush is shown here in a three-man presidential debate with Bill Clinton and Ross Perot in 1992 on Washington University's campus. (Photo Courtesy Washington University Archives.)

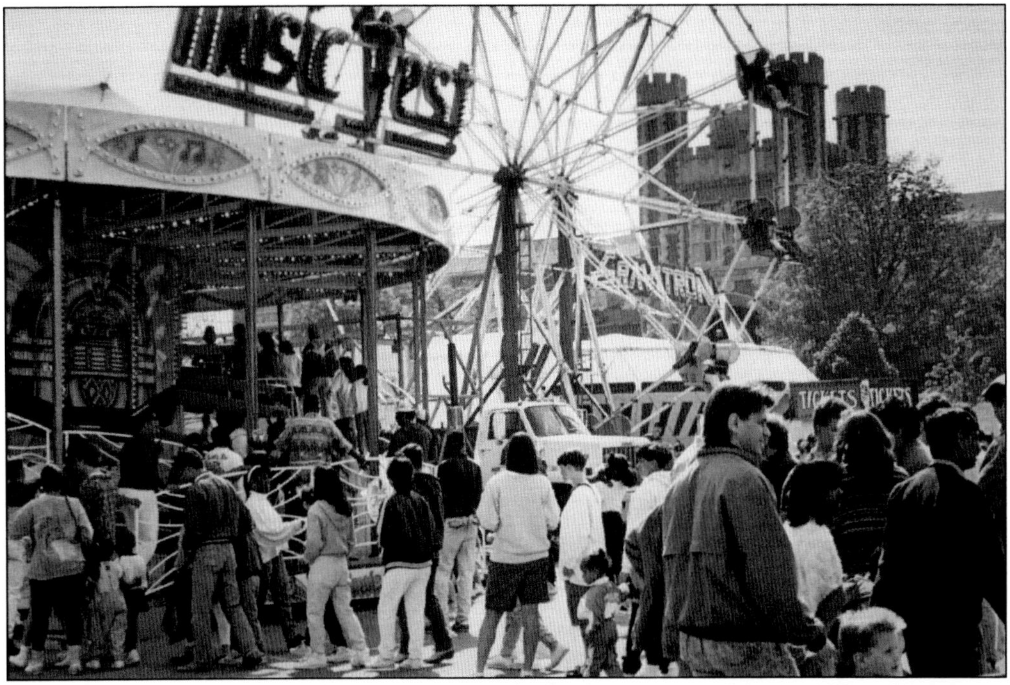

Thurteene Carnival, an annual University event, had its beginning on May 9, 1907, at "Younnivee Surrkuss" the proverbial grandfather to the modern-day event. Through the years, the event has undergone several name changes to reach its present title. Today, Thurteene Carnival is the largest and oldest student-run carnival in the nation. Nearly 40 student organizations take part in the two-day event. (Photo Courtesy of Washington University Archives.)

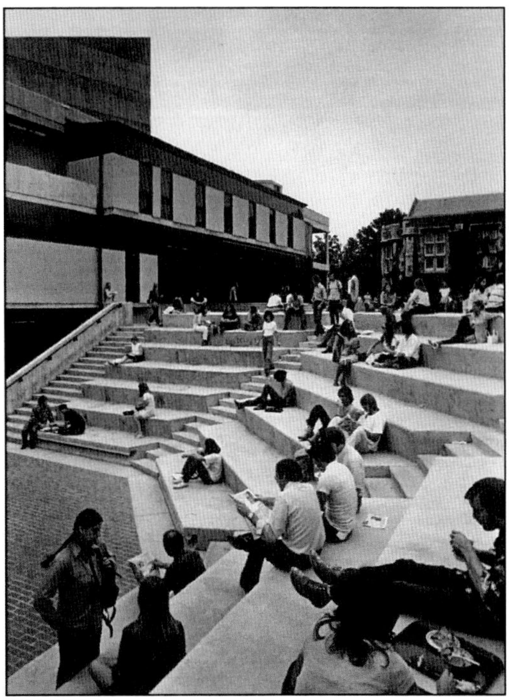

Students find Bowles Plaza at Mallinckrodt Center a peaceful place to study, relax, and enjoy an afternoon. (Photo Courtesy of the Washington University Archives.)

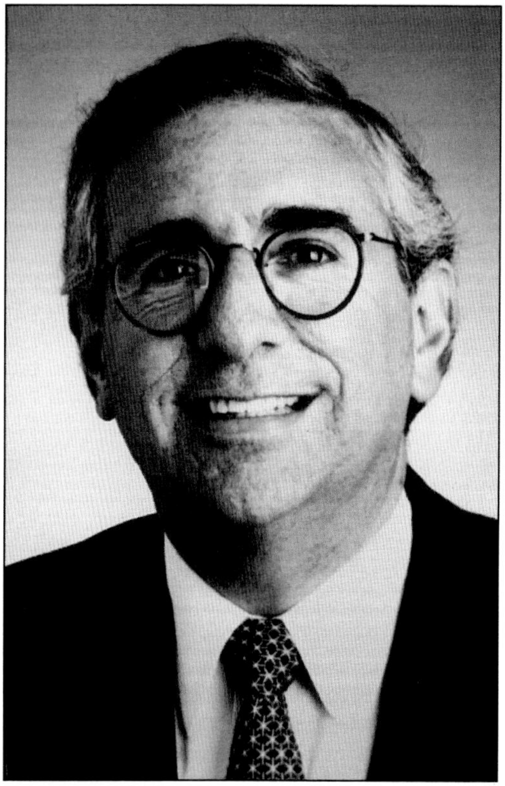

Arthur Zetcher, CEO of Talbots International, a 1958 University City High School alumnus and Washington University Trustee, is one of the many University City School District alumni who have succeeded at Washington University. During the decade of 1924-34, one tenth of the district's graduates who attended the University's College of Liberal Arts were given certificates of exceptional scholarship and 12 percent of the district alumni at that time were elected to Phi Beta Kappa. The University's alumni includes successful men and women from every walk of life. (Photo Courtesy of the Arthur Zetcher and Washington University Archives.)

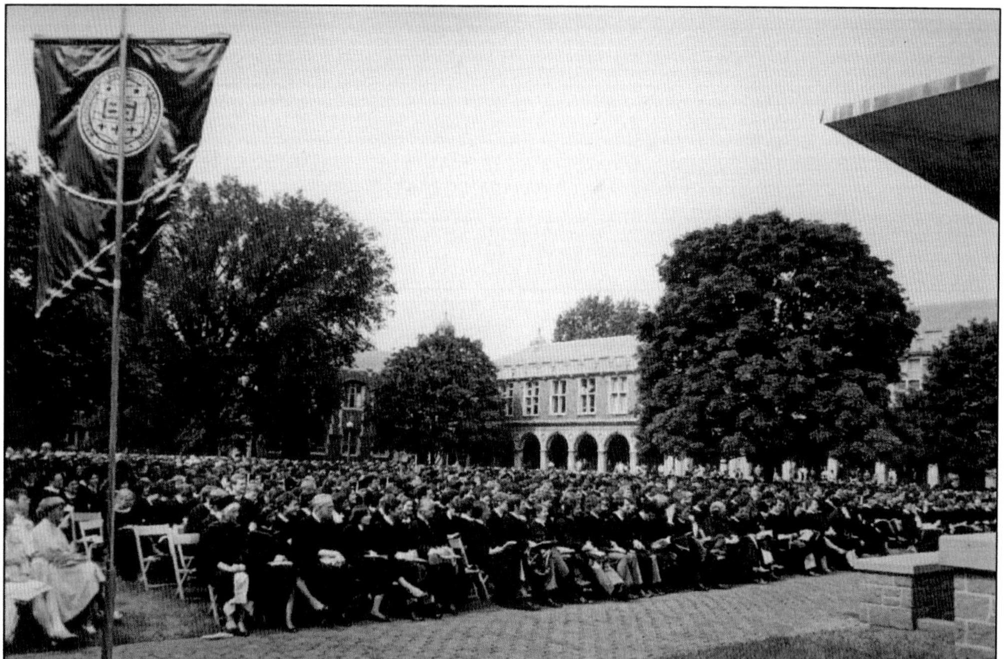

The University Quadrangle for years has been a landmark for activities, programs, and spring graduations for thousands of students each year. (Photo Courtesy of Washington University.)

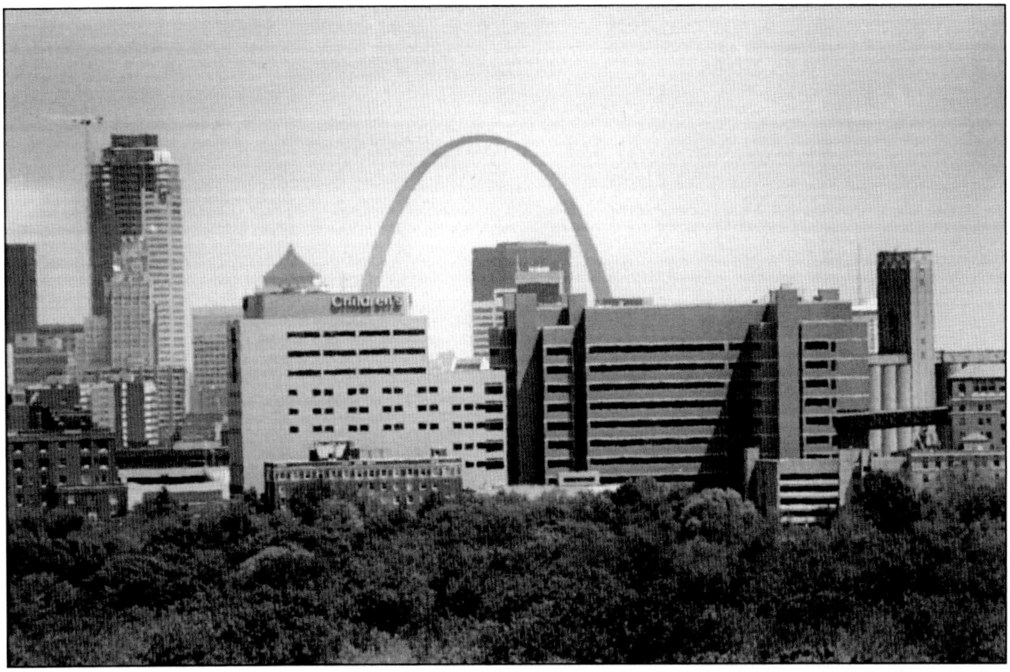

At the eastern end of Forest Park is the University's 59-acre Medical Campus which includes the School of Medicine and associated hospitals and institutes of the Washington University Medical Center. Seventeen members of the University's staff have received the Nobel Prize in physiology or medicine. (Photo Courtesy of the Washington University Archives.)

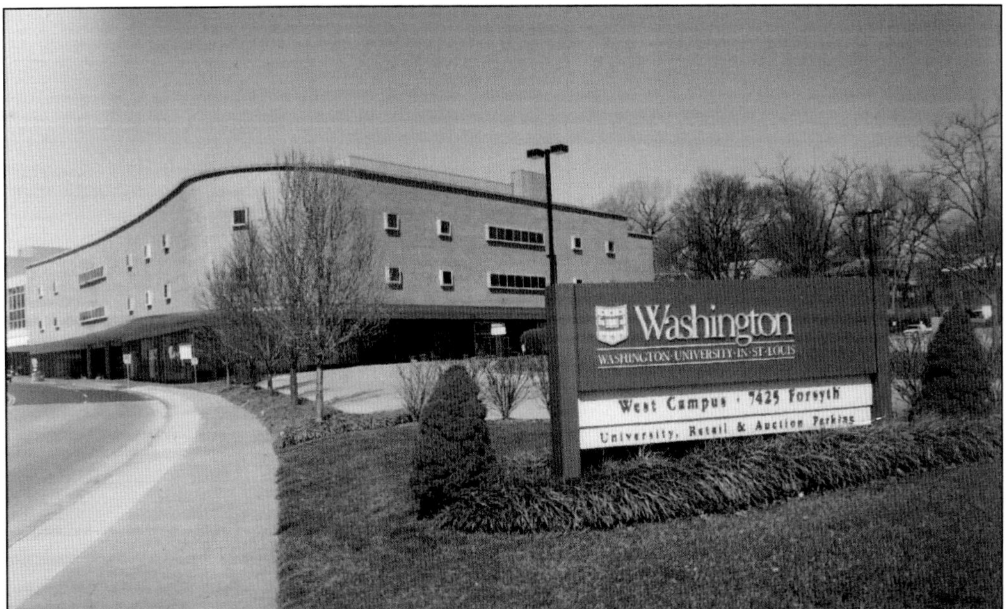

The West Campus on the eastern edge of Clayton is the latest campus addition. It is the home of the University's archives, campus publications, and a few independently owned businesses. (Photo by John A. Wright.)

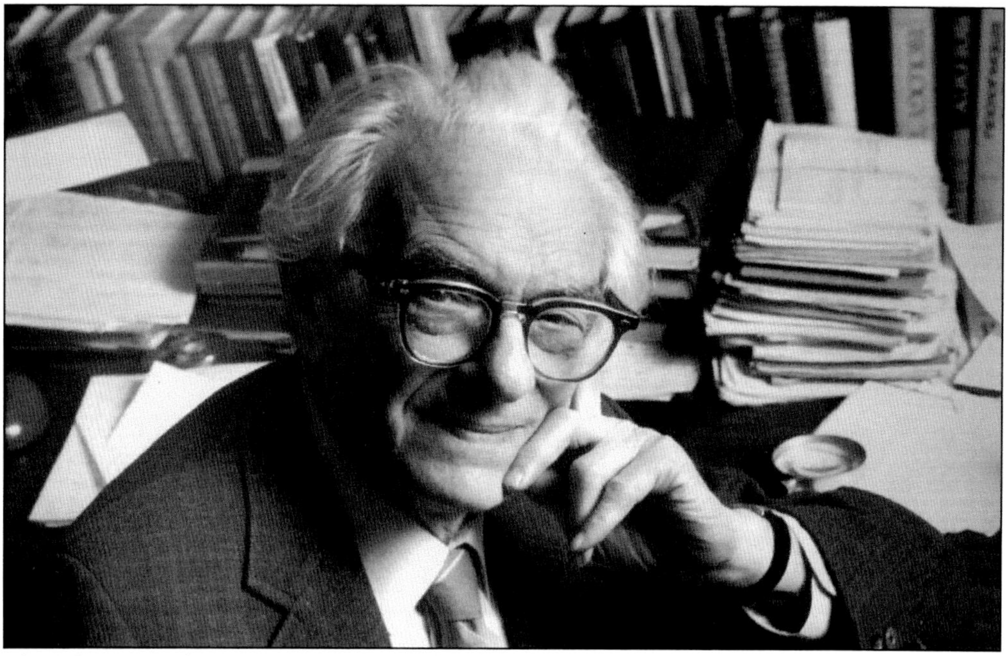

The University has many internationally known Nobel Prize winners and accomplished educators on staff. Many give a great deal without recognition such as Victor Hamburger, pictured here: Many believe he was overlooked in 1987 by the Nobel Prize Committee for the Medicine Award. The award went to Levi Montalcine, professor emeritus of Biology at the University and Stanley Cohen, a biochemist at Vanderbilt, for discoveries made nearly 40 years earlier in Hamburger's laboratory. (Photo Courtesy of Washington University Archives.)

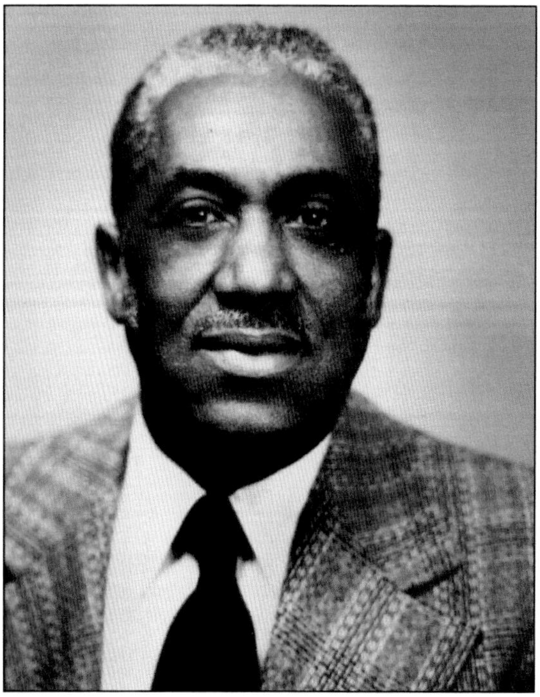

University City resident, John Ervin, in 1968 became the first African-American Dean at Washington University. He served as dean of the University College from 1968 to 1977, and served on the National Advisory Council on Extension and Continuing Education from 1976 to 1983. In Ervin's honor the University established the John B. Ervin Scholars Program to assist African American students attending Washington University. (Photo Courtesy of Ladorn and Jacqueline Ervin Creighton.)

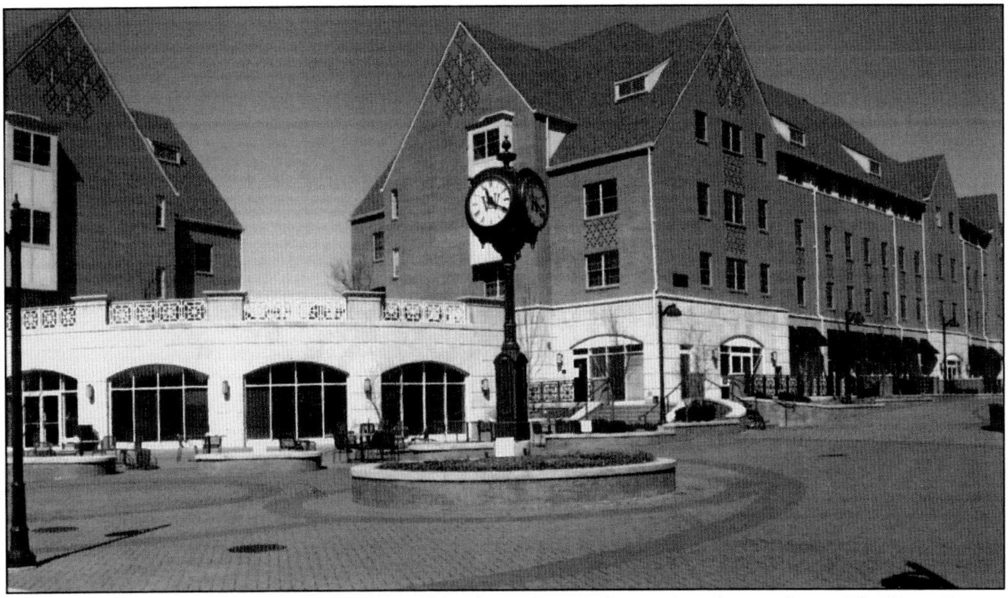

The "South Forty' Campus at Big Bend Boulevard with large, lovely residential halls, is home to over 2,000 undergraduate students. The nickname "the South 40" was given because it is located on 40 acres south of the hilltop campus. When Chancellor Ethan A.H. Shepley created the campus, it moved Washington University from a predominately local University to one with a majority out-of-state student body. (Photo by John A. Wright.)

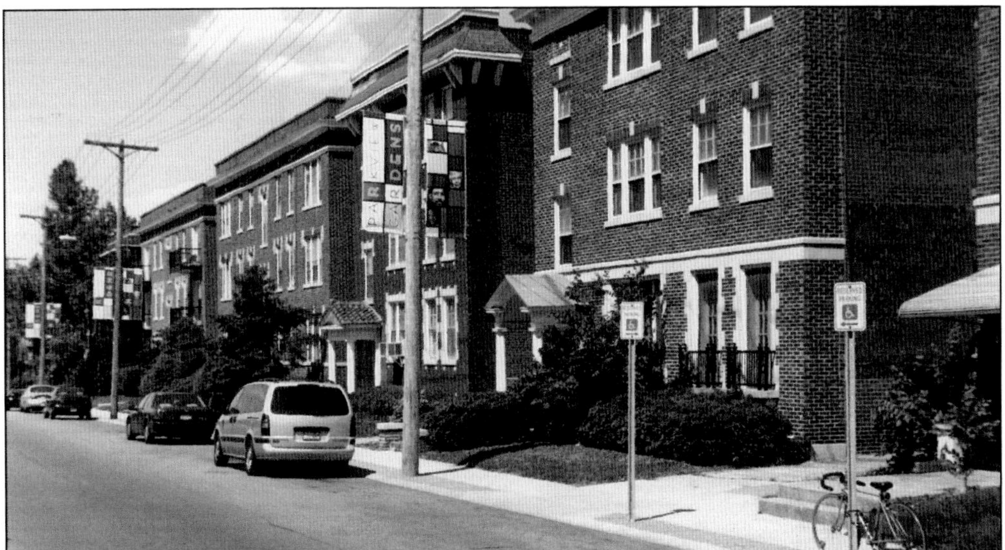

Washington University has a great investment in University City. It is the largest of University City's tax-exempt owners with 68 residential properties, three vacant parcels, and four properties used for education. The University for many years has had an interest in two of the largest of the residential properties with more than 100 apartments. The University City Loop area is the home away from home for many Washington University students. The University provides transportation for the students to and from the University to the Loop. (Photo by John A. Wright.)

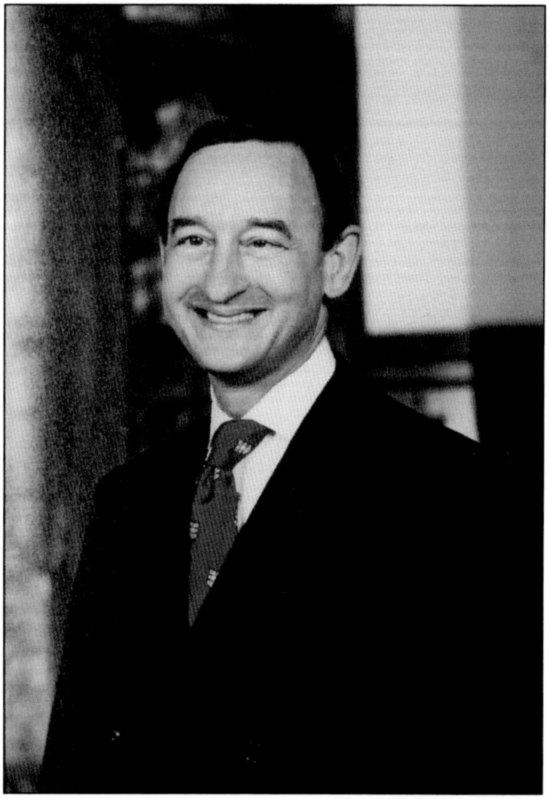

Internationally known Mark S. Wrighton, came to the University in 1995 as chancellor. His accomplishments after assuming the chancellorship include more than a two-fold increase in undergraduate applications, more than 100 new endowed professorships for faculty, a redesigned Arts and Sciences curriculum and newly created programs, biomedical engineering, American Culture studies, and the completion of 16 new buildings, with another 11 either under construction or planned in the next few years. (Photo Courtesy of Washington University Archives.)

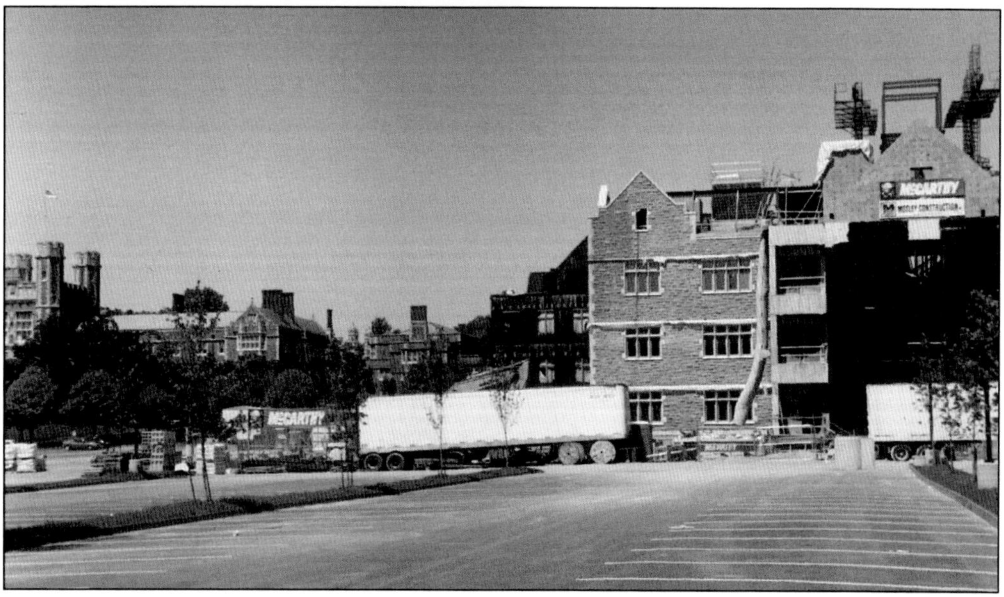

In 1998, under Mark Wrighton, the University publicly launched a billion-dollar campaign, which it has already surpassed, to build resources for student scholarships, professorships, other endowed program support, and new buildings. As the University's reputation grows, student interest in attending the school has climbed dramatically. As example, nearly 21,000 applications for 1,280 openings were submitted for the fall 2001 entering class. (Photo by John A. Wright.)

Postscript

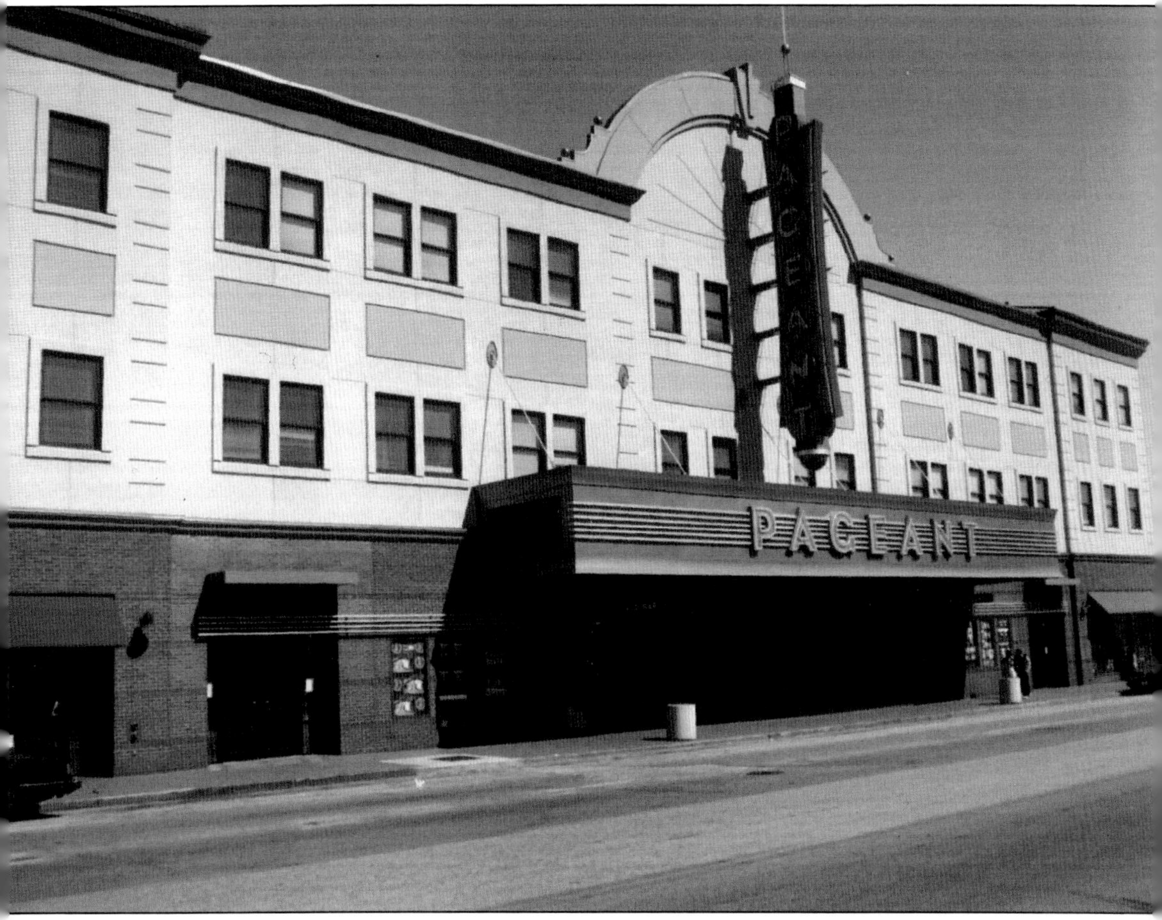

New growth and development throughout University City is a testimony to the spirit of the community. Evidence of this spirit, is the city's revitalization along Olive and Delmar Boulevards into the City of St. Louis. This growth and development also attests to the realization of the dreams and hard work of the people of University City, who refused to let the community be destroyed by the red-lining carried on by real estate agents and nay-sayers of the 1960s, '70s, and '80s.

University City has emerged stronger for its diversity as can be seen in areas such as the Loop. This area serves as a gathering place for neighbors, business people, and the faculty and students from nearby Fontbonne College and Washington University. The atmosphere and offerings of the Loop such as the array of international restaurants, galleries, and shops draw people of all cultures and walks of life. (Photo by John A. Wright.)

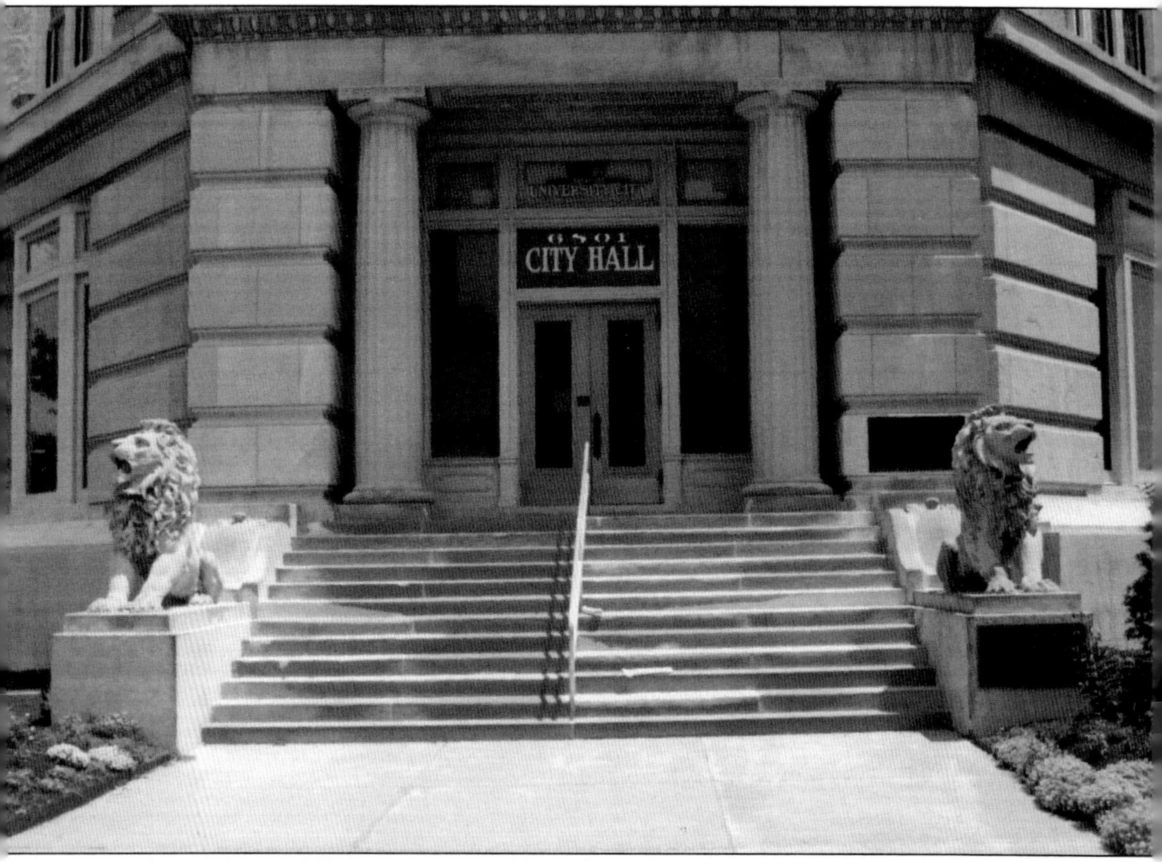

As the residents of University City take pride in the city's success, they are aware, like the proud lions that guard City Hall and watch over Delmar Boulevard, that they can not rest and must be ever vigilant as they work together to move the city to a higher level of success. (Photo by John A. Wright.)

Selected Bibliography

Harris, Nina. *Legacy of Lions*. University City. The Historical Society of University City, 1981.

Little, Judy. *University City: Landmarks and Historic Places*. University City, Historic Preservation Commission of University City, 1997.

Longo, Jim. *A University City Album*. University City, The Citizen's Committee for the Seventy-Fifth Anniversary, 1981.

Morse, Sidney. *The Siege of University City the Dreyfus Case*, University City, University City Publishing Company, 1912.

School District of University City. *The Romance of a Quarter-Century of Education 1911–36*, School District of University City, 1936.